THE SCHOOL
OF JESUS

Other Books By the Author

Man Needs God, An Interpretation of Biblical Faith.

The Beginning of Eternal Life, The Dynamic Faith of Thomas Aquinas, Origins and Interpretation.

Dimensions of Faith.

The Origin and Evolution of the Priesthood, a Return to the Sources.

The Heresy of Monasticism. The Christian Monks: Types and Anti-Types.

An Overview of Christian Education
Yesterday and Today

THE
SCHOOL
OF JESUS

James Mohler, S.J.

ALBA · HOUSE   NEW · YORK

Library of Congress Cataloging in Publication Data

Mohler, James A
    The school of Jesus.

    Bibliography: p.
    1. Religious education—History. I. Title.
BV1465.M6   207'.1   72-11835
ISBN 0-8189-0262-0

Nihil Obstat:
    Edward Higgins, O.F.M. Cap.
    Censor Librorum

Imprimatur:
 +James P. Mahoney, D.D.
    Vicar General, Archdiocese of New York
    November 10, 1972

The nihil obstat and imprimatur are official declarations
that a book or pamphlet is free of doctrinal or moral error.
No implication is contained therein that those who have
granted the nihil obstat and imprimatur agree with the
contents, opinions or statements expressed.

Designed, printed and bound in the U.S.A., by the Fathers and
Brothers of the Society of St. Paul, 2187 Victory Blvd.,
Staten Island, N.Y. 10314 as part of their communications
apostolate.

Acknowledgments

Cambridge University Press, for quotes from **Fénelon on Education,** H. Barnard, ed.

Catholic University of America Press for quotes from the **Fathers of the Church** series, R. Deferrari, ed.

Columbia University Press for quotes from L. Thorndike's **University Life and Records in the Middle Ages.**

Cornell University Press, for quotes from M.L.W. Lainster's **Christianity and Pagan Culture in the Later Roman Empire.**

Crowell-Collier, New York, for quotes from A. Farrell's **The Jesuit Code of Liberal Education** and E. Fitzpatrick's **La Salle, Patron of All Teachers.**

William Eerdmans Publishing Company, Grand Rapids, Mi., for quotes from **A Select Library of Nicene and Post-Nicene Fathers.**

Harvard University Press for quotes from **Loeb Classical Library.**

National Council of Churches of Christ for quotes from the **Revised Standard New Testament.**

Oxford University Press for quotes from W. Jaeger's **Early Christianity and Greek Paideia** and R. Ruether's **Gregory of Nazianzus** and H. Danby's **Mishnah.**

Paulist/Newman Press, New York, for quotes from the **Ancient Christian Writers** series.

Random House, New York, for quotes from **Basic Writings of St. Thomas Aquinas,** A. Pegis, ed.

H. Regnery, Chicago, for quotes from **Thomas Aquinas, The Teacher, The Mind,** J. McGlynn, ed.

Russell and Russell, New York, for quotes from C.J.B. Gaskoin's **Alcuin**

Sheed and Ward, New York, for quotes from H. Marrou's **A History of Education in Antiquity,** J. Danielou's **Origen,** and L. Daly's **The Medieval University.**

SPCK, London, for quotes from W.D. Davies' **Paul and Rabbincal Judaism.**

World Publishing Company, New York, for quotes from C. Montefiore and H. Loewe's **A Rabbinical Anthology.**

Contents

Abbreviations

ACW   **Ancient Christian Writers, J. Quasten et al, eds. New York, Paulist/Newman.**

AF   **The Apostolic Fathers, R. Grant, ed., New York, Nelson.**

ANF   **The Ante-Nicene Fathers, A. Roberts and J. Donaldson, eds., New York, Scribners.**

DOB   **Dictionary of the Bible, J. McKenzie, New York, Crowell-Collier.**

FOC   **Fathers of the Church, R. Deferrari, ed., Washington, Catholic University Press.**

LCL   **Loeb Classical Library, Cambridge, Harvard University Press.**

NCE   **New Catholic Encyclopedia, New York, McGraw-Hill, 1967.**

NPNF   **A Select Library of the Nicene and Post-Nicene Fathers, Second Series, P. Schaff and H. Wade, eds., Grand Rapids, Eerdmans.**

PL,PG   **Patrologiae Cursus Completus, J-P. Migne, ed., Paris.**

SC   **Sources Chrétiennes, H. DeLubac and J. Danielou, eds., Paris, Cerf.**

LIST OF ILLUSTRATIONS

Introduction

RELIGIOUS education today is under fire as never before. In Roman Catholic tradition, the bishop's position as official teacher of the church is being challenged. Religious teachers, fed up with the problems of compulsory catechetics, are leaving their orders or going into more relevant social work. Financially plagued Christian schools are closing on all levels. Heavily taxed parents, unable to support one school system, let alone two, are questioning the value of religious education. Christian colleges, lacking church support, are being priced cut of existence by vast, tax-supported state schools.

Is religious education relevant today? Historically most advanced religions have been educatory, especially after they develop moral codes and sacred writings. And if they are not educatory, they are nothing at all. Both Judaism and Christianity are teaching religions. Beginning with the school of Jesus, splitting shortly into the schools of James, Paul, Matthew, John, etc., continuing through Justin, Hippolytus, Origen, Basil, the two Gregories, Augustine, Cassiodorus, Columban, Alcuin, Aquinas, Ignatius of Loyola, Angela Merici, John Baptist De La Salle, John Carroll and many others, the torah of Jesus has been taught and interpreted to each new generation. Each attempted to make the sacred and eternal truths relevant in the language of secular time, whether that be Hebrew, Aramaic, Greek, Latin, Neo-Platonism, Aristotle, Quintilian or whatever.

The languages and mores of today all but defy the religious teacher: existentialism, phenomenology, language analysis, process, Neo-Hegelianism, secularism, personalism, and the new electronic media. And the religious teacher tries harder to express the sacred truths in the new languages and zeitgeist philosophies and the new media, attempting to bridge the gap between the eternal and the transitory, the sacred and the profane.

There have been many fine sociological, psychological and

educational studies of religious teaching today, but perhaps a neglect of the essence of religious education and its relationship to secular teaching. How did we get where we are today with a vast system of religious schools, ranging from kindergarten to university? Do we need all this? What about the battle of the catechisms? And the relationship of the Christian teacher with his bishop? Who has the right to educate—church, state or parents?

We hope in this book to examine the Christian teacher, beginning with his prototype the Jewish rabbi, then proceeding from Jesus and Paul down to Ignatius of Loyola, John Baptist De La Salle and the modern scene. Perhaps in our search of Christian pedagogy we may find something of value to help our life situation today, for though he lives in different secular times, the Christian teacher is an existential replica of the Master. And as such, he must close the breach between the Rabbi Jesus and the modern student, seeking a common language of expressing the eternal truths to today's generation.

THE SCHOOL OF JESUS

1. **Third century synagogue at Capernaum. Jesus taught in its predecessor.**

1

WHO ARE THE GUARDIANS OF THE TOWN? THE TEACHERS OF THE BIBLE AND MISHNAH. (T.J. Hag 1, 7, f.76c)

THE TEACHING of ancient truths and their new interpretations to the present generation of disciples has always been an essential part of religion. Although we are interested primarily in the development of the Christian teacher, we should first see something of his predecessor and model, the Jewish rabbi.

One of the chief duties of the Jewish priesthood was teaching, but this was not the same as that practiced later on by rabbis. "They (Levites) shall teach Jacob thy ordinances and Israel thy Law" (Dt 33:10). Thus it is the duty of the Levites to teach customary laws (*mispatim*) to the people and to give them instructions and decisions (*torot*) of God according to his Covenant. From the eighth century to the exile the priests gave torah to the people (Hos 4:6; Dt 31:9,26; Jer 2:8; Ezk 7:26)—decisions of what is right or wrong, what is to be done in worship, ritual and the Sabbath observances, etc.[1]

By the time of Hosea (8:12) the priestly torah concerning the sacrifices is already written down. The Deuteronomic tradition has Moses entrusting the written law to priests, a corpus of divine directives and laws deriving from Yahweh's covenant with Israel (Dt 31:9). Torot of Dt 33:10 are accompanied by *mispatim* (customary laws). Yet these are not spot decisions made by the priests themselves and unrelated to the divine norm. No, the customary laws flow from and are dependent on the Covenant.

---

1. A. Cody, **A History of the Old Testament Priesthood**, Rome, PIB, 1969, pp. 116-17. This section depends on Cody.

This tradition of torah and mispat grows as new responses are given to problems of law, crime, ethics, ritual and morality. Originally the priestly responses may have been a simple yes-no oracle at the casting of lots, though later solutions were sought in the body of law and tradition. Cody writes:

> The torah giving of a later period is indeed a teaching function, but it consists of little more profound than handing down statements on the conformity or non-conformity of a given course of action with a given norm.[2]

But the proper teaching function in Israel fell not to the priest, but rather to the wise man, the *hakam*, who knew the torah and the traditions of the fathers. Although some wise men may have been priests, their teaching was based on their wisdom and not on their priesthood. This is an important point which we shall see later.

In a sense the prophets also taught their disciples and the people. But rather than reciting or explaining torah, they spoke directly through divine inspiration. "Thus speaks Yahweh."

A. SCRIBES & RABBIS

In the exile the teachings of Law and prophets were redacted and taught by priest-scribes. And just as Samuel instructed his followers, so Ezra, the priest-scribe taught his disciples torah. At least initially most scribes seem to have come from the levite class.

Of course, the father of the family traditionally instructed his sons in the Law and the prophets (Kid. 30 A), but this was augmented by the schools. Gradually the *bet ha-midrash*, became established in post-exilic Israel so that by the first century it was common alongside the synagogue *(bet ha-keneset) and* the primary school *(bet ha-sefer)*. The first *bet ha-midrash* of record was taught by Abtalion and Shemiah. One of their pupils

2. **Ibid.**, p. 118.

was young Hillel. The Shammaites and Hillelites argued whether the *bet ha-midrash* should be exclusively for the wise and well-born youths or for all. The Hellelites won and the *bet ha-midrash* was open to all. And the addition of 400 extra chairs earned the school the title of *yeshibah* (sitting, academy). Although some of scholars of the *bet ha-midrash* were married (Ber 17a), it seems that most were teen agers *(bahurim)*. Though usually associated with the synagogus, the *bet ha-midrash* ranked higher (Meg 26b, Ber 64a). By the year 70 AD there were 480 synagogues in Jerusalem, with primary schools for the study of Scripture and *batte ha-midrashot* for teaching law and tradition.

The academy was also called *bet torah*. Torah can mean either Law or teaching, illustrating the two-fold function of the academy, as a *yeshibah* or house of learning and also a sanhedrin or *bet din* (court) (R.H. 31a, b). And the rabbis were often elders of the sanhedrin, judging local cases, with their students sitting in front, observing.

The dual function of the academy is seen especially in Jerusalem where the Great Sanhedrin and the Great Bet ha-Midrash were held in conjunction in the temple hall. Paul and perhaps Jesus may have studied there. The disciples were able to learn the Law at first hand and their presence insured that the democratic process would be preserved in the courts. Leading scholars often became teachers in the academy and judges in the sanhedrin.

The zuggoth scholars oversaw the Jerusalem academy until 70 AD when it moved to Jabneh, where it continued to flourish as the leading court and school in Judaism. But even it is not the greatest, for the highest school of all is the heavenly academy. And those who faithfully attend the earthly *bet ha-midrash* will be welcome in the next world where God himself teaches righteousness.

The *bet ha-midrash* at Jabneh was called "The Vineyard" either because it was located in a vineyard, or because it was built in a semi-circle shape as a vineyard (Ket 4, 6). At any rate, this became the common name of the *bet ha-midrash*. "Let us get up early to the vineyards" (Song of Songs 7, 12). An interesting parable was told by R. Zera at the funeral of R. Abin, a young scholar who had been a rabbi only eight years.

A king had a vineyard in which he employed many laborers, one of whom demonstrated special aptitude and skill. What did the king do? He took this laborer from his work, and strolled through the garden conversing with him. When the laborers came for their wages in the evening, the skillful laborer also appeared among them and he received a full day's wages from the king. The other laborers were angry at this and protested: 'We have toiled the whole day, while this man has worked but two hours. Why does the king give him the full wage, even as to us?' The king said to them: 'Why are you angry? Through his skill he has done in two hours more than you have done all day.' So it is with R. Abin ben Hiyya. In the 28 years of his life he has attained more in the Torah than the others attain in 100 years (Yer Ber 2:8).

Let us now see something more of the Jewish teacher. By New Testament times, the scribes, knowledgeable in Law and wisdom, were often known as teachers or rabbis. Most were Pharisees. Rabbi (my master) is a typical title of respect of the disciple for his master. Presidents of the Great Sanhedrin as Gamaliel I, Johanan be Zakkai were called Rabban. Rabbis of the Talmud were not like modern rabbi-ministers who have taken on a lot of the trappings and functions of contemporary clergy, but they were essentially teachers of Torah and Mishnah to their disciples and to the community. They could also be a community official as the *nasi, ab bet din,* or local judge, as we have seen. Gradually because of their superior knowledge of the Law, the rabbis replaced the elders in the ruling and judging sanhedrins. In general, though, it seems that the rabbis tried to avoid office, for when he assumes the robe of office (tallit), he assumes the burdens of the community (Exod R. 27:9).

Yuda Nesiah, exilarch of Babylonia (c.200, AD), sent Rabbis Hiyya, Assi, and Ammi to the cities of Israel to teach Torah and Mishnah. But when they came to a city and found no rabbis, they called for the elder-guardians. When the presbyters arrived, the Rabbis asked, "Are these the guardians of the town? They are its destroyers." Then the people asked who the real guardians were. They answered, "The teachers of the Bible and the Mishnah. For unless the Lord guard the city, the watchman wakes but in vain" (T.J. Hag. I, 7, f76c; Pes. K. 15, 120b-121a). The elder guardians are more negative, preserving the laws of the city against violation, while the rabbis are positive-teaching proper moral conduct which should make the work of the guardians unnecessary.[3]

In general, the rabbis were self-supporting, but had tax privileges and exemptions from public works. In earlier times the rabbi worked at his trade for 1/3 of the day, while studying torah the rest. Later rabbis worked more and studied less. But the rabbis felt strongly that work and study should go hand in hand. For example, Rabban Gamaliel III:

> Excellent is the study of the Law together with worldly occupation, for toil in them both puts sin out of mind. But all study of the Law without (worldly) labor comes to naught at the last and brings sin in its train. And let all that labor with the congregation labor with them for the sake of heaven for the merit of the fathers supports them and their righteousness endures forever (Ab 2:2).

The rabbis were often impressive figures, dressed in long white robes and gold-trimmed cloaks. And they were honored by their disciples even more than their own parents (Kid. 32b; ab 6:3).

The rabbi or *hakam* lectured to his *talmidim* in the *bet ha-midrash* or *yeshibah*. He rarely spoke in public except to explain the laws and customs before a great feast. The rabbi, then, is neither priest nor administrator, but primarily a teacher and judge, explaining Torah in the schools, synagogues and san-hedrins. Some Jewish sects had special instructors as the Essene mebaqqer, teaching the sectaries the Law and the rules of the community, separating the sons of light from the sons of darkness (SR 9:12-26).

Besides the scholarly rabbi teaching in the *bet ha-midrash*, there was the preacher rabbi, the *maggid* or *haggadist*, who taught the multitudes, answering their questions in haggadic manner. An example of this may be seen in the Passover haggadah told in answer to the questions of the youngest. Sometimes the *maggid* began with a passage from Scriptures *(petibah)* (Sotah 41A) Because of the popular nature of his discourse, the *maggid* often

3. See C. Montefiore and H. Loewe, **A Rabbinical Anthology,** Cleveland, World, 1963. p. 138. In general, rabbinical quotes are from Montefiore and H. Danby's **The Mishnah,** Oxford, 1967 and **Soncino, Babylonian Talmud,** London.

attracted large crowds in contrast to the small band of students who surrounded the scholarly *dashan* to learn halakah. Some rabbis, e.g. R. Jeshuah, R. Meir and R. Isaac combined the qualities of both.

B.   TORAH

The chief mission of the Jewish rabbis is to study, teach and preserve the Torah. The Torah, as its author, is eternal, pre-existing not only Moses and Abraham, but even the creation of the world (Zeb 116a). Moses entrusted the Torah to Joshua and the Elders who passed it down through the prophets and the Great Synagogue to the Zuggoth scholars. The rabbis' task is to judge deliberately, teach disciples and build a fence around the Torah (Ab 1:1). But the fence is not to make the Torah monolithic, rather to preserve it from harm and keep it open for contemplation. More specifically, the fence or hedge is the oral torah of the rabbis,—warnings, applications, interpretations in order to make the Law more relevant. But the fence should never overshadow that which it guards, lest it fall in and crush it (Ab. R.N. [Vers II] 1:2a).

Study of the Torah increased greatly with the destruction of the temple, first in the exile, then at a much greater pace after the 68 and 138 AD millennial catastrophies. Now the Law replaces the temple as a vehicle of sacrifice and atonement. "When the temple is not there, what shall atone for you? Busy yourselves with the words of the Law, for they are the equivalent of sacrifices and they will atone for you" (Tan. B. Ahare Mot. 35a).

Learned scholars of the Law, the Haberim, are often contrasted with the ignorant Am ha-Aretz, although at a later date the Haberim did not hesitate to take members from the Am ha-Aretz.

Words pertaining to study and teaching dominate Jewish thought. For example, torah (teaching, law), haber (companion or colleague), rabbi (teacher), hakam (wise man), mishnah (repetition), gemara (completion), tanna (teacher), amora (speaker), talmud, (teaching, learning), yeshibah (academy), and the most important root LMD which can mean either study or teaching showing the close interrelationship between the two.

Since Torah is God's teaching, man's highest possible occupation is studying it. Thus it must take precedence over all other occupations. Poverty and humiliations are little to endure in order to study Torah. For example, R. Nehorai put aside all worldly occupations to teach his son Torah. Other vocations man cannot follow when he is old, "But the Law keeps a man from evil in his youth and gives him an assured outlook in his old age" (Kid 4:14). One must be willing to undergo pain and even death for the Torah (Ber 63b).

Although in general Jewish tradition frowned on celibacy as against Genesis and required the teacher of children to be married (Kid 4:13), study of the Torah took precedence even over marriage and the family. Thus R. Simon b. Azzai, a second century tanna, seems to have been celibate, answering taunts with "What shall I do? My heart desires Torah; let the world be maintained by others" (Yeb 63b). Other rabbis left their families for extended periods of study in the academy. "Disciples (of the Sages) may continue for thirty days against the will (of their wives) while they occupy themselves in the study of the Law" (Ket 5:6). Indeed Akiba stayed away from his wife and family for 24 years. And R. Samuel b. Ammi said, "If a man does not show himself cruel towards himself, his children and his household as a raven (to its young) he does not succeed in acquiring Torah" (Lev. R. 19:1).

Moreover, the disciples should not be troubled with family problems (Kid 29b).

> Our rabbis taught: if one has to study Torah and to marry a wife, he should first study and then marry. But if he cannot (live) without a wife, he should first marry and then study. Rab Judah said in Samuel's name: The Halachah is: (A man) first marries and then studies. R. Johanan said: (with) a millstone around the neck, shall one study Torah! Yet they do not differ: the one refers to ourselves (Babylonians); the other to them (Palestinians).

It would seem that while the young local scholars remained single, those who came from abroad first married and provided for a family before leaving to study in the Palestinian schools.

Rabbinical marriage to the Torah, or perhaps more accurately to the Shekinah, may mirror that of Moses and the continence of the priests before the Shekinah in the temple. Later Christian trends in continence and celibacy may be descendents of rabbinical marriage to the Torah.

Torah study even took precedence over prayer and charitable works, provided there were others available to perform them (Sab 10a).

But is Torah that great? Is not the priest or the king greater than the scholar? The Torah is greater for it is acquired by 48 qualifications whereas only 30 are required for royalty and 24 for priests. The scholar must be practiced in: audible study, distinct pronunciation, discernment of heart, awe, reverence, meekness, cheerfulness, ministering to the sages, attaching oneself to colleagues, discussion with disciples, sedateness, knowledge of the scriptures and mishnah, moderation, resignation, love, no boasting, bearing others' yokes, "by being composed in one's study, by asking and answering, hearing and adding thereto, by learning with the object of teaching, and by learning with the object of practicing, by making one's master wiser, fixing attention upon his discourse, and reporting a thing in the name of him who said it" (Ab 6:6).

These are the rules which guided the rabbis and their disciples in acquiring Torah. Notice the rapport between the rabbi and his talmidim and the collegiality of the haburah. The scholar ministers to the sages, attaching himself to his colleagues and discussing with his fellow disciples. Torah is not gained in isolation but with the haberim. No man can be a judge in his own case, but with the help of others he can progress (Ber 63b). Even prominent rabbis learned much by discussing with their talmidim (Ta'an 7a). When two haberim study Torah together, the Shekinah rests between them (Aboth 3:3). The colleges of haberim studying Torah day and night, keeping the Law strictly, some remaining continent while in academy, remind one of the collegiality of the Qumran sect and later Christian monks.

But it is not enough to study Torah, although this is a most worthy thing. No, one must also teach it to others. "If a man teaches the son of his fellow student the Torah, the scripture accounts it to him as if he had created him" (Sanh 99b). Thus the rabbi is sometimes called Ab (Father or Source) (Pirke Aboth; Mt 23:8-12).

R. Johanan said "He who learns Torah and does not teach it, is like a myrtle in the desert" (R.H. 23a).

In general, the rabbis had a good rapport with their disciples. The give and take of their schools typified LMD.

As a little wood can set light a great tree, so young pupils sharpen the wits of great scholars. Hence said R. Hanina: "Much Torah have I learned from my teachers, more from my colleagues, but from my students most of all" (Ta'an 7a).

As today, all kinds of disciples came to study under the rabbi. They are described graphically in Pirke Aboth (5:12, 14, 15).

There are four types of disciple: swift to hear and swift to lose—his gain its cancelled by his loss; slow to learn and slow to lose—his loss is cancelled by his gain; swift to hear and slow to lose—this is a happy lot; slow to hear and swift to lose—this is an evil lot . . .
There are four types among them that frequent the House of Study: he that goes and does not practice—he has the reward of his going; he that practices but does not go—he has the reward of his practicing; he that goes and also practices—he is a saintly man; he that neither goes nor practices—he is a wicked man.
There are four types among them that sit in the presence of the Sages: the sponge, the funnel, the strainer, and the sifter. "The sponge"—which takes in at this end and lets out at the other; "the strainer"—which lets out the wine and collects the lees; "the sifter"—which extracts the coarsely-ground flour and collects the fine flour.

The rabbis taught their disciples not only by word, but also by example. Thus they were in a sense living torahs, humble, chaste, with mutual honor between students and teachers.

A teacher should hold his pupil as dear as he holds himself. The honor of a fellow student should be as precious to a man as the honor of his master, and the honor of his master should be as precious to a man as the fear of heaven. (Mek 2, Amalek, Beshallah 1, p. 178)

The scholars in their intense study and zeal for the Law were tempted beyond their strength by the yetzer ha-ra (evil inclin-aation). Perhaps their continence escalated their appetites. For example, R. Hiyya b. Ashi who thought that he fell when tempted by a courtesan (actually it was his wife in disguise), went home and sat in the oven (Kid 81b).

Modesty and humility were the hardest virtues for a scholar. *Scientia inflat.* But the true scholar is recognized by his humility.

> One coin in a bottle rattles; a bottle full of coins makes no sound. So the scholar who is the son of a scholar is modest; the scholar who is the son of an Am he-Aretz trumpets his konwledge around (Bab M. 85b).

Wisdom and goodness must be coupled. If there was anything the Pharisaic scholars feared it was hypocrisy. "A disciple of the wise whose inside is not as his outside, is no disciple of the wise; he is an abomination" (Yoma 72b). The Talmud draws the types of Pharisees graphically from the "shoulder Pharisee" carrying his good deeds on his shoulder for all to see to the "bruised Pharisee" who cracks his head on a wall to avoid looking at a woman, to the "God-loving Pharisee" who resembles Abraham.[4]

The scholar's conduct should reflect his wisdom, especially concerning money, drinking, temper, dress and speech. "Four things are unseemly for a scholar: to walk out at night, to smell of scent in the street, to be among the last to enter the synagogue, to dally much with the Amme ha-Aretz". He should be quiet and proper in eating, drinking, bathing, anointing, tying his shoes, gait, dress, voice and charity (Der. Er. Z. 5, 2, 3; 6, 1; 7, 2). Moreover, he should be modest, humble, eager and bright, submissive, beloved, gentle, God-fearing, not taking pleasure in the things of the world. Seated at the feet of the wise, he should ask and answer properly (Der. Er. 2, 1, 1).

The rabbi must teach Torah by words and example. But the teaching of children is the most important thing. Even in those days adult education was seen to be a contradiction in terms. But with those who are still in their formative years, education is of prime importance. Thus the great Metatron, high angel of God, sometimes identified with Logos, Enoch or the Great Scribe, teaches Torah to the children (Ab. Zar. 3b). Those who

---

4. Montefiore and Loewe, **op. cit.**, pp. 487-88.

faithfully teach scripture and mishnah to children will sit at God's right hand (Pes. K. 180a).

The children are God's anointed and their teachers are like gardens flourishing by the river side (Tan. D. B. El p. 116) and the pupils are the blossoming flowers (Pes. R. 29b). The Shekinah accompanies them (Lam. R. 1, 33 on 1:6). Boys should be sent to school at the age of 6 to 7. There should be one teacher for every 25 boys and both knowledge and exactness should be considered in their hiring (Bab. B. 21a). Mothers acquire merit by sending their children to learn Torah in the synagogues and their husbands to study in the schools of the rabbis (Ber 17a).

C. INTERPRETATION

What method did the rabbis use in their teaching? One of the chief means was a probing (midrash) of the original text of the Torah to find its application for the day. This could be either halakah when a law was involved or haggadah when the non legal aspects of tradition were being discussed. Sometimes midrash defined more precisely the biblical law. Or if there were no law, a new one might be drawn up to fit the present circumstances, for example; the institution of the synagogues, the feast of Hanukkah, and the rabbinical tradition itself.

Whereas collections of haggadah were made early, the writing down of halakah was not allowed. Why not? R. Johanan responds: "The writing down of halakot is equal to the burning of the Torah" (Temurah 14b). It would seem that any rival collection of law would lessen the value of the original Torah given by the Lord to Moses. Thus a clear distinction was kept between the written Torah of God and the oral torah of man. Also some of the Rabbis felt that the writing down of laws and blessings would destroy their spontaneity and stop their evolution. As Loewe writes:[5]

The leader in prayer had certain subjects assigned to him to be al-

5. Ibid., p. 131.

luded to in a certain order. The phrasing was, within certain limits, left to him. Similarly, the codification of law was held to imperil the continuance of living and expanding law.

The law code was never meant to be a monolithic seal on all future developments.

Although haggadah was valued by the rabbis as a teaching device which swayed the hearts of the simple people, it never attained the importance or the binding force of the halakah. By the beginning of the second century midrashic books began to be edited in the Academy at Jabneh: Mekilta (Exodus), Sifra (Leviticus), Sifre (Numbers and Deuteronomy).

As Judaism spread throughout the diaspora and as Hebrew became more of a liturgical language since Aramaic was the official language of the Persian empire, translations, targumim, became an important part of rabbinical teaching. And these were not just literal translations but rather attempts by the Jews of every generation to interpret scriptures, applying them to their own situation. This gave rise to many degrees of interpretation. For example, Philo's allegories, and the retelling of the ancient stories with new embroidering added. Embroidery was one of the principal methods of haggadic midrash. As Bowker points out[6] the Dead Sea Scrolls give many examples of scriptural exegesis of the time.

> The methods found in the Scrolls include verse by verse commentary (e.g. 1QpHab, 4QpNah); extension of scripture by producing works purporting to come from biblical figures (e.g. Enoch, Moses, the Twelve Patriarchs); retelling of a biblical narrative (e.g. Jubilees, the Genesis Apocryphon); imitation of scripture, by producing works modeled on accepted scriptural books (e.g. 1QH, The Psalms of Joshua, the Prayer of Nabonidus); anthologising scripture, by collecting related passages and linking them together with brief notes and comments (e.g. 4QTest, the Messianic Anthology); and the application of the Mosaic law to contemporary situations (e.g. the Commentary on Biblical Laws).

All these methods of making the ancient scriptures relevant were

6. Bowker, **The Targums and Rabbinic Literature**, Cambridge, 1969, p. 6.

found not only at Qumran but throughout Judaism. As Bowker points out[7], the task of interpretation was not so much to point out what Judaism was in olden times, not what it had been, but what it was to become. Obviously the answers differed with different schools of thought. Although the Pharisaic-Rabbinic interpretation would eventually dominate, among the rabbis themselves there were disagreements.

The translator or methurgeman in the synagogue followed the Hebrew reader, who read one verse at a time, and from the prophets not more than three. The main job of the methurgeman was to make the text meaningful to the congregation. Thus the Targums lie half-way between translations and a free telling of the biblical story, interpreting it to make sense to his hearers. The written Targums: Onkelos, Pseudo-Jonathan, and Fragment Targum summarize the traditional and most widely accepted interpretations of the scriptures.

Besides Midrash and Targum, another product of rabbinical teaching is the Mishnah (shanah—repeat or study), edited by Judah the Prince (3c), but based on other collections, some going back to the first century. The Mishnah is divided into six main topical Sederim covering: agriculture and prayer, festivals, women and marriage and family, injuries, holy things, and cleanliness.

The Mishnah was at first repeated and handed down orally by the disciples of the rabbis. The Aramaic of shanah is tana. Hence the tannaim who taught from 10-220 A.D., ending in the final redaction of the Mishnah by Judah the Prince. Principal rabbinical schools were at Jerusalem, then Jabneh (68-), Sikhnin (135-). Other schools were at Usha, Tiberias, Sepporis, etc. Since most mishnoth were short, supplementary comments were required (Tosefta).[8]

About 220 the rabbinical center of learning shifted to Babylon where an academy was founded by Abba Areka, a disciple of Judah the Prince at Sura on the Eupretes. Other academies were

---

7. **Ibid.**, p. 8.
8. However, the Tosefta may be earlier than Mishnah in form and layout. See Bowker, **op. cit.**, p. 63.

also founded where Mishnah was studied by the Amoraim or speakers, Babylonian teachers who completed the Mishnah by writing the Gemara, both together forming the Talmud (Teaching, study). There are two versions of the Talmud, the Palestinian or Jerusalem edited by the Tiberias rabbis (3-5c) and the Babylonian (4-5c).

Whereas the Palestinian teachers were called Rabbi, the Babylonians were called Rab or Mar. Babylonian teachers had more authority and their decisions bore more weight because Babylonian Jews lived in more homogeneous groups and were allowed more autonomy than those in Palestine under the severe Roman rule.

The fifth century marks the end of the era of great teachers with the decline of the Jewish community in Palestine and the abolition of the office of patriarch. Likewise the persecution of the Jewish communities in Babylon in the fifth century by the Sassanian kings brought an end to the rabbinical schools there.

The aim of all rabbinical studies, whether Midrash, Targum or Mishnah[9] was to interpret scripture for each succeeding generation. The Bible itself sanctions this (Dt 17:8-12). An abundance of forms is found in rabbinical literature, running the gamut from embroidery, to miracle stories, legends, parables, wisdom sayings, etc., all used to help make the Jewish traditions more interesting and more relevant for the disciples and common people. Constantly examples are drawn from their daily lives, whether from the household, the fields, trades, etc.

Past traditions had shown that the Law is not absolute, but must be modified or even suspended if the need arose. Ultimately the authority to guide life cannot be a written text, but the living interpreter of the texts.[10] When Moses had requested absolute truths on which to build tradition, the Lord answered, "There are no pre-existent final truths in doctrine and law; the truth is the considered judgment of the majority of authoritative interpreters in every generation" (Sanh. Yer. 4:2). This

---

9. Mishnah texts are not necessarily connected with Scripture.
10. See R. Ben Zion Bokser, **Wisdom of the Talmud**, New York, Citadel, 1962, p. 7.

has been the prime function of religious and ethical teachers down through the millennia, namely, not a mere repetition of ancient truths, but the new authoritative interpretation for each successive generation.

Naturally different schools of interpretation arose from the different rabbis and it was the job of the Talmud to try to correlate these. Two famous rabbinical schools were those of Hillel and Shammai. Also there were often widely divergent views between the Pharisees, Sadducees, Essenes, Baptists, Zealots, etc. It was this basic Jewish pluralism that allowed the followers of the Christian Way to remain within the fold of Judaism until the second century when Christianity became largely a Gentile religion.

But did not the constant arguing (rab) of the rabbis confuse the people? R. Berechiah compares their parries to a ball tossed about by girls at play. "So it is when the sages enter the house of study, and are occupied with the Law. One says its meaning is this, and another says its meaning is that. One gives such an opinion, his fellow a different one" (Pes. R. 8a). But all opinions ultimately come from one shepherd, Moses, who received the Torah from God. Sometimes the Bat Kol (heavenly voice) corroborated a rabbi's opinion (Bab. M. 59b; Ta'an 25b).

Controversies, rabbinical or otherwise, tend to perdure simply because they usually involve basic human paradoxes such as the problem of evil. But controversy has its purpose.

> The truth unchallenged and not revitalized by arguments tends to lose its influence. The most fecund controversy is the conflict between the Old and the New. It will endure till Elijah's coming, to turn the hearts of children to the fathers. Until he comes, the struggle must continue, the effort to reconcile progress and tradition. Only so can the equipoise be kept. Otherwise, 'The earth will be smitten with the curse' of indifference. 'These and those are each, the words of the living God' ('Erub. 13b)[11]

But it would seem that despite its controversies, or perhaps because of its controversies, the study of Torah is sufficient and

---

11. Montefiore and Loewe, op. cit., p. 656.

that, therefore, there is no need of Gentile learning. This was a problem particularly in the diaspora where Jewish and Hellenist, Babylonian or Egyptian cultures confronted each other. Syncretism was inevitable. The Jews feared Hellenization as apostasy after their experiences under Antiochus Epiphanes. The Gemara seems more broad-minded about foreign learning and later rabbis such as Judah the Prince seemed more tolerant of Greek (Bab. K. 83a). The synthesis of Jewish traditions with foreign elements by men like Philo and Maimonides represents a further interpretation and adaptation of the Torah which is at bottom the basis of Talmudic study.

The Jewish traditions of study, learning and teaching, stretching almost 900 years from Ezra to the final redaction of the Talmud could not but have an impact on the early Christian Jewish teachers, in particular its founding rabbi, Joshua b. Jose, whose talmud, interpreting the Torah in his own inspired manner, formed the basis of the new religion called Christianity.

2

RABBI, WE KNOW THAT YOU ARE TRUE, AND TEACH THE WAY OF GOD TRUTHFULLY, AND CARE FOR NO MEN: FOR YOU DO NOT REGARD THE POSITION OF MEN (Mt 22:16)

JESHUA B. JOSE (Jesus son of Joseph) was a first century Galilean rabbi whose teachings, handed down by his talmidim, are recorded in the Christian gospels. What was his relationship with contemporary Judaism? How well known was he? What training did he have in the Torah? These and other questions pertain to the historical Jesus. We can gain some knowledge of Jesus and his teachings from the gospels, although they are usually linked with interpretations to fit the life situation of the early church.

A   EARLY LIFE OF JESUS

Jesus probably studied in the synagogue grammar school from his sixth to thirteenth year, the year of his bar mitzvah, as his confreres. We know very little of his early years except for an isolated discussion with the rabbis at the temple school in Jerusalem. When his parents found him there, listening and asking questions, he responded that they should have known where to find him. "Did you not know that I must be in my Father's house?" (Lk 2:49). Although some might interpret his answer as a little impudent, Jesus may be stressing the importance of Torah in his Father's house over all else, even over his parents. It was at the age of thirteen, or sometimes a year or two later that the Jewish boy went to the bet ha-midrash, sometimes even forsaking his family for the study of the Torah. In a real sense the rabbis are considered his new parents, superior to his natural mother and father. (Kid 32b; ABG:3).

Since we have little information about Jesus' hidden life, we might conjecture that he may have continued his studies with the Jerusalem rabbis as Paul did. In fact, ancient Talmudic tradition (B. Sanh. 107b; B. Scot. 47a) has Jesus studying under R. Joshua B. Perahyah, leading Pharisee and President of the Sanhedrin at the time of John Hyrcanus, who drove Joshua out of office.

The story in Sanhedrin 107b illustrates the rabbinical saying "Ever let the left hand repel and the right hand invite, not like Elisha who repulsed Gehazi with both hands and not like R. Joshua B. Perhayah who repulsed Jesus (The Nazarene) with both hands." It seems that Rabbi Joshua fled the wrath of John Hyrcanus to Egypt with his disciple Jesus. There he excommunicated Jesus for improper conduct. At length he seemed willing to take him back, but Jesus misunderstood. Then seeing Jesus in idolatry, R. Joshua warned him—"Repent." Jesus replied: "Thus I have received from thee, that every one who sins and causes the multitude to sin, they give him not the chance to repent." And a teacher has said, "Jesus the Nazarene practiced magic and led astray and deceived Israel."

Perhaps there was a tradition that Jesus studied under the Pharisaic rabbis, some of whom may have belonged to the school of Joshua B. Perahyah, but rejected some of their teachings, leading the people astray. We know that the Pharisees accused Jesus of this in the gospels. The anachronism of Jesus studying under Joshua, several generations earlier, is not too unusual for Talmudic chronology.[1] Wherever Jesus studied, it was most likely not at a *bet ha-midrash* near home (Mk 6:2ff; Mt 13:54ff; Jn 7:15).

In the gospels we find Jesus as a disciple of John in the Jordan Valley, where John directed a charismatic eschatological

---

1. Editions of the Talmud after the 16th century edited out the passage about Joshua and Jesus. See L. Laible and G. Dalman, **Jesus Christ in the Talmud, Midrash and Zohar**, Cambridge, 1893, p. 41; R. I. Herford, **Christianity in Talmud and Midrash**, Clifton, N.J., Reference Book Publishers, 1966, pp. 50ff.; **Pirke Aboth, The Ethics of the Talmud**, New York, 1966, p. 27.

community. John was a prophet-teacher whose teachings (Is 40:3) reflect the Qumran monks. Although there is no reference to John, or to Jesus, in modern rabbinical literature, John may have been in earlier editions as Jesus was. Moreover, Josephus has a lot of respect for him (Ant. 18, 5, 2). John, as many people of his time, felt that the messianic age was near. In preparation he exhorted the people to virtue, justice, piety, and baptism as a sign of repentance. Both John and the Pharisees joined repentance with the kingdom.

When John was imprisoned by Herod, Jesus proceeded North to Galilee with some of John's disciples, preaching the message of repentance. "The time is fulfilled, the kingdom of God is at hand; repent and believe in the good news" (Mk 1:14-15). Gathering more disciples, he began to teach.

The process of becoming a rabbi in Palestine in the first century is rather hazy, but may have involved a recognition of the disciple's knowledge by some external sign on the part of his master, for example, the laying on of hands *(semikah)* (Yer. Sanh. 19a). Did not John recognize Jesus' superiority in the Law, designate him as the expected Messiah, and delegate him to carry on his preaching of the approaching kingdom? There are times in the gospels when John is unsure of Jesus' mission (Mt 11:2-6; Lk 7:18-23), and not all of his disciples followed Jesus (Mk 2:18; Acts 18:25 19:3). Also it would seem that the Jews did not associate John with Jesus (Origen, *Contra Celsum* 1:48; Josephus, *Ant.* 18, 5, 2).

B. TEACHING

Whatever Jesus' relationship to John the Baptist, he is a teacher in his own right. But was he a Torah scholar in charge of a bet ha-midrash, dedicated to turning out experts in the Law? Certainly many admitted his superiority in the Law. And his disciples, as most Jewish laymen of the time knew Torah from their primary school study. They recognized Jesus as a rabbi of superior knowledge and leadership, not so much as a bet ha-midrash scholar, but rather as a wandering maggid preacher.

Jesus taught throughout Palestine, although centering his

apostolate in Galilee. His school was not just a closed ring of disciples, but also attracted the laity: the Am ha-Aretz, trades-men, fishermen, tax-collectors, housewives, etc. He preached not only in the synagogues, but in the open, as a maggid. Jesus is frequently described as preaching, proclaiming *(kēryssien)* (Mk 1:38; Lk 4:18, etc). The *kēryz* (KRZ) was not unknown in Jewish tradition. Sometimes he is the herald of the bet din, proclaiming rabbinical decisions to the people. Other times he is the amora or meturgeman, repeating and explaining the rabbi's words to the people in the synagogue.

Kērussien can also mean to preach and, indeed Jerome and Luther usually translate it this way. It is contrasted with *didas-kein,* the exposition of scriptures in the synagogue or bet ha-midrash. *Kéryssien* can be for sinners, for the Am he-Aretz in the streets, byways and fields. Jesus seemed to combine the preaching of the *kēryx,* "The kingdom of heaven is here" with the haggadah of the maggid and is less like the scholarly dashan of the bet ha-midrash, although at times he showed the character-istics of both, mixing haggadah and halakah.

Following rabbinical tradition, Jesus demanded no money for his teaching, but was supported by his own work and that of his disciples, plus the aid and hospitality of friends. This is why we find him frequently with his disciples fishing, plucking grain, visiting in the homes of friends. Although the gospel does not show Jesus practicing his trade of artisan after the beginning of his public life, it would fit the tradition if he continued to work while teaching.

Of course, Jesus taught the Law, and he taught in the rab-binical manner using parables, legends, wisdom sayings. His main purpose paralleled that of the rabbis, namely, to make the Law relevant to his hearers by applying the homey haggadah of the good shepherd or the lost groat.

He discussed many of the problems of their daily lives: mar-riage, divorce, clean and unclean, Sabbath, etc. It is possible that Jesus' disciples memorized some of his sayings much the same way that the disciples of the other rabbis did. Thus an abundance of his quotes come up in early Christian literature. Collections of these could have been made, for example, the

Sermon on the Mount. But as Davies points out[2], the scriptural exegesis in the New Testament differs from that of the rabbis in that parts of the Old Testament are applied to the life of Jesus. If there was an anthology of Messianic quotes among the Essenes, which seems highly probable, these Old Testament state-ments and prophecies may well have been applied to Jesus by his followers. So the constant refrain in the gospels "As it was written" or "In order that the Scriptures might be fulfilled."

Jesus had numerous exchanges with the Pharisaic scholars. But this is in the best of rabbinical tradition. Two Jews, two views. In many ways he took a more lenient side, especially concerning the rigid purification rules of the haberim. Most of Jesus' audience may have been from the Am ha-Aretz, the simple people of the land, who were turned off at the elaborate regulations of the Pharisees. Though the Pharisees were concerned with making the Law relevant for the common people, their very insistence on the weighty agrarian and purity laws and their fear of con-tact with the Am ha-Aretz widened the split between the two groups.

As Moore comments[3] every sect has its peculiarities and special practices and because of these considers itself superior to the others.

> Worse than this displacement of values by emphasis on the different peculiarities is the self-complacency of the members of such a party or association, and the self-righteousness that comes of believing that their pecularities of doctrine or practice make them singularly well-pleasing to God. With this goes censoriousness towards outsiders, which often presumes to voice the disapprobation of God.

The Pharisees seem to have had some of this superiority, even placing their study over or prior to the performing of good deeds.

Jesus challenged this superiority complex of the Pharisees as many of them did themselves. As Montefiore writes,[4] Jesus

2. W. D. Davies, **Sermon on the Mount**, Cambridge, 1966, p. 132.
3. **Judaism in the First Centuries of the Christian Era**, Cambridge, Mass., 1927-30, vol. 2, pp. 160-61.
4. Montefiore and Loewe, **op. cit.**, p. 484.

broke away from the Pharisaic tradition of keeping aloof from the non-observers, placing his priorities on seeking out sinners, healing, consoling, etc.

The Pharisaic haber spent most of his time in the Bet ha-Midrash, studying Torah, though he would serve on the local sanhedrin or administer relief to the poor. Jesus, on the other hand, taught, at least in the beginning, in the synagogue itself. It would seem that any qualified male could read or even teach in the synagogue. The archisynagogue would call upon a male member of the congregation to read and/or interpret the passage. Sometimes one would read while another would explain.

For example, at Nazareth Jesus was given the book of Isaiah to read:

> The Spirit of the Lord is upon me, because he has anointed me to preach good news to the poor. He has sent me to proclaim release to the captives and recovering of sight to the blind, to set at liberty those who are oppressed, to proclaim the acceptable year of the Lord. (Is 61:1-2)

As customary Jesus sat down to explain the passage. "Today this scripture has been fulfilled in your hearing" (Lk 4:21). But he was not received in his own country and they even threatened him with death. Increasing hostility of his enemies forced Jesus to teach in more out of the way places, such as Caesarea Philipi, and Transjordan. "The crowds gathered to him again; and again, as his custom was, he taught them" (Mk 10:1).

How did he teach?

> And they went to Capernaum and immediately on the sabbath he entered the synagogue and taught, and they were astonished at this teaching. For he taught them as one having authority and not as one of the scribes (Mk 1:21-22).

Maly[5] compares the authority *(exousia)* of Jesus with that of the rabbi *(resut)* to impose a binding decision, underlining the two-fold rabbinical function of teaching and judging. Jesus'

---

5. **Jerome Biblical Commentary**, Englewood Cliffs, Prentice Hall, 1968, 42:13.

authority seems even on a higher level for it comes from the Father (Jn 8:26, 29; 14:26).

Jesus not only taught and judged, he also healed. Historically teaching and healing have always gone together. The teacher is basically a healer and vice versa. The title doctor was and is used of both teachers and healers. The rabbis were teacher-judges, but also health officers of the community making sure the health laws and purification rules were observed. The Talmud gives many examples of rabbis healing the sick. Jesus healed many *(therapeuein)* and he passed on this power to his disciples, along with that of teaching and judging (Mt 10:8; Lk 10:9; Jas 5:14-15).

But let us get back to the teaching of Jesus. There is an interesting contrast between the earlier, simple teachings of Jesus and Hillel and later rabbinic scholasticism with its sophistication and precedent citations. Certainly Jesus, as Hillel, uses Scripture, but at this time there is not yet a mishnaic tradition to quote. Jesus taught independently, as most of the rabbis did. He followed neither of the two main rabbinical schools of the time, namely, those of Hillel and Shammai, though he sometimes leaned towards the latter (Mt 19:9). A good example of Jesus' authority and independence is the "I say" quotes (Mt 5:21-).

> You have heard that it was said to the men of old, "You shall not kill; and whoever kills shall be liable to judgment." But I say to you that every one who is angry with his brother is liable to judgment. Whoever insults his brother shall be liable to the council . . . (Mt 5:21-22).

Jesus is not abrogating the Law, but in good rabbinical tradition explaining it, applying it, expanding it, specifying it, fulfilling it. The Law is imperfect and unfinished. And Jesus is trying to bring it to completion.

Jesus, as some of the other rabbis, taught in parable form *(mashal)*, and, indeed, this is the only way one can teach simple people, leading from the known to the unknown. Some parables are found in the Old Testament (e.g. 2 Sam 12:1-14; Ezk 19:10-14). Jesus' and maggid parables usually answer a question by a disciple, using something familiar to draw out a comparison.

Gospel parables include stories such as the Prodigal Son and similes "The kingdom of heaven is like a field."

Many feel that the church adapted the parables of Jesus applying them allegorically to her life situation. For example, in Mark 4:1-20, the parable of the sower (Mk 4:1-9) probably reflects the original words of Jesus, while 4:10-20 is the interpretation of an early Christian homilist, comparing the seeds to Christians who have been tempted by Satan, the shallow and rootless who fall in persecution, those choked by worldly desires, and finally those who hear the word and accept it.

Often when the parables were retold in the early church, details were changed to make them more relevant. For example, types of houses, fields, agriculture, artisans described would fit better into the hearers' background, whether Hellenist, Roman, etc. This type of adaptation is, of course, the essence of good teaching and must be a constant process to keep the parable relevant. For if his purpose is to lead the hearer from the known to the unknown, the teacher cannot start with an example unknown to his disciple. Some parables were abbreviated, eliminating irrelevant material for the same purpose. McKenzie (DOB 636) supposes that the primitive church may have had a collection of parables of Jesus which were used as need arose in the homilies where they were expanded or placed in a relevant setting.

But despite adaptations, Jesus' basic themes remain the same: the approaching kingdom of God, the arrival of the new era, *(kairos)*, God's mercy to the penitent sinner, the coming judgment, faith, discipleship, his passion and death, and the last days. These are eternal themes and so quite adaptable to whatever times and circumstances.

Of course, no parable, no matter how apropos, will be accepted by a non-believer.

> To you has been given the secret of the kingdom of God, but for those outside everything is in parables; so that they may indeed see but not perceive, and may indeed hear but not understand; lest they should turn again and be forgiven. (Mk 4:10-12)

Docility is a prerequisite for even the best of parables.

At any rate, Jesus makes good use of parables, which could

2. Roman school scene. Teacher with boys reading. Stone relief from the third century. Note box with wax tablets. (Trier Archeological Museum)

be classified broadly under haggadah. Probably he was one of the first rabbis to make wide use of parables. Some of his stories appear in rabbinical literature probably indicating that both Jesus and the rabbis drew from a common stock of folk stories and wisdom sayings. For example the story of the king's banquet (Mt 22:1-14; 25:1-12; Lk 12:35-41) is reflected in Johnatnan b. Zakkai's parable.

> A king once invited his servants to a banquet without indicating the precise time when it would be given. Those who were wise remembered that things are always ready in a king's palace, and they arranged themselves and sat by the palace gate attentive for the call to enter, while those who were foolish continued their customary occupations; saying: 'A banquet requires great preparation.' When the king suddenly called his servants to the banquet, those who were wise appeared in clean raiment and well adorned, while those who were foolish entered in soiled and ordinary garments. The king took pleasure in the wise, but was full of anger at those who were foolish, saying that those who had come prepared for the banquet should sit down and eat and drink, but those who had not properly arrayed themselves should remain standing and look on. (Shab 153a)

In Matthew's account, the errant guests are bound hand and foot and cast into outer darkness (Mt 22:13), while in Johanan's story they merely have to stand by, an interesting contrast. Another Matthean story, that of the vineyard workers (Mt 20:1-6) is reflected in Yer Ber 2:5c, as we have seen, though the applications differ, namely, the death of a young rabbi in the Talmud story and the late coming Gentiles rewarded the same as the Jews in the Kingdom in Matthew. The last will be first, and the first last.[6]

Although Jesus used haggadah to attract the simple people, he also taught applications of the Law, halakah. He argued with the Pharisaic rabbis frequently over the Sabbath, marriage, taxes and purification laws. Sometimes his interpretations were more lenient than those of some of the Pharisees. For example, his response to those who challenged his disciples for picking

---

6. For other examples of parables common to Jesus and the Talmud see G. Dalman, Jesus-Jeshua, Studies in the Gospels, New York, KTAV, 1971, pp. 225ff.

grain on the Sabbath. "The Sabbath was made for man and not man for the Sabbath" (Mk 2:27). He also did not hesitate to heal on the Sabbath, asking rhetorically, "Is it lawful on the Sabbath to do good or to do harm, to save a life or to kill?" (Mk 3:4). But while lenient in disciplinary matters such as fasting and Sabbath regulations, Jesus could be strict in his interpretations of the essentials of the Torah. For example, the "I say" passages (Mt 5:21ff), as we have seen.

Jesus' views of the Law were by no means radical for opinions similar to his may be found among the other rabbis. For example, some, along with Jesus, felt that it was legal to heal on the Sabbath. As his rabbinical confreres, Jesus wanted to make the Law relevant for the people who had by and large rejected it or at least ignored it. The Pharisees in their enthusiasm to preserve the Law by building a fence around it had alienated the Am ha-Aretz.

Jesus seemed to plot a middle course between the lax Am ha-Aretz and the over-observant Pharisees. But, as we have seen, there were all shades of Pharisees. And certainly not all were unreasonable in their observances. From the challenges to Jesus' disciples about their uncleanness and Sabbath laxness, we may gather that Jesus and his followers pursued the line of reason more acceptable to weak human nature. Christianity started out as a religion of the weak and, despite periodic rigorist groups, often eschatological and sometimes heterodox, it would remain such.

Yet Jesus obeyed the Law, in general, observing the Sabbath in the synagogue, going to the temple for the feasts, offering sacrifice. Moreover, he respected priests and the traditions of his Fathers. But Jesus, as Paul did later, put a heavy stress on the interior law of love which must be the motivating force behind all external law.

Jesus' teachings are contained in summary form in the Sermon on the Mount (Mt 5-7), which is more than anything else a mishnah of Jesus, compiled, perhaps by the school of Matthew from a multiplicity of remembrances. Of course, the mishnah of Jesus is applied to the various life situations of the early Christian communities.

Davies feels[7] that the Matthew school, seeing Jesus as the New Moses, leading the New Exodus for the New Israel, may have used the Sermon on the Mount as an oral torah with five divisions reflecting the Pentateuch. But Jesus' torah is not new in the sense of abrogating the old, but rather an interpretation and completion. Matthew's Christ on the mountain is a teacher of righteousness instructing in messianic torah, a messianic interpretation of the old Law. Although Matthew is hesitant to use the term "New" of Jesus and his doctrine, later in the first century John spoke of "New Commandment". Davies senses[8] that the Sermon on the Mount is the deliberate formulation of the Christian moral ideal and tradition at a time when the Mishnah was being formulated in Judaism.

C. DISCIPLES

We have examined briefly the teachings of Jesus, now let us see something of his disciples. Discipleship is essential to the rabbinical tradition for no man is a teacher without disciples. Both teacher and scholars are engaged in the learning process, LMD. Though in many ways Jesus' disciples differed from those of the other rabbis, they were certainly men of the Book.

What was the age of Jesus and his disciples? Rabbi Judah b. Tema (2c) gives us a clue (Nez. 5:21).

At five years (one it fit) for the Scripture, at ten for the Mishnah, at fourteen for (the fulfilling of) the commandments, at 15 for the Talmud, at 18 for the bride chamber, at 20 for pursuing (a calling), at 30 for authority . . .

It would seem that with a firm foundation in Torah, a boy went to study under a rabbi at the bet ha-midrash after his Bar Mitzvah. Rabbis could be ordained at 20. Could Jesus and his disciples have followed this pattern? Some of the disciples were

7. Sermon on the Mount, pp. 30-32.
8. Ibid., p. 90.

over 18, for it seems that Cephas was married and Matthew was a tax collector. But it is possible that the others may have been younger (bahurim). One pericope (Lk 3:23) gives Jesus' age as 30. Was this to impress Luke's Gentile audience? What did Jesus do during the ten years between 20 and 30? Was marriage required for all teachers or only for those teaching children? (Kid 4:13). There are many questions still to be examined. But it would seem that many passages from the gospels could be more easily explained if the disciples were teen agers. For example, leaving their fathers and boats, plus their impetuosity, enthusiastic rivalry, utter devotion to their master. And, indeed, Jesus calls them children, a term of endearment used by the rabbis of their young disciples (Jn 21:5).

Jesus' disciples are called to a life long commitment, leaving family and home. "If any one comes to me and does not hate his own father and mother, and wife and children and brothers and sisters, yes, and even his own life, he cannot be my disciple." (Lk 14:26). As we have seen the disciples of the rabbis gave up all including their families for Torah study, revering their masters as superior to their parents (Kid 32b; Ab 6:3). Here "hate" means a preference of one over the other.

The devotion of the Christian disciples to their master in some ways resembled that of the disciples of the rabbis, though none of the latter seem to have claimed for their masters the messiahship. And Jesus demanded loyalty even to death. As the other disciples, Jesus' served him, preparing his way, providing transportation, washing his feet, preparing his meals, etc.

Jesus taught Torah and Mishnah to his followers, and as the students of the other rabbis, they may have committed both to memory, and, perhaps later written collections were made. At any rate, the mishnah of Jesus, applied to the life of the early church, ends up in the gospel form following roughly the chronological life of Jesus. And this seems to be a basic difference from the Jewish Mishnah. As far as we know now, there were no written collections of mishnah from individual rabbis, but rather the mishnaic tradition included the sayings of many teachers.

As we have seen, Jesus is a traveling rabbi. His first followers seem to have been disciples of John the Baptist (Jn 1:35). Jesus continued to gather disciples and the gospel describes him teaching large crowds (Lk 6:17; 19:37; Jn 6: 60). Some of them left all to follow him (Mt 10:37ff; Lk 14:26ff).

Jesus often made use of the vineyard parable to describe himself, his disciples, and the kingdom. Did this have any bearing on the rabbinical usage which compared the bet ha-midrash to a vineyard? For example, Matthew 20:1ff could refer to the admission of later disciples into Jesus' school and their position vis-a-vis the original followers (Also Mt 21:28ff; Mk 12:1ff, Lk 13:6; 20:9ff; 1 Cor 9:7). In John (15:1ff) Jesus himself is the vine and his disciples are branches. And the Father is the vinedresser who prunes off the unfruitful branches. The disciples must abide in their master's teaching. "I am the vine, you are the branches. He who abides in me and I in him, he it is that bears much fruit. For apart from me you can do nothing" (Jn 15:5).

As with the other rabbis' disciples, Jesus' are being trained to teach others. In Matthew (10:5) he forbids them to teach the Gentiles and Samaritans. "Preach (kēryssete) as you go. saying 'The kingdom of heaven is at hand' " (Mt 10:7), healing, raising the dead, etc. They are to go without money or extra clothing. Moreover, Jesus predicts persecutions, floggings, reflecting the experience of the early church (Mt 10:16-23).

And his disciples are not to use the honorific titles of the Pharisaic teachers such a rabbi, abba, moreh.

> But you are not to be called rabbi, for you have one teacher and you are all brethren. And call no man father on earth, for you have one Father who is in heaven. Neither be called masters, for you have one master, the Christ. He who is greatest among you, shall be your servant. Whoever exalts himself will be humbled, and whoever humbles himself will be exalted. (Mt 23:8-12)

The early Christian community adhered strictly to this instruction with Jesus as *The* Master and all others his disciples. And in their teachings they imitate what their master taught them. "A disciple is not above his teacher, nor above his master; it is enough for the disciple to be like his teacher, and the servant like his master" (Mt 10:24-25).

When Jesus' disciples are on missionary journeys, they are often called apostles, in the full sense of the Jewish *selihim*, with the complete delegated authority of their master to teach, heal, cast out demons, etc. In a word, wherever they go, they act in lieu of the Master. The Jewish high priest or nasi had similar apostles and rabbinical missionaries are mentioned in both the New Testament (Mt 23:15) and in the Talmud (T.J. Hag. 1, 7, f.76c).

The Twelve consituted Jesus' special haburah, an inner circle of disciples. The minimum number for a haburah was ten. Probably the number twelve reflects the twelve tribes of Israel. Some, as McKenzie (DOB, 47), say that Jesus did not use the title, apostle, at all. In accord with Jewish tradition it is generally used of the disciples when they are on the missions.

There is no question of the teaching and judging authority of the Dozen in the early church. The authority which Jesus had received from the Father, he passes down to them.

> All authority in heaven and on earth has been given to me. Go, there-fore, and make disciples (matheteusate) of all nations, baptising them in the name of the Father and of the Son and of the Holy Spirit, teaching (didaskontes) them to observe all that I have commanded you; and lo, I am with you always, to the close of the age (Mt 28:18-20.)

And, as we have seen, Jesus also passes on the power to preach (Mk 6:12; Mt 10:7), judge (Mt 16:19; 18:18) and heal (Mt 10:8; Lk 10:7). With authority (exousia), the Dozen haberim presided over the primordial academy, teaching and distributing goods to those in need (Acts 2:42f; 4:34-37). They instruct and perform signs and wonders in Jesus' name (Acts 5:12, 40). And they lay hands on assistants to help in the temporalities so that they can spend more time preaching and teaching (Acts 6).

The apostles act in college at Jerusalem (Acts 8) and to-gether with the elders rule and judge the whole church in sanhe-drin (Acts 15:2, 4, 6, 22f; 16:4). If we can draw any comparison with Jewish customs, the disciples, or the talmidim scholars are generally considered on a higher plane than the administering elders. For this reason, increasingly the sanhedrins of ruling elders were made up of the scholar rabbis. The position of James in the Jerusalem church we will not discuss here, but his leader-ship would seem to be based on his close relationship to Jesus.

When the apostles came to choose another member of the haburah, he had to be someone who had been a disciple of Jesus from the very beginning at the baptism by John (Acts 1:15-26). This is what discipleship means, to sit at the feet of the master through the whole course. This is why the early Christians sometimes questioned Paul's apostolic authority, for he was not a disciple of Jesus in the ordinary sense.

The initial haburah, The Dozen, is the very foundation of Christianity. With the authority of their rabbi, they preach, heal, call for repentance in view of the kingdom. Teaching others, they extend the original haburah, even accepting Gentile proselytes as disciples. Thus the school of Jeshua spreads, discipleship is enlarged and others assume the apostleship to spread the word.

Though his disciples and their disciples would, in turn, teach, forming schools of interpretation as James, Peter, Mark, Paul, Luke, Matthew, John, each with his own view of the Master, Jesus would always remain The Teacher of Christianity. All others, no matter how learned and eloquent, would remain his disciples.

He who has disciples and whose disciples again have disciples is called "Rabbi"; when his disciples are forgotten (i.e., if he is so old that even his immediate disciples belong to the past age) he is called "Rabban"; and when the disciples of his disciples are also forgotten, he is simply called by his own name (Tosefta to 'Eduyot [end]).

3

MEN OF ISRAEL, HELP! THIS IS THE MAN WHO IS TEACHING AGAINST THE PEOPLE AND THE LAW AND THIS PLACE (Acts 21:28)

A. SAUL OF TARSUS

ONE OF THE later disciples of Jesus who although he had never studied at the feet of the Master, yet became one of his most enthusiastic apostles, was Saul of Tarsus. Saul differed from the other disciples insofar as he was a diaspora Jew, born in Tarsus and a Roman citizen by birth. Yet he was trained in Torah in the temple school at Jerusalem. So by birth and circumstances he became the ideal preacher and teacher to the Gentiles. By trade he was a tent-maker, weaving them out of the strong black goat's hair.

Saul was a strict Pharisee. We can only conjecture about his early life. But he probably attended grammar school in Tarsus, then proceeding to Jerusalem at Bar Mitzvah to sit at the feet of the great Gamaliel, grand son of Hillel. "Educated according to the strict manner of the Law of our fathers, being zealous for God" (Acts 22:3).

To study in Jerusalem was indeed a great privilege for here the top scholars were as Jesus himself had experienced (Lk 2:46-50). Only outstanding local rabbis and judges were tapped for the Great Sanhedrin there (Sanh 17a, 88b; Tos Hag 2:9). The Great Sanhedrin, 70 in number, sat in a semi-circle around the Nasi or High Priest with two or three scribes in attendance, and three rows of scholars in front, from whom it was customary to choose the new elders (Sanh 36b, 37a).

Saul was one of the leading scholars of his era. This we can judge not only by his superior knowledge of the Law, but also by his remarks to the Galatians. "I advanced in Judaism beyond

many of my own age among my people, so extremely zealous
was I for the traditions of my Father" (Gal 1:14). Also his
discipleship under Rabban Gamaliel, de facto if not de iure, the
head of the Sanhedrin, and his close association with the Sanhedrin in responsible positions mark him out as a comer (Acts
7:58-8:1; 9:1-2).[1]

Saul, then, is a top scholar, a doctor of the Law, and if not
a member of the Sanhedrin, at least in line for such a honor. His
mission to Damascus, more than anything else, underlines his
position vis a vis the Sanhedrin.

> But Saul, still breathing threats and murder against the disciples of
> the Lord, went to the High Priest and asked him for letters to the
> synagogues at Damascus so that if he found any belonging to the
> Way, men or women, he might bring them bound to Jerusalem. (Acts
> 9:1-2; 26:9-11)

There are some who would doubt any jurisdiction of the Jerusalem Sanhedrin over the diaspora communities at this time. But
we know that diaspora apostles collected tithes for the temple.
Philo calls them *hieropompoi* (*Legation to Gaius*, 216).

So there seems to be some influence of the Jerusalem Sanhedrin over the diaspora communities in the first century. Saul's
mission would corroborate this. Was Saul an apostle of the
Sanhedrin? Though he is not called one, he has many of the pre-
rogatives including letters from the High Priest, authorizing him
to act in his place and power to imprison any synagogue members
who were following the Christian Way. The Babylonian Exilarch
also had similar apostles. This much we can say, that if Saul
is an apostle of the Sanhedrin, he is one of its outstanding men.
His discipleship under Gamaliel certainly would have been no
hindrance to his promotion, especially within the Pharisaic
establishment.

On his way to Damascus Saul was converted to the Way
of Christ. His excellent training in the Pharisaic doctrine, including belief in the resurrection, may have paved the way

---

1. See. J. Klausner, **From Jesus to Paul**, Boston, Beacon, 1961, p. 311;
C. Montefiore, **Judaism and St. Paul**, London, 1914, pp. 58-129.

for his belief in the risen Christ. Saul always claimed that he had been instructed by Christ himself in some mysterious way. Thus he was a true disciple, although he had never sat at his feet as the other apostles had done. Barnabas befriended Saul and brought him to Antioch where his rabbinical training was put to use by the nascent church.

Acts 13:1-2 talks about the prophets and teachers of the Antioch church. Besides Saul and Barnabas, are mentioned Symeon the Black, Lucius of Cyrene and Manden, a member of the court of Herod the tetrarch. Are two different offices described in the Antioch church, namely, prophets and rabbis? When the gospels speak of scribes and Pharisees, they usually mean Pharisaic scribes.

The rabbis felt themselves to be the successors of the prophets by way of the Great Synagogue and the zugoth scholars (Pirke Aboth 1:1).[2] In Paul prophecy, teaching and apostleship overlap. Actually prophecy and teaching have much in common. Both the prophet and the teacher speak to the people, either speaking for God or interpreting his word. The prophet speaks from inspiration, while the teacher instructs from his wisdom. " 'Touch not mine anointed, and do my prophets no harm' (1 Chron 16:22). The former are school children, the latter, rabbis" (Sab 119b). Furthermore, we know that most of the Jewish apostles were rabbis.

Were the prophet-teachers of Antioch a small haburah, perhaps including a few more to bring the number up to ten? They studied Torah, worshiped the Lord *(leitourgountōn autōn)* and fasted. Under the inspiration of the Holy Spirit, Paul and Barnabas were set aside as apostles with a laying on of hands. This would seem to be a type of ordination or at least a passing on of authority. The rabbis ordained their disciples in a similar manner. Paul and Barnabas set out to preach the gospel of Christ in Cyprus, Perga, Antioch of Pisidia and the cities of Lycaonia (Acts 13 & 14).

As Jesus did, they started out preaching in the synagogues.

2. See L. Finkelstein. **New Light from the Prophets**, New York, Basic Books, 1969.

Thus Christianity is not preached as a religion separate from Judaism, but as a Way, sect or heresy. But there was jealousy over the popularity of Paul and Barnabas, who promptly responded:

> It was necessary that the word of God should be spoken first to you. Since you thrust it first from you, and judge yourselves unworthy of eternal life, behold we turn to the Gentiles (Acts 13:46).

B. THE GENTILES

Whether to preach to the Gentiles was a big issue in the early church. There are parallels in contemporary Judaism's discussions over proselytes. Did Christ mean to preach to non-Jews and if so, should they be made to keep the Law? Certainly the messianic kingdom includes the Gentiles (Ps 2). In Matthew we have both commands. "Go nowhere among the Nations" (Mt 10:5) and "Go, therefore, and make disciples of all nations," baptizing and teaching (Mt 28:19). The two paradoxical views have never been adequately explained. Perhaps the first command gives the words of Jesus, while the second is an interpretation of the early church in the light of the decision of the Jerusalem Christian sanhedrin (Acts 15). As we have seen, this is rather typical of gospel methodology, that is, making applications of Jesus' teachings in the name of the Master. In other words, what would the Master say if he were here now? It would seem that if Jesus had been crystal clear on the conversion of Gentiles, there would have been no need for debating it in the early church. Despite the objections of some Pharisees, the Jerusalem Christian sanhedrin under James ruled that Paul's Gentile converts would only have to observe the Noachian precepts. And their baptism was sufficient without circumcision.

The decision was written in the form of an apostolic letter to be carried by Paul and Barnabas, Judas and Silas. Paul traveled throughout Asia Minor and Greece, including Cilicia, Lycaonia, Phrygia, Galatia, Macedonia, then to Rome and perhaps Spain.

Paul's work was cut out for him, namely, preaching to the Gentiles (kerygma) and teaching his convert proselytes (didache).

Some say that Judaism was popular in the first century, with many seeking to become proselytes and others living the Torah as Fearers of God. And the Pharisaic missionaries were zealous for converts among the Gentiles (Mt 23:15; Acts 15:1). Rabbinical missionary activity may have been sparked by the belief that the messianic age was imminent and the Gentiles would share in it along with the Jews. Although some rabbis as Paul did not require the repugnant circumcision for their converts, many of the Pharisaic missionaries from Palestine insisted upon it because of trouble that they had had with backsliding and even subversive Gentile proselytes. Palestinian zealot pressure may have been a factor, too.

Paul's most successful work seems to be among the Gentile Fearers of God who were attracted to his non-circumcision type of Judaism.[3] Paul preached the way of Christ and his Torah, to die with Christ and be born again with him in the waters of Baptism. The idea of resurrection was not foreign to many of the contemporary mystery religions and we know that the Pharisees believed in it. When Paul's Christians rise with Christ it is into a New Israel, a new community or church, united to Christ in his mystical body. Christ is the New Moses leading his people through the new Exodus. The Paschal liturgy of Baptism is well known. Paul compares the Christian Way to the New Passover with Christ as the Paschal Lamb (1 Cor 5:6-8), or as the Rock in the desert giving supernatural drink (1 Cor 10:1f). As Davies comments,[4]

> The story of the 'Old Israel' is treated as parallel and yet continuous with the 'New Israel'. The Exodus of the 'Old Israel' is reenacted in the experience of the 'New'. And 1 Cor 10:1-5 is to be regarded as a midrash.

And further,[5]

3. See Bamberger, **Proselytism in the Talmudic Period**, New York, KTAV, 1968, pp. 38ff.
4. W. D. Davies, **Paul and Rabbinic Judaism**, London, SPCK, 1958.
5. **Ibid.,** p. 108.

Paul was the kerux not of a new mystery but of a new Exodus and all that it implied. Dr. Dodd has made us familiar with the nature of the kerygma of the Apostle as of the early Church. It was the proclamation of certain events, but no mere events, rather events charged with meaning. And Paul's doctrine of the individual Christian is that he is one who has made his own these external events that he proclaims.

As the Christian dies and rises with Christ in Baptism, his eucharist is not a mere remembrance, but the presence of the living Christ.

If the new Christian is reborn and risen with Christ in the New Israel, his old sinful self must be completely dead and his new life reflect the Torah of Christ. Davies[6] names three factors which affected the lives of the early Christians, namely, Pentecostalism, Gentile anti-nomianism and second adventism. Paul warned against the dangers of all three, placing his stress instead on proper moral conduct in the new life of conversion to Christ.

Especially as the hope of the second coming faded, the Church had to place more stress on the here and now of daily ethics. As Davies comments,[7] it was not sufficient for Paul just to be a *kerux* announcing the death and resurrection of the Christian with Christ. No, he had to be their rabbi, *didaskolos*, instructing them in the race of life (Phil 3:4; Gal 2:2). This was the basis of the Christian *didache* as it was also in the Jewish. Judaism was and is a system of monotheistic ethics with its 613 laws as means to establishing the kingdom, the good, moral society. Ethical problems kept popping up in Paul's churches, and he usually solved them by letter, the most practical manner of teaching for a traveling rabbi.

At bottom, Paul's Gentile converts had to obey the Noachian precepts (Acts 15:28-29). In the new messianic kingdom there will be no difference between Jew and Gentile. Though the Gentile Christians had once been *gerim* and *nokrim*, strangers and foreigners, now "you are fellow citizens with the saints and members of the household of God" (Eph 2:19).

6. Ibid., p. 111.
7. Ibid., p. 112.

Paul's *didache* to the newly converted Gentiles reminds one of the instructions of the rabbis to proselytes. Both the proselyte and the Christian convert are as new-born children. Paul prefers "new creation" (1 Cor 5:17; Gal 6:15; Eph 4:24). Jewish proselytes had a threefold rite: circumcision, baptism and sacrifice. Also instructions were given at this time (B. Yebamoth 47a). Jewish catechisms such as the Essene Damascus Document and Scroll of the Rule, the *derek eretz* and others may well underlie the Christian ones such as Paul's in Ephesians and Colossians, and also Didache, the Epistle of Barnabas and the Mandates of Hermas.

Parallel passages in New Testament documents give evidence of a common Christian catechism built on the Jewish synagogue model. For example: 1 Pet 1:3-4:11; Col 3:8-4:12; Eph 4:22-6:18; Jas 1:1-4:10. Davies[8] parallels Col 3:8-4:12 and Eph 4:22-6:18.

> But now put them all away: anger, wrath, malice, slander, and foul talk from your mouth. Do not lie to one another, seeing that you have put off the old nature with its practices and have put on the new nature, which is being renewed in knowledge after the image of its creator (Col 3:8-10).

> Put off your old nature which belongs to your former manner of life and is corrupt through deceitful lusts, and be renewed in the spirit of your minds, and put on the new nature, created after the likeness of God in true righteousness and holiness.

> Therefore, putting away falsehood, let every one speak the truth with his neighbor, for we are members of one another. Be angry, but do not sin; do not let the sun go down on your anger . . . (Eph 4:22-26).

And another comparison:

> Wives be subject to your husbands, as is fitting in the Lord. Husbands, love your wives, and do not be harsh with them (Col 3:18-19).

> Be subject to one another out of reverence for Christ. Wives be subject to your husbands, as in the Lord. For the husband is the head of the wife as Christ is the head of the church, his body, and is himself its savior. As the church is subject to Christ, so let wives also be subject in every thing to their husbands. Husbands love your wives,

---

8. **Ibid.**, p. 122ff.

as Christ loved the church and gave himself up for her . . . (Eph 5:21-25).

Other parallels of: new birth, putting off, worship, submission and resistance can be found in 1 Pet 1:1-4:11 and Jas 1:1-4:10. The similarity of order and content in the hortatory parts of these epistles implies that there was a common catechetical tradition, probably synagogal, from which they drew.

That these instructions were related to Baptism is pointed out by Davies.[9]

> The putting off of evil would be fitly symbolized by the stripping off of garments before immersion; the command to stand morally would correspond to standing up in the baptismal service after prostration in prayer and the references to the taking of milk of the word is probably connected with the ritual act of giving the baptized a drink immediately after immersion.

Paul, then, is a rabbi, a *didaskalos,* teaching his converts from a common fund of catechesis similar to the other rabbis. Though Paul echoed the torah of Jesus—as the other rabbis—he felt free to voice the teaching in his own manner. But the words of Jesus form a common source for Paul, the synoptic gospels and the Agrapha of the Lord.[10]

For example, Rom 12:14 "Bless those who persecute you; bless and do not curse them" echoes Mt 5:43 "But I say to you, love your enemies and pray for those who persecute you." Rom 14:10 "Why do you pass judgment on your brother" mirrors Mt 7:1 "Judge not, that you be not judged." Rom 14:14 "I know and am persuaded in the Lord Jesus that nothing is unclean in itself" is similar to Mk 7:15 "There is nothing outside a man which by going into him can defile him." Other parallels may be found in 1 Thes 4-5 and Col 3-4. Davies feels[11] that there may have been a collection of Jesus' sayings from which Paul drew.

For example, 1 Cor 7:10 "To the married I give charge, not I but the Lord, that the wife should not separate from her hus-

9. **Ibid.,** p. 129.
10. **Ibid.,** p. 138.
11. **Ibid.,** p. 140.

band" parallels Mark 10:12 "If she divorces her husband and marries another, she commits adultery." Also 1 Cor 11:23 "For I received from the Lord what I also delivered to you" and 1 Cor 7:25 "Now concerning the unmarried I have no command of the Lord." Indicate that certain directions of Jesus were either memorized or perhaps committed to writing. Most of the citations are halakah: marriage, divorce, etc. Following rabbinical tradition, Paul quotes the precedent of the Master to help in the making a legal decision. Most of Paul's halakic decisions were by letter which would be normal for such a traveling apostle.

As we have seen, the early Christian kerygma was soon supplemented by didache. We see this in the evolution of the synoptics where the kerygmatic gospel of Mark is soon supplemented by the Q collection of the teachings of Jesus, redacted into Matthew's gospel. Paul from the beginning taught the torah of Jesus.[12] This passing on of the torah of the Master is the very basis of the apostolic tradition.

For Paul Jesus is the Law, just as for the Jews Moses had been the Law. But when Paul identifies the Law with Jesus, is this not oral torah, which rather than abrogating the written Torah of Moses, complements it? Without this new law of the Spirit of Jesus Christ, the old Law appears to be just a measure of sin. Thus by permitting transgression, Law makes sin unfold itself to man, making him conscious of sin and so seeking salvation.

> The law of the Spirit of life in Christ Jesus has set me free from the law of sin and death. For God has done what the law, weakened by the flesh could not do. Sending his own Son in the likeness of sinful flesh and for sin, he condemned sin in the flesh, in order that the just requirement of the law might be fulfilled in us, who walk not according to the flesh, but according to the Spirit (Rom 8:2-4).

The law of Christ Jesus is love and all other regulations are just footnotes. This love is personified in Jesus who gave his life out of love for us. As a living torah, Jesus Christ is a model for his followers. The old Law is not dead, but updated, made relevant by the oral torah of Christ. Therefore, the Christian should

---

12. **Ibid.**, p. 143.

not depend on the Law of Moses for justification, but rather trust in Christ Jesus and his torah.

Paul's principal theme in Galatians and Romans is the antithesis between the Law of Moses and trust in Jesus Christ. It seems that Christian Pharisees under pressure from the Palestinian zealots had been preaching the necessity of circumcision in Galatia. But the Galatians had been converted to Jesus Christ not by the works of the Law, which they probably did not even know, but by trust in the Spirit. "Does he who supplies the Spirit to you and works miracles among you do so by works of the Law, or by hearing with trust?" (Gal 3:5).

Abraham was justified by his trust in Yahweh, not by works of the Law. So all descendants of Abraham are men of trust (Gal 3:6-9). Following Jewish tradition which makes Abraham the father of proselytes, Paul tells his converts they are sons of Abraham. Trust and faith in the torah of Jesus Christ has completed and fulfilled the old Torah (Gal 3:23-25). No longer slaves, they are now sons of God in Christ. And as adopted sons of God and brothers of Christ, they are coheirs of the testament given to Abraham and Christ by the Father (Gal 2-3). And this testament is to be shared by all nations, Jews and Gentiles (3: 8-9, 14), since all receive the benefits equally through Christ (3:14, 22).

Another analogy is drawn between the Law and the pedagogue (3:23-). The Law is a pedagogue training the youngster until he comes of age. Before he attains his maturity, the son is as a slave, under the slave-pedagogue. Having been a slave of sin, the Christian through his faith and trust in his God, attains adopted sonship. Paul is not against the Law, but wants to show that it is an instrument of the Father to train his child for sonship, to be worthy of his eternal inheritance.

Once the Christian is adopted through baptism, he is freed from the tutelage of the Law (2:18-19; 3:13; 4:4-9). He becomes a completely new person, his old self done away with in his baptismal rebirth (2:20; 3:27-29). Now he is justified (3:26), heir of Abraham (3:29), adopted son of God (3:26). It is through trust in Jesus Christ, God's Son and trustee, that the Christian receives the inheritance of the testament, eternal life.

Paul's convert now lives in Jesus Christ. As a newborn

brother of Christ, the new Christian should imitate him in all things, doing everything *in* Christ (2 Cor 2:17, 19; Phil 2:1, 4:2; Rom 16:22, 16:8) even to imprisonment in Christ (Phil 1:13) and death in Christ (1 Cor 15:18). *Brotherhood* expresses more than any other word the close relationship between the Christian and Christ. He joins the haburah of Jesus (1 Cor 1:9). Not only are all Christians brothers of Jesus Christ, but by this very fact are brothers in Christ (Col 1:2). United in Christ, all are members of his body. Now no longer are they Jew and Gentile, male and female, slave or free. All are one in Jesus Christ (Gal 3:28-29). So when one member suffers, all suffer; when one rejoices, all rejoice (1 Cor 12:12-31).

To become more like Jesus Christ, their teacher and model, they put on Christ (Gal 3:27), partake of him, belong to him (Rom 7:4, 19-20). They are crucified with Jesus Christ to the world (Rom 6:7; Gal 2:19f). They suffer with their new brother Christ in order to be glorified with him (Rom 8:17). As brothers, they share both his sufferings and joys (Gal 2:20-21; 4:19). In a word, the convert not only puts on Christ, but Christ enters into his heart and he becomes one with Christ.

But what did one have to believe in order to become an adopted brother of Jesus Christ, to belong to his haburah? First of all, to believe that he is the Messiah and that God has raised him up (Rom 10:9) and that in Jesus we are delivered from our sins and raised up for righteousness. Not only did the new Christian believe in Jesus as the new living torah, but had to live in him, modeling his life on the Master in every way as a true disciple.

C. PAUL—APOSTLE

We have seen Paul as the Christian rabbi, teaching the torah of Christ. But he was also an apostle. Jewish apostles were known at the time, including the Pharisaic, Palestinian and Babylonian missionaries from the Nasi or Exilarch. But what kind of apostle was Paul? Clearly he is a Pharisaic apostle. And he may have been an apostle of the Nasi in his mission to Damascus. But what was he after his conversion? He was commissioned by the Antioch church and confirmed by the Christian sanhedrin in Jerusalem under James, the Lord's brother.

As some feel that Paul resembled the Jewish rabbi in his teaching, so he may also have mirrored the traveling Jewish apostle: judging (1 Cor 5:1-13), reconciling (2 Cor 1:23-2:11), admonishing not to take differences to the secular courts (1 Cor 6:1-8). He settles marriage problems (1 Cor 7), exhorts not to eat meat offered to idols (1 Cor 7), cautions about abuses during the meal accompanying the Eucharist (1 Cor 11:17-33), raises funds for the Jerusalem church (1 Cor 16:1-4; 2 Cor 8-9).

Although he did not have a letter from the Nasi as he had on his Damascus mission, he did have one from his Christian Nasi, James (Acts 15:30). When the Corinthians asked to see his apostolic letter, he told them that he did not need one. Christ himself had appointed him.

> You yourselves are our letter of recommendation, written on your hearts, to be known and read by all men. And you show you are a letter from Christ delivered by us, written not with ink, but with the Spirit of the living God, not on tablets of stone, but on tablets of human hearts. (1 Cor 3:2-3)

But it was not only the Corinthians who challenged Paul as a rabbi-apostle. At Perga, he exhorted them in the synagogue concerning Christ and his resurrection,—"When the Jews saw the multitudes, they were filled with jealousy, and contradicted what was spoken by Paul and reviled him" (Acts 13:45). And Gentiles accused him of disturbing the city and blaspheming, when he was trying to uphold morality (Acts 16:16; 19:23).

In Achaia some of the Jews attacked Paul before the tribune Gallio, saying, "This man is persuading men to worship God contrary to the Law" (Acts 18:13). But Gallio responded, "If it were a matter of wrong-doing or vicious crime, I should have reason to bear with you, O Jews. But since it is a matter of questions about words and names in your own Law, see to it yourselves. I refuse to judge these things" (Acts 18:14-15). Of course, Gallio was right for questions of the Law were to be handled in the local sanhedrins and not taken before the Roman courts (1 Cor 6:1-8).

It seems that the main group to oppose Paul were the Palestinian Pharisees, who, perhaps under the pressure of the Zealots were tightening up the rules for admitting proselytes, insisting on circumcision (Acts 15:1; Gal 3-). They seem to be of the same persuasion of the Asians who accused him of bringing Gentiles into the temple. "Men of Israel, help! This is the man who is teaching men everywhere against the people and the Law and this place. Moreover, he also brought Greeks into the temple, and he has defiled this holy place" (Acts 21:28). The Roman officials, protecting Paul from the crowd, brought him to Caesarea and eventually to Rome.

In general, Paul's liberal torah, adapted to the needs of his Gentile converts, was rejected by the strict Pharisees in a period when there seems to have been a withdrawing or at least a restricting in the policy of proselytizing.

As a rabbi and an apostle, Paul had disciples, such as Luke, Timothy and Titus, but he preferred them to consider themselves rather disciples of Jesus, then of himself or of Barnabas or Apollos.

> What I mean is that each of you says "I belong to Paul" or "I belong to Apollos" or "I belong to Cephas" or "I belong to Christ." Is Christ divided? Was Paul crucified for you? Or were you baptized in the name of Paul? I am thankful that I baptized none of you, except Crispus and Gaius, lest any one say that you were baptized in my name. (1 Cor 1:12-14)

Early Christian tradition, as Jewish, looked upon the baptizer as the father of the newly born convert, in a sense replacing his earthly father of his previous life. Paul was afraid of factions developing among the early Christians, some following one rabbi, others, another. In fact, there were Pauline and Petrine schools in the early church. And it would not be long before various sects broke off to follow their own teacher's interpretation of Christ. The only solution is to consider Christ, *The* Teacher of Christianity, as Moses is *The* Teacher of Judaism. All other masters are really disciples of the Lord, who are trying to make his teachings relevant for their own particular time and place.

Thus Paul never used the title of teacher *(didaskolos)* of himself or of his associates. Usually he called his co-workers *adelphoi* or *synergoi* which could be related to the Jewish *haberim*. Nor did he call those whom he instructed disciples *(mathétai)*, although frequently enough he uses the rabbinical name *tekna* (children) (1 Cor 4:17; 4:14; Tit 1:4; Gal 4:19).[13]

Though he never used the title, Paul was always the Jewish rabbi who had converted to be disciple of Christ. As Davies writes:[14]

> Both in his life and thought, therefore, Paul's close relation to rabbinic Judaism has become clear. And we cannot too strongly insist again that for him the acceptance of the Gospel was not so much the rejection of the old Judaism and the discovery of a new religion wholly antithetical to it, as his polemics might sometimes pardonably lead us to assume, but the recognition of the advent of the true and final form of Judaism. In other words, the advent of the Messianic Age of Jewish expectation.

Paul's teaching tradition was important to the early church. Both the Torah of Moses in the LXX and the Torah of Jesus in the gospels were taught along with Paul's interpretations of both. Moreover, Paul's rabbinical treatises on ethics as seen in Ephesians (4:22-6:18) and Colossians (3:5-4:12) where the new man is contrasted to the old, are echoed in the two ways of Didache (1:1-6:2) and the Letter of Barnabas (18:1-21:9), and the Mandates (26-49, esp 36) of Hermas.

Both kerygma and didache would play an important part in the early church as long as adult conversions continued to be the practice. Also while disputes with pagans and dissident Christians continued, apologetics would remain in the forefront. In a word, for several centuries, the Christian teacher, either lay or cleric, would have his work cut out for him.

---

13. See E. Ellis, "Paul and His Co-Workers," NTS, July, 1971, pp. 437-52.
14. W. D. Davies, **op. cit.,** p. 324.

4

AFTER THE PRAYER, LET THE TEACHER LAY HANDS ON THEM AND PRAY AND DISMISS THEM
(Hippolytus, *Apostolic Tradition*, 18-19)

SO FAR WE have seen Jewish rabbinical tradition with two outstanding teachers, Jesus and Paul, instructing in the Christian Way. Though Jewish educational methodology was important to the nascent church, including Mishnah, Gemara, Targum, Derek Erez, etc., as Christianity split away from Judaism to become the church of the Gentiles in the West, it was natural for Gentile teachers and educational methods to succeed the Jewish. Christian rabbinical traditions were kept alive in the East much longer. But by the second and third centuries, Western Christian teachers are not so much rabbis, as Roman grammarians, rhetors and philosophers, professional men hired to teach the catechumens the books of their new religion.

A. ROMAN EDUCATION

Education in the early days of Rome had been largely within the family circle where the children were taught respect for the law, customs, religious piety and morality. And even after schools were started, the lessons were practical, stressing: reading, writing, numbers and morality including the virtues of piety, love of country, justice, honesty and gravity.

Roman education was influenced by the Hellenist system and included three divisions: ludus, grammar school, and rhetoric. Although there were government efforts to bar the Greek influence, still many of the teachers were Greek, some of whom were slaves. Higher schools for the aristocrats were bilingual.

The grammar school teacher, *Litterator,* was also called

Primus Magister or *Magister Ludi*. School was often held in a shop fronting on the Forum, with the master seated on his *cathedra* on a raised dias, facing the students and aided by a *hypodidaskalos*. As Marrou comments,[1] "In Rome as in Greece, schoolmastering remained a despised occupation, the lowest of all professions, *rem indignissimam,* tiring, arduous and badly paid." By the third century a magister would need 30 pupils to equal the pay of a mason or a carpenter. This only attracted applicants from the lower classes; slaves, freedmen, or others of humble beginnings. The main subjects of study were reading, writing and some numbers. Discipline was severe, although it was mitigated by Nero's time.

At the age of 11 or 12, boys and girls of the upper classes went on to the grammarian's school, usually another shop along the Forum. The *Grammaticus* who taught the classics was paid four times as much as the primary teacher, but not much more than a skilled artisan so that upper class men were not attracted. The *Grammaticus* used the Greek teaching methods, stressing the theory of good speech and the study of the classical poets. Grammar, letters, syllables, words, and parts of speech were examined. By the end of the first century Quintilian favored the study of the older classical immortals: Virgil, Terrence, Sallust and Cicero,—the Latin Quadriga. The exposition included: *praelectio,* an explanatory reading by the master; a reading by the pupil; finally an *enarratio* or exposition or crisis of the passage.

In general, the Roman educators followed the Greek *egkyklios paideia,* (encyclopedia) known in Latin as the liberal arts, but the scientific side was slighted. For example, Quintilian allowed little time for science, spending most of his energy on grammar. Marrou writes[2] that although there were teachers of mathematics, geometry and music in Rome, they taught only a few who were inclined to these subjects.

Once the toga of manhood was received at the age of 15,

---

1. H. Marrou, **A History of Education in Antiquity,** New York, Sheed and Ward, 1956, p. 267.
2. Marrou, op, cit., p. 282.

the scions of the upper classes proceeded to the school of the rhetor to learn the art of oratory. Although top rhetors as Quintilian earned four times the salary of a grammarian, by the time of Diocletian, most rhetors earned only 250 denarii a month per pupil, 50 more than the grammarian, but still not enough to attract leading men. Moreover, many students, as today, were reluctant to pay. However, in the late empire rhetors attained high office in both church and state. Certainly among the educators, a generally low class, the rhetors were the highest. But as Marrou says[3] it was not usually their teaching that brought them to public attention, but their leadership in writing, administration and politics.

The rhetors also taught in the Forum, and perhaps as early as Hadrian the state supplied *exedras, auditoriums* for them. The methodology of the rhetors is based on Greek tradition going back to the Sophists. Cicero claimed that rather than stressing exercises and methodology, the rhetor's education should be based on a broad culture including: philosophy, law and history *(De Oratore)*. With this broad background one would have a good understanding of human nature as a basis for oratory. Quintilian agreed. But, in general, Roman rhetors followed the advice of neither Cicero nor Quintilian. Law was for specialists, and philosophy and history received comparatively little attention.

There was no Latin rhetoric as such, but rather an imitation of the Greek, making imaginary speeches on a subject given by the teacher, for example: kidnapping, family situations, laws, etc. Marrou comments,[4]

> The coming of the empire and the loss of political "liberty" from the time of Augustus onwards had caused Roman culture to model itself on Hellenistic culture, and the higher eloquence became, not political eloquence, but the disinterested aesthetic eloquence of the public lecturer.

Roman education more closely resembled the Greek with a view

3. **Ibid.**, pp. 254-55.
4. **Ibid.**, p. 288.

to acquiring an ideal humanism removed from technical and utilitarian problems.

Marrou remarks:[5]

> Real life is not the sole source of inspiration. There is also imagination, there is the great event. And indeed these subjects had a peculiar destiny that in the West took them far beyond the confines of the academic world, for they lie beyond the development of the tales or stories that began to appear in the Middle Ages in Latin, like the Gesta Romanorum, or in the vernacular. They are one of the sources of the romantic tradition in modern European literature.

Not to mention Western aretology and hagiography throughout the ages.

Actually this idealized rhetorical training would produce many lawyers and both civil and church leaders. Whereas the Greeks tended to specialize more in philosophy and medicine, the Romans gravitated more to law.

Rome gave the Greek culture, including education, to the world-to the Danube, Gaul, Spain, Africa and Britain. Elementary schools were everywhere, with grammar and rhetoric schools in the main centers. At that the masses were not reached in the hinterlands where native languages were still spoken. Some of the main educational centers were: Gaul: Limoges, Bordeaux, Marseilles, etc; Africa: Carthage; Italy: Rome, Naples and Milan.

Gradually the Roman government assumed more responsibility in educational matters. For example, Vespasian gave tax and other exemptions to teachers. But they had to fix a maximum figure for many were seeking the doctor's *cathedra* as a tax dodge. Students also had privileges. Vespasian endowed chairs of Greek and Latin rhetoric in Rome. Later Marcus Aurelius endowed one chair of rhetoric and four of philosophy (Platonists, Aristotelians, Epicureans, and Stoics) in Athens.

Municipal schools were common by the time of Pliny. Municipal teachers were hired by the city council *(Ordo)* after they had shown them their *probationes* (c.f. Augustine, *Con-*

5. Ibid.

fessions 13:33). Fifth century teachers who had completed twenty years with distinction were designated counts of the first order.

As Marrou writes,[6] aristocratic and educated culture was the special prerogative of the senatorial classes of the great landed proprietors. And the classical tradition was kept alive in them, despite invasions and other reverses.

> It was in vain that the **clarissimi** left the cities at the end of the third century and tried to settle down on their country estates in the **villae**, their country houses becoming true castles. They remained men of letters and intellectuals.

Even when the emperors became plebians from the third century on and the rude Barbarian leaders invaded, they still respected classical learning and culture. As family traditions weakened, more and more the preservation of culture fell upon the schools.

But we are concerned primarily with religious education especially Christian education. Early Roman family education was fundamentally concerned with morals and religious practice. As schooling became formalized outside the family circle, less stress was placed on these basics.

B. EARLY CHRISTIAN PAIDEIA

There was a tradition of Christian *paideia* going back to Jesus who experienced the *paideia* of his Father along with his sonship (Lk 23:16, 22; Heb 5:8). In *Hebrews* 12 the Christian as a brother of Christ is chastised in virtue of his adopted sonship.

> It is for discipline (**eis paideian**) that you have to endure. God is treating you as sons (Prov 3:11-12). For what son is there whom his father does not discipline (**paideuei**)? If you are left without discipline, in which all have participated, then you are illegitimate children and not sons (Heb 12:7-8).

6. **Ibid.**, p. 309.

Paideia, as Bertram writes (TWNT 5, 622) "is what God does to us if we submit to him." Thus we join Christ in submitting to the Father's *paideia*. And this is a better and stronger *paideia* than that of the Law. Although in the beginning it brings pain, later comes joy (Heb 12:11).

The Book of Revelation (3:19) also links the Father's love with his paideia. Paul had suffered this fatherly training (1 Cor 6:9; 2 Cor 11:23). And he admonishes Christian fathers to bring up their children in *paideia kai nouthesia kuriou* (Eph 6:4). This is the essence of Christian paideia, namely, the Lord educating through the earthly father, teacher or community. This is the message of the Pastorals and of Clement (1 Cor 21:8; 56:1-16).

Christian education, though it may have used some of the methods of Greek and Roman paideia, was basically different. At least in the beginning, it stressed moral and disciplinary training by parents and community, educating for the heavenly reward. Later, under the influence of the *didaskoloi* more interest was shown in doctrinal teaching.

As Western Christianity left its Jewish milieu and became almost totally a Roman and Gentile religion, the Christian teachers less resembled the rabbis and more and more mirrored the Roman rhetors and philosophers. For example, the *didaskoloi* who taught the catechumens, preparing them for Baptism. Most of these teachers were professional men, either rhetors or philosophers, hoping to supplement their meager incomes. Later many Christian bishops would be drawn from this class and teach from the episcopal cathedra.

Christianity, as Judaism, is a religion of the book, an intelectual religion as opposed to the mystery cults of Isis or Mithra. To many it seemed to be a philosophy. The LXX, the Gospels, Paul's letters, catecheses like Didache were studied in preparation for Baptism.

Christian teaching could not but be affected by Hellenism. To begin with it was preached and taught in Greek. The gradual Christian adaptation of Greek and Latin educational methodology is a good example of the cultural osmosis of the time. Christians accepted the basic Hellenist humanism and built upon it, for clearly one had to be a man before he could become a Christian. Indeed, Christianity seemed to flourish best when it could build upon a culture such as Hellenism.

Although there was an inevitable syncretism, on the other hand, there was a clash between the two religions, that is, the cult of the Muses and Christianity, the Academy and the Church. Whatever reservations the early church had concerning pagan cult and culture, it had to be open to the Hellenist education because Christianity is a book religion. But the pagan authors were always secondary, and a preparation for reading the gospels (Jerome, L 21). Even Tertullian who thought that the teaching of the pagan classics was incompatible with Christianity, allowed children to attend the schools in order to learn to read and write. But the child should be weaned from paganism by religious training at home and in church, counteracting the poisons of the pagan schools (Idol. 10).

But some Christians taught as grammarians or rhetors, e.g. Origen and Gregory of Nyssa. It seems that the Christian teachers sometimes twisted the pagan authors to fit their own beliefs, bringing on Julian's order forbidding Christians to teach in the Roman schools (362) (C.Th. 13, 3, 5), which was abrogated two years later. But, in general, the Christian teachers used the same methodology and texts as the pagan teachers. Sometimes the Christian pupils would draw a † at the top of each page of their work.

Let us now look at a few early Christian teachers who had their own schools for the training of catechumens in the fundamentals of the Christian religion. For example, we find Justin, a Samaritan philosopher, teaching in Rome in the second century. Trying various philosophies, he settled on Platonism, whose idealism and spirituality many Christian thinkers would find compatible with the gospels. Platonism lay the groundwork for Justin's conversion to Christianity, the true philosophy.

Justin opened a school of Christian philosophy in Rome about 150 above a certain Martinus near the Timotian Bath. There he dialogued with other philosophers, both Christian and pagan. As other schools, Justin's had its famous students as Tatian and Irenaeus and produced its own literary tradition.

Although philosophy was not as popular with the Romans as with the Greeks, there were some other philosophy teachers in Rome.

Justin was basically an apologist, refuting the slander of atheism, immorality and disloyalty hurled at the Christians by the Romans. It is true that the Christians have a different God than the Romans, another moral code and a heavenly kingdom instead of an earthly one, but all of these are true in contrast to the false Roman ones. In his dialogue with Trypho Justin is careful to point out Christianity as the true philosophy, and Jesus Christ the true Messiah predicted by the prophets, and also the true Logos of Hellenism. History is consummated in Christ. Christianity is not just one philosophy among many, but *The* Philosophy, Truth itself. Justin saw both Judaism and Platonism as laying the groundwork for Christianity.

Hippolytus was another Roman Christian philosopher towards the end of the second century. As Justin, he taught a Logos theology, yet his trinitarianism was primitive, with the Logos appearing as a facet of God, while the Spirit seemed to be even less. There was a justified fear of Logos theology in the early church. In fact, it was kept out of the Nicaean creed out of fear of Arianism or Ditheism. Hippolytus in his attempt to synthesize Christianity with Greek philosophy, succeeded only in weakening the former.

Dix comments on the situation in Rome in the second century:[7]

> The genius of the Roman church was religious, not speculative. It sought always to confine its requirements simply to **credenda**, to the facts for belief, and so far as possible to leave the explanations of these, the theology, a very wide latitude. Its method was always to set complementary truths side by side with hardly a pretense of reconciliation, to declare that this and this is the faith, and that all metaphysical systematization which cannot find full room for each of these facts is thereby ruled out as defective, and then to leave the matter at that. If the doctrines so established appear contradictory, that is the affair not of the hierarchy, but of the theologians.

7. Hippolytus of Rome, **Apostolic Tradition,** London, SPCK, 1968, p. xxiii.

But the theologian must begin from the *terminus a quo* that the church has defined. Episcopal doctrinal decisions tended to favor the beliefs of the simple laity. Really the arguing and contesting of the didaskoloi never concerned the Christian laity any more than the wrangling of the rabbis bothered the simple Jewish lay folk. Much of Christian theology as with much of the Talmudic discussions seem to have been written more for the doctors themselves. Many early fathers including Tertullian (Prax 3) and Clement of Alexandria (Strom 1. 1. 18. 2). not only complained that the laity had no interest in their speculations, but that they actually tried to put a stop to them.

Liturgy, rites and prayers were the *forte* of the layman. And although these were based on belief and doctrine, *lex orandi est lex credendi*, in general, he could not have cared less and so was indifferent to the musing of the theologians. So the bishops, the guardians of the flock, tended to favor the side of the simple, uncomplicated lay man in their disputes with the learned doctors.

Hermas speaks eloquently against false teachers in Rome in the second century. One does not believe in repentance after Baptism (Mandate 4). And another teaches doublemindedness as a false prophet (Mandate 11). Though they sit on the *cathedra*, they are empty. The true prophet and teacher who has the Spirit is gentle, quiet, humble. He refrains from evil and worthless desires; he is needy and does not speak for himself, but only when God wishes him to speak.

On the other hand, the false prophet and teacher,

> That man who thinks he has the Spirit elevates himself and wishes to have the seat of honor. And right away he is bold and shameless and talkative, and lives in great luxury and in many other pleasures and accepts pay for his prophesying.

He avoids the assembly of the righteous, associating only with the duplex, telling them what they want to hear. But he is speechless when he comes into the assembly of the righteous (Mandate 11).

In Similitude 9:22 Hermas has more to say about false teachers:

> From the fifth mountain, the one with green vegetation and was

rough, are such believers as these: they are faithful, but slow to learn and self-determined and pleasing themselves, wanting to know everything and yet they know nothing at all. Because of this self-determination of theirs, understanding has left them and foolish stupidity has come into them. But they praise themselves for having understanding and wish to be teachers on an official basis, though foolish as they are. So because of this haughtiness many, by exalting themselves, have been ruined, for self-determination and over-confidence are a great demon. (AF 6:150)

Some of these repented, while others continued to live in evil.

The tension between the elder guardians preserving the apostolic tradition for the laity and the teachers and philosophers speculating on new ideas would be a continual life situation in the church; and perhaps this polarity between the old and the new is the very tension of life itself, which is constantly and often painfully adapting to new environmental conditions. And unless it adapts it surely must die according to the inexorable law of nature.

When a teacher was excommunicated for holding an opinion that was too far out, his disciples usually followed him out. Moreover, he continued to teach in his *didaskaleion* as before. One of the basic problems here was that the Christian church was not as yet allowed to have its own buildings for teaching. Thus the only way for Christian teaching to continue was by private teachers in their own *didaskaleia*. These were professional men, either rhetors or grammarians, and were usually paid by the catechumens or by a patron and not by the church.

We have seen Justin's and Hippolytus' philosophical schools in Rome. Others were set up by Tatian, Justin's disciple, by Rhodon, the two Theodoti, Praxeas, Epigonus, Clemones and Sabellius. Soon there would be other schools in Alexandria, Caesarea, Antioch, Edessa, Nisibis and elsewhere. But there was a fear of having the church split up into schools or heresies. Harnack comments.[8]

As a direct counterpoise to the danger of having the church split up

---

8. **Mission and Expansion of Christianity**, New York, Harper, 1962, pp. 357f. For the use of **hairesis** to denote Greek school classes, see Marrou, **op. cit.**, pp. 110, 386.

3. **Roman teacher and boy with parents. Stone funeral monument of the third—fourth century. Teacher has box with volumina. (Arlon, Belgium, Museum)**

into schools, and the gospel handed over to the secular culture and the acumen and the ambition of individual teachers, the consciousness of the church finally asserted its powers, and the word "school" became a term of reproach for a separatist ecclesiastical community.

Thus: the Marcionite school, Theodotian, Sabellian, etc. But the Christian teachers would maintain their position alongside the ordained clergy until such a time when presbyters and episcopals would be drawn more and more from their ranks, by the end of the third and the beginning of the fourth century.

Let us see for a moment how the Christian teachers operated in Rome. Hippolytus describes it well in his *Apostolic Tradition* (16). The *conversi* went to the home or shop of the teacher for instruction. "Those who came forward for the first time to hear the word shall first be brought to the teachers (at the house) before all the people *(laos)* come in." They must bring Christian witnesses to their character and sincerity. Slaves could attend with the permission of their masters. But no possessed person *(energumen)* was allowed to enter until he had been cleansed. Since this is basically an intellectual exercise, any lightheadedness would only spoil it for all concerned.

The early Christians were most careful on admissions and kept neophytes segregated as their Jewish contemporaries did. Especially in times of persecution there was fear of infiltration and subversiveness.

Each time the teacher finishes his instructions, let the catechumens pray by themselves apart from the faithful. After the prayer let the teacher lay hands on them and pray and dismiss them. Whether the teacher be an ecclesiastic or a layman, let him do the same. (18-19)

It seems that while the teaching of the pagan catechumens was done by the lay *didaskoloi,* the instruction of the faithful was pursued by the clergy at their daily chapter (33). "The God-fearing man should consider it a great loss if he does not go to the place in which they give instruction and especially if he knows how to read" (35). For the Holy Spirit dwells in this assembly where instructions are given in morals and faith (35). And if an instruction is not given, the faithful should read a holy book at home.

We have seen the Roman teachers, but there were also

Christian *didaskoloi* elsewhere in the empire. In the beginning they were generally associated with prophets and apostles. Often they were professional rabbis or *magistri*. For example, the Eastern *Didache* speaks of the traveling teachers.

> Thus, whoever comes and teaches you all the aforesaid things, receive him. And if the teacher himself turns aside and teaches another didache, which undermines the aforesaid, do not listen to him. But if his teaching fosters righteousness and knowledge of the Lord, receive him as the Lord. (11:1-2) (AF 3:169)

These traveling teachers paralleled the peripatetic Jewish rabbis of the time.

Not any one could be a teacher, but only those qualified (Jas 3:1). So non-teachers who exhort make it clear that they are not doctors. Thus Barnabas' letter, "And now, not as a teacher but as one from your very midst, I will point out a few things which will enable you to rejoice in the present circumstances" (1:8). Some reluctance to claim the *cathedra* might have been due to reverence for Christ as *The* Teacher of Christianity. Even Ignatius of Antioch speaks, not as a teacher, but as a fellow disciple of Christ (Eph 3:1).

A Pseudo-Clementine Epistle on Virginity warns those who seek to be teachers, quoting Paul (1 Cor 12:29):

> Let us, therefore, fear the judgment which awaits teachers, for a severe judgment will those teachers receive "Who teach, but do not" (Mt 23:3), and those who take upon them the name of Christ falsely, and say: we teach the truth, and yet go wandering about idly, and exalt themselves, and make their "boast in the mind of the flesh." (Col 2:18) (1, 11)

These men teach frivolously, leading others into error. But if you have the gift of teaching, bless God, and serve your spiritual brothers for their edification.

But the true teachers were highly respected and often ranked with the charismatics. Tertullian places them second only to the martyrs (De Praescr. 3). Cyprian seems to include them among the elders (L 29). Epiphanius describes them as standing alongside of the elders (Haer 42:2). There was certainly a rivalry between teachers, presbyters and bishops and an overlapping in which some teachers were chosen as bishops.

C. EDDESSA AND NISIBIS

We mentioned earlier that Christian rabbis in the Jewish tradition continued to teach on the Eastern fringes of the Empire. Let us now take a closer look. As we have seen, Babylonia and then Persia were centers of Jewish learning from the time of the exile, producing such outstanding scholars as Hillel and Nathan. The main centers of learning in Babylonia in Tannaitic times were Nehardea and Nisibis. While Palestine was besieged by troubles in the first and second centuries, Babylonian schools grew unmolested. In the third century two outstanding Palestinian rabbis, Abba Areka (Rab) and Samuel brought Babylonian scholarship to a high point, Samuel in Nehardea and Rab in Sura. The greatest product of these schools is the Babylonian Talmud completed around the year 500.

Meanwhile the Christian school of Judaism was also thriving in Eastern Syria and Babylonia, principally Osroene and Adiabene. Eusebius (HE 1, 13, 1-22) claims that Abgar, the king of Edessa wrote to Jesus who sent him his disciple Thaddeus. This tradition may be a product of the school of Edessa under Abgar IX the king in the second century.

Another version has the school of Thomas located at Edessa, writing the *Psalms of Thomas* (2c), the *Acts of Thomas* (3c), and possibly the *Gospel of Thomas* (2c). The relationship of the school of Edessa with Jerusalem may be gauged by the large place that James has in the *Gospel of Thomas*. Other works of this school may have been the *Odes of Solomon* (1c) and the *Gospel of Truth*.[9]

The origins of the Christian school of Edessa are, indeed, hazy, but may originate from Jerusalem led by Jesus' disciples, Thaddeus or Thomas or both. On the Eastern borders of the empire, Edessa had contact with many oriental peoples. Thus the school of Edessa is called the school of the Persians.

The Syrian Tatian, Justin's disciple and leading promoter of encratist asceticism, may have returned here from Rome in

---

9. J. Danielou, **The First Six Hundred Years**, New York, McGraw-Hill, 1964, p. 46f.

the 170's to write his popular *Diatessaron*. Bardesanes (154-222), friend of Abgar IX, hymnologist, philosopher and perhaps astrologer, also was from Edessa. Moreover, the Syrian *Peshitta* (2c) may originate from the school there.

Ephrem the Syrian is sometimes associated with the Edessa foundation, coming there from his school in Nisibis in 363 when the emperor Jovinian ceded that city to the Persians. Ephrem appears as the *mepasqana*, expositor or commentator and head of the school.[10] Among other works, he composed a commentary on Tatian's *Diatessaron*. The Edessa interpretation of scriptures seemed to balance between Antiochene literalism and Alexandrian typology.

After Ephrem's death (373), the school's reputation continued to grow under his disciples with the number of "brothers" in studies ever increasing. Other famous teachers who were elected *mepasqana* of the school were: Qiyore, Rabbula, Ibas, and Narsai. It seems that some of the scholars were called to be presbyters and bishops.

Students at Edessa began with a study of the psalter, plus instructions in reading and writing. Then they began the books of the Bible and commentaries by Ephrem and later Theodore of Mopsuestia. That the head man of the school is the *mepasqana* indicates the importance of exegesis. In this respect it parallels the midrash schools. By the fifth century, Greek philosophy was studied along with history, geography and astronomy. Some famous teachers were Hiba, Kumi, Proba, M'ana, translating the Greek fathers and philosophers into Syriac, especially Theodore of Mopsuestia.

The split over the diophysite movement in the fifth century would destroy the school. Rabbula, bishop of Edessa, sided with Cyril of Alexandria against the diophysites and Antiochene theology. Narsai, *mepasqana* of the school and follower of Theodore and Nestorius, was forced to leave for Nisibis (451) where he was welcomed by the Persians. Other diophysite teachers and students would follow. And the school of Edessa was closed by Bishop Cyrus II in 489.

10. A. Voobus, **History of the School of Nisibis**, Louvain, 1965, pp. 7ff.

Narsai was offered the headship of a small school in Nisibis founded by Semon Garmuia and supported by the bishop Bar Sauma. Narsai's group is typical of many early Christian schools or heresies, which when declared heterodox were forced to move elsewhere, but continued to flourish in their new locale.

The site of the new school was a camel stable and caravansary near the church and the bishop's house. The school at Nisibis was modeled on that of Edessa. So by examination we might get glimpses into earlier practices. Because of the migration from Edessa, the school of Nisibis started out with a good reputation for scholarship. As at Edessa the head of the school was elected from the teachers and was called *mepasqana* or *rabban,* sided by an elected assistant, *rabbaita,* and an advisory council called "outstanding brothers."

Among the teachers were some known as *maqreiane,* readers or lecturers, *mehageiane* who gave a firm foundation in reading and a *sepera* or scribe to teach writing. As with the Persian Jews, the teachers were often called *Mar.* Grammar, philology and exact reading of the liturgical chants were taught. Some philosophy was studied, but the main thrust was biblical exegesis with the principal exegete as head of the school as at Edessa.

The schools of Nisibis and Edessa resembled monasteries and may reflect Syrian asceticism and perhaps some rabbinical customs of the time. We have already seen some parallel terminology: *mespasqana, rabban, mar,* the central position of exegesis. It seems that the teachers and students also lived in community. And students were required to remain celibate while in studies and hand over their possessions to the community.[11] Discipline under the *rabbaita* was strict even to beating and expulsion. Students learned the Nestorian doctrines over a three year course and sometimes there were as many as 1000 in attendance at the height of the school. Meanwhile officials kept an eye on their pupils even during vacations, warning them against going into Byzantine territory.

Narsai was forced to leave his school for a period of six years in which he lived in the monastery of Kephar Mari. The

11. A. Voobus, **op. cit.,** p. 110.

jealousy of the wife of Bar Sauma over Narsai's popularity may have been a cause.[12] If this is true, it might be another example of the rivalry between bishops and teachers in the early church. When the rift was healed, Narsai returned but moved his residence far from the episcopal domicile. But his theological enemies did not rest.

Some of Narsai's illustrious successors were Abraham, Johanan de Bet Rabban and Henana. For 200 years Nestorian alumni of the school filled the sees of Persia and Nestorian missions spread as far as China. Eventually it was succeeded by rival schools in Seleucia-Ctesiphon and Baghdad.

Having seen the Syrian and Persian schools on the Eastern borders of the empire, let us return to Alexandria and its school of catechetics which stressed the Greek rather than the Jewish paideia, but which also centered around exegesis especially under its illustrious head, Origen.

12. Ibid., p. 116.

5

ANYONE CAN CELEBRATE SOLEMN LITURGICAL FUNCTIONS BEFORE THE PEOPLE, BUT THERE ARE NOT MANY MEN WHO LEAD HOLY LIVES AND KNOW A GREAT DEAL ABOUT CHRISTIAN DOCTRINE, MEN OF PROVED WISDOM AND UNDOUBTED CAPACITY FOR TEACHING OTHERS THE TRUTH ABOUT THINGS (Origen, *Homily 6 on Leviticus*, 6)

THE CATECHETICAL school at Alexandria is one of the first attempts at organized Christian education. And it produced many famous teachers such as Clement, Origen, Dionysius, Peter, Athanasius, Didymus and Cyril. Practically from its inception Alexandria had been a great intellectual center with a famous library built by Ptolemy I in the Brucheion and developed by Ptolemy II (3c, bc). By the first century it contained 700,000 rolls, but was partially destroyed by Aurelian in 272 AD. Ptolemy I also built the world-renowned Museum which was to be' to science and literature what the schools of Athens were to philosophy. The Museum was a college of scholars under the leadership of a priest of the Muses, subsidized by the government. Here were developed systematic studies of literature, philology, textual criticism and library science, encompassing most of the Greek classical literature.

A. CLEMENT OF ALEXANDRIA

Into this milieu came the Jewish and Christian scholars with their attempts, to synthesize Hellenistic learning and religious culture, yet fully aware of the dangers of paganism. Founded by Pantaenus (180) the Christian catechetical school of Alexandria flourished under his successor Clement who was knowledgeable in philosophy, science and letters. One purpose of the catechetical school seems to have been to correct errors taught at the pagan Museum. But there was an exchange between the two schools, with pagans attending the Christian academy, while Christians, as Origen, studied under the great Ammonius Saccas at the Museum.

Clement argued against the Gnostic teachers of Alexandria who wanted to use certain pejorative elements from Hellenism and heterodox Judaism in their speculations. Yet he followed the way pioneered by Philo in trying to show the basic compatibility of revelation and Hellenist philosophy. His three main works are: *An Exhortation to the Greeks, the Pedagogue, and Stromateis* or *Carpets*. In his *Exhortation* (189) he asks the Greeks to see the truth and beauty described by their poets and philosophers as fulfilled in the true Logos, Jesus Christ. Urging them to abandon their idolatry for the Word of God, he points out the absurdity of pagan myths, cruelty of sacrifices, and the stupidity of the images. The philosophers and poets have already seen this and so helped pave the way for the Truth of Christ.

In his *Pedagogue* or tutor, he shows those who have accepted Christ that he is their Tutor. "The Tutor, being practical, not theoretical, his aim is thus to improve the soul, not to teach, and to train it up to a virtuous, not an intellectual life" (1:1) (ANF).[1] As the pedagogue has charge of children, so we are God's adopted children through Baptism and he treats us with kindness or severity as we show need.

Books Two and Three of the *Pedagogue* stress practical morality with a Stoic influence. As we know, moral problems were frequent topics of early Christian teachings in the Gospels, Paul and the Fathers. For Clement morality is living according to the Logos who is *The* Pedagogue by word and example. Three Stoic virtues in particular that he stresses are: self-sufficiency, frugality and apathy.

Clement originally intended to have his trilogy cover three areas, namely: exhortation, training and teaching. However, he

---

1. Clement's quotes are from the **Ante-Nicean Fathers,** vol. 2.

preferred to follow the model of the day in his third work, *Stromateis*, or *Carpets*, which is not a systematic study but rather hits various questions of the day at random. First of all, he underlines the compatibility of Christianity and Greek philosophy.

The works of the philosophers were written under God's providence (Stir 1:1). "First, even if philosophy were useless, if the demonstration of its uselessness does good, it is yet useful" (1:2). Philosophy is a gift of God to the Greeks and can be a handmaid to theology.

> The preparatory training for rest in Christ exercises the mind, rouses the intelligence, and begets an inquiring shrewdness, by means of the true philosophy, which the initiated possess, having found it, or rather received it from Truth itself. (1:5)

Philosophy concerns itself with speculation, the performance of precepts, and the formation of good men. The Gnostic, the true philosopher, seeks God in order to know him as far as possible. This is the highest speculation because it seeks to penetrate the greatest of mysteries. This is true wisdom from which right conduct can never be separated (2:10).

Philosophy gives only an imperfect knowledge of God, but it prepares the way for perfect knowledge. "So there is no absurdity in philosophy having been given by divine providence as a preparatory discipline for the perfection which is by Christ" (6:17). Philosophy is a gift of God to the Greeks as Law was his gift to the Hebrews, both preparing the way.

Clement writes of the true Christian Gnostic as opposed to the false Gnostic. The true Gnostic seeks God, trained in Christian knowledge, pursuing good for its own sake.

> We are then to strive to reach manhood as befits the Gnostic, and to be as perfect as we can while still abiding in the flesh, making it our study with perfect concord here to concur with the will of God, to the restoration of what is the truly perfect nobleness and relationship to the fulness of Christ, that which depends on our perfection. (4:21)

The Gnostic aims for likeness to Christ and God, but first he has to attain purity of heart. "Mildness, I think, and philanthropy and eminent piety, are the rules of gnostic assimilation" (7:3). Controlling his passions and practicing every virtue, the Gnostic is open to the Gnosis, receiving from the

> Only-Begotten the express image of the glory of the universal King and Almighty Father, who impresses on the Gnostic the seal of the perfect contemplation according to His own image; so that there is now a third divine image, made as far as possible like the Second Cause, the essential Life, through which we live the true life; the Gnostic, as we describe him, being described as moving amid things sure and wholly immutable. (7:3)

The true Gnostic is a pupil of the Lord, devoting all his energies to learning and acquiring the knowledge he desires.

> Striving, then, to attain to the summit of knowledge (Gnosis), decorous in character, composed in mein, possessing all those advantages which belong to the true Gnostic, fixing his eye on fair models . . . he therefore loves not all the good things of the world, which are within his grasp, that he may not remain on the ground, but the things hoped for as to be apprehended. (7:11)
>
> The Gnostic, consequently, in virtue of being a lover of the one true God, is the really perfect man and friend of God, and is placed in the rank of son. For these are the names of nobility and knowledge, and perfection in the contemplation of God; which crowning step of advancement the gnostic soul receives, when it has become quite pure, reckoned worthy to behold everlastingly God almighty "face" it is said "to face," for having become wholly spiritual, and having in the spiritual church gone to what is of kindred nature, it abides in the rest of God. (7:11)

In a word, the Gnostic is a perfect man, self-controlled, faithful, helpful to others, prayerful, teaching others by his example, lover of God and man, self-restrained, charitable, longsuffering and forgiving, a pupil modeled on the life and teachings of the Master.

In all three of Clement's works we see him striving for relevance, first trying to wean the Greeks away from their false gods, but at the same time honoring their philosophy as a way to Christ, going from the known wisdom of the ancients to the unknown mysteries of Christianity, with Christ as the true Logos and Christianity as the true philosophy. About the year 202 Clement was forced to leave Alexandria in the persecution of Septimius Severus.

B. ORIGEN

Clement was succeeded at the catechetical school by Origen, an Alexandrian grammarian, whom Pope Demetrius placed in charge of the school when he was only 18. Despite dangers of the persecution, Origen was still a popular teacher. He soon felt that his grammarian's profession was incompatible with his sacred studies, even selling his library of pagan authors. He lived abstemiously like a philosopher; if he had been born a century later, surely he would have been a monk.

Many famous people came to study under Origen including Plutarch, Serenus, Heraclides, Hero, another Serenus, Herais, Basilides, etc. In the beginning he taught preparatory subjects as dialetics, physics, mathematics as well as philosophy and theology. But he soon devoted his full time to theology and Scripture, while his pupil Heraclas took over the introductory courses. At the same time, Origen attended Ammonius Saccas' lectures on Platonism at the Museum.

Origen's school was probably held in his home or else in a shop as the Roman teachers did. Subsidized by his friend Ambrose, he employed copyists and secretaries to help in his scriptural work. Most of his students were catechumens, although others were welcome including pagan philosophers.

As his predecessor, Origen saw the usefulness of pagan philosophy, once it had been purged of its errors. Although he sampled many philosophical systems with his students, they did not settle on any one, but took what was useful from each. In the persecution of Caracalla, Origen fled to Caesarea in Palestine to teach and preach.

This is the period when the bishops are rising as the chief teachers of the church, as we have seen in Rome. Although Origen had been a member of the *didaskoloi*, an extra-clerical college of teachers, he subsequently went to Palestine to be ordained, perhaps foreseeing that to remain an effective teacher, he would have to adopt the clerichood.

It seems that there was a rivalry between the clerics and the teachers until eventually more and more presbyters and bishops were chosen from among the *didaskoloi*. From the beginning the elders had been good family men of some influence in the community, but who did not necessarily excel in learning. So *did-askoloi* had to be hired to instruct the catechumens. Also the teaching of rude and unlettered catechumens did not appeal to many of the hierarchs.

For Origen the *didaskoloi tēs ekklēsias* are an order parallel to the priests (Homily 14 on Genesis; Homily 2 on Numbers). Sometimes when a *didaskolos* became too popular, feelings of jealousy were aroused in the clergy. Origen was opposed by the uneducated Pope Demetrius who was shocked that Origen had preached in the Caesarean church in the presence of the bishops, though still a lay teacher. But Alexander, bishop of Jerusalem, and Theoctistus, bishop of Caesarea, defended this policy.

> Where there is found persons suited to help the brethren, they are invited to preach to the people by the holy bishops. For example: in Laranda, Euelpis by Neon; in Iconium, Paulinus by Celcus; and in Synnada, Theodore by Atticus, our blessed bishops. And it is likely that this happens in other places also without our knowing it. (Eusebius, HE 6, 19, 18)

This early church custom may reflect Jewish synagogal practice in which any qualified male could be chosen by the archisynagogue to address the congregation.

Originally, as we have seen, the teacher was an office separate from the presbyters who were principally administrators and judges, acting in college, while the rabbis conducted the schools. By the third and fourth centuries the sanhedrins, both Jewish and Christian contained many rabbis. This in itself may have been a factor in restricting the independent teacher. Harnack points out another reason, namely, that since many of the teachers were Hellenist philosophers, there was a danger of syncretizing the gospels away. But a further and more compelling reason was:

> The episcopate with its intolerance of any office that would not submit to its strict control and allow itself to be incorporated in the simple and compact organization of the hierarchy headed by the bishop.[2]

Origen himself gives another reason in his *Contra Celsum* (3:9). Now that the upper classes are coming into the church,

2. Harnack, **The Mission and Expansion of Christianity**, p. 361.

the office of teacher has taken on a new prestige, which it definitely did not have in the days of persecution. The teaching no longer only involved instructing the unlettered lower classes, but included the more delightful task of initiating the well educated and the wealthy into the Christian mysteries. More and more the bishops themselves would be drawn from these classes.

The Christian teachers, as Origen, attracted many pagans to their lectures, much as a modern inquiry class, for this was the logical place to go to find out about the new religion. Both Clement and Origen taught Christianity to the pagans as the true philosophy, but not necessarily incompatible with their own Stoicism and Platonism. Both men used their learning to attract men of letters to the faith.

The brilliant Origen was intolerant of ignorant clerics who were mere liturgical functionaries. "There are not many men who lead holy lives and know a great deal about Christian doctrine, men of proved wisdom and undoubted capacity for teaching others the truth about things" (Homily 6 on Leviticus, 6)[3]. Origen's ideal, writes Danielou[4]

> Was the "Doctor" who was at once a man of deep spiritual life, a speculative thinker and an exegete. It can be seen emerging in the second century from the raw material provided by the lives of the gnostic **didaskoloi** and attained its ideal realization in Origen himself.

Homily on Leviticus (4) compares the Doctor of Scripture to a priest.

> The priest who takes away the skin . . . is the man who removes the veil of the letter from God's word and reveals the members—the spiritual meaning—behind. These members, this inner meaning of the word, he puts down not just anywhere, but on the altar; the place he puts them in is raised above the ground and holy. In other words, the men he reveals God's mysteries to are not the undeserving, whose lives are base and earthy, but those who are God's altars, those in whom the divine fire, continually consuming the flesh of the victim, never ceases to burn. It is on men like that that the victim of the holocaust is placed and divided limb from limb. The man who divided the victim limb from limb is the one who can systematically explain and show with the proper distinctions what degree of spiritual pro-

3. J. Danielou, **Origen**, New York, Sheed and Ward, 1955, pp. 44ff.
4. **Ibid.**, p. 45.

gress is involved in touching the fringe of Christ's garment and what in washing his feet with one's tears and wiping them with the hair of one's head . . .

Anyone who can reason about that spiritually and see the distinctions involved—any **didaskolos** of that kind—may be considered to be the priest who divides the victim limb from limb and puts it on the altar.

Origen is explaining his own rationale in Scripture study. The Christian *didaskolos* must be careful to give proper food to each class of the church: beginners, advanced and gnostics, just as Jesus taught differently to sinners, faithful and apostles.

The doctor is now a priest who has living souls for altars, to whom is presented the living logos as spiritual food. The doctor uncovers the logos hidden under the letter of the Scriptures, presenting to each soul the facet he needs. The Levitical priesthood has been succeeded in the New Law by the spiritual doctor. But what of the clerical priesthood?

As Origen sees it, the church is the hierarchy of the faithful in their various degrees of holiness, grouped around the spiritual master, rather than the ecclesiastical community grouped around its bishop.[5]

In Homily 9 on Leviticus (1) Origen places the stress on the spiritual priesthood of all believers. It is upon this basis that the priestly doctor builds. And the food must be in proportion to the believers: solid food for the men, milk and vegetables for the women, children and proselytes (Homily 9 on Joshua, 9). The spiritual *didaskolos* can by his very spirituality penetrate the hidden spiritual meaning of the mysteries, which are hidden behind the veil of his conscience and should not be readily shown to non-believers. Thus when he is instructing the *competentes* he should hold back some of the secret wisdom (Homily 4 on Numbers, 3).

All are not worthy of the priesthood or the doctorate. It often happened that people of low and worldly mind entered the higher ranks of the priesthood or the professor's chair. Often more spiritual Christians may be found in the lower ranks of the ministry and among the laity (Homily 2 on Numbers, 1). Origen

5. **Ibid.**, p. 48.

places great emphasis on the holiness of both priest and doctor. It is not enough to teach, but one must also do. This is the very basis of the *didaskolos* going back to Jesus and Paul, both of whom taught by word and example.

We have seen how Pope Demetrius of Alexandria took umbrage at Origen's preaching at Caesarea. Fifteen years later he would take even more umbrage at his ordination by the Palestinian bishops without Demetrius' permission and despite Origen's eunuch-hood—both against early church customs. Eusebius (HE 6. 8, 4) claimed that Demetrius was jealous of Origen's success as a scholar and teacher. If so, this would not be the last time that ignorant and jealous administrators would try to silence successful teachers and writers. At any rate, Origen was excommunicated by the Alexandrian synod and deprived of his priesthood (231).

So he set sail for Caesarea where he was invited to start a new school of theology by the bishop. His school followed the Alexandrian plan, starting with an introductory philosophical exhortation, then a preparatory training including: logic, dialectic, natural science, geometry and astronomy, and finally ethics and theology. In other words, the old *egkyklios paideia* of the professional *didaskoloi* with the addition of morals and religion based on Scripture.

Gregory the Wonderworker, one of Origen's students at Caesarea has left us with a farewell speech describing the school. He fell under Origen's spell.

> Being most mightily smitten by this love, I was persuaded to give up all those objects or pursuits which seem to us befitting, and among others even my wasted jurisprudence. . . . And in my estimation there arose but one object, dear and worth desire—philosophy, and that master of philosophy, this inspired man. (**Panegyric of Origen**, 6)

But not all were equally laudatory of Origen's scholarship. The ignorant taunted him that he was wasting his time in his efforts to make the Word relevant for his disciples.

> The ignorant, among other faults, have this worst fault of all, that of regarding those who have devoted themselves to the word and teaching as vain and useless. They prefer their own ignorance to the study and toil of the learned, and by changing titles, they call the exercises of

the teachers verbiage, but their own unteachableness or ignorance,
simplicity. (Homily on Psalm 36; 5:1)

Actually the teaching and learning of Origen probably affected
a small minority of Christians. As today, the bulk of the Christians, both at Alexandria and Caesarea cared little for the in-
tricacies of exegesis and theologizing. In general, only the upper
classes passed beyond the ludus into grammar and rhetoric
schools and so could appreciate Origen's work.

Let us look for a moment at the teachings of Origen, trying
at the same time to see him as a *didaskolos* in a period when the
didaskoloi were free to speculate and syncretize Greek philosophy
and the Christian gospels, for not yet had Christian theology become concretized by episcopal synods and creeds, and not yet had
the episcopals reserved to themselves the doctor's *cathedra*.

First of all Origen orientated all of his studies towards the
Book:

> In order that what the sons of the philosophers say about geometry
> and music and grammar and rhetoric and astronomy, that they are
> the handmaids of philosophy, we may say of philosophy itself in re-
> lation to Christianity, (Letter to Gregory, 13:1)

Origen leaned towards Plato and sometimes it led him into difficulties such as the pre-existence of the human soul.

Some feel that his use of allegories in his interpretation of
Scripture led to subjectivity. His Scripture studies and teaching
occupied the foremost place in his work. For example, his *Hexepla*
edition of the Old Testament is a monumental attempt at
establishing a critical text. Also he wrote scholia, homilies and
commentaries on Scripture. Scripture for Origen is not something written only for the people of past ages. No, it is the living
word of God addressing man today. The relationship between the
Old and the New Testament is seen through allegory.

Origen teaches three scriptural senses, namely, historical,
mystical and moral, which correspond to man's three parts:
body, soul and spirit and the three grades of perfection. In
Scripture the historical is found intermingled with the impossible,
but often a superior spiritual sense is hidden in these passages.
Origen was one of the first demythologizers. For example, he

writes of Mt 4:8 where the devil takes Jesus up on a high mountain to see the kingdoms of the world.

> The careful reader will detect thousands of other passages like this in the gospels which will convince him that events which did not take place at all are woven into the records of what literally did happen. (On First Principles, 4, 3, 1)

The Book of Genesis is filled with these myths, but the man of discernment can perceive the hidden spiritual meanings (4, 3, 5).

As the rabbis, Origen defends the literal interpretation of Scriptures, but also the hidden spiritual meaning. A key problem in these early days especially in Alexandria was the relationship of Christianity to Judaism. Steering between the Jewish literal interpretation of the Old Testament and the Gnostic rejection of it, Origen takes a middle path by his allegorical interpretation. Philo, of course, had paved the way. For Origen the Law is a preparation for the gospels; thus the Old Testament is a tutor or pedagogue, preparing man for the Master. Moses is dead, but Jesus lives on (Homily 10 on Leviticus, 1; Homily 2 on Joshua, 1).

Origen saw the mystery of Christ hidden in the forest of the Scriptures, to be released by the Scripture scholar who can grasp the hidden analogies and allegories. To the Gnostic the Old Testament myths are foolishness, while the Jews, holding to a literal interpretation of the Law, see no value in the Law of Christ. The task of the Scripture scholar never ends for the more he explains the mysteries, the more he uncovers new ones (Homily 9 on Genesis, 7).

Besides his Scriptural work, Origen also engaged in apologetics *(Against Celsus)* and dogma *(On First Principles)*, laying the foundation stones for the development of dogma, using Greek philosophy, Scripture and Christian tradition in his early attempt at a Christian synthesis. Along this same line both Clement and Origen are the founders of Christian philosophy. Though the Greeks already had a theology, Clement and Origen's approach was new. As Jaeger comments[6]

6. W. Jaeger, Early Christianity and Greek Paideia, Oxford, 1961, p. 47.

New was the fact that philosophical speculation was used by them to support a positive religion that was not itself the result of independent human search for the truth, like earlier Greek philosophies, but took as its point of departure a divine revelation contained in a holy book, the Bible.

As the pagan Platonists in the schools of Longinus and Plotinus explained the myths of Homer, so the Christian scholars sought to explicate the biblical myths and anthropomorphisms. Contemporary Greek philosophers had attacked the Christian myths just as their ancestors had opposed the Greek myths. By explaining the spiritual sense which lay behind the literal one, Origen saved the Christian paideia and its biblical foundation much as the Stoics had done with Homer's theology.

Jaeger points out[7] that both Clement and Origen followed the Greek distinction between the knowers (gnostic) and the believer (pistic), with the gnosis on the higher level. This is the very basis of Gnosticism is its many forms, with its secret knowledge not available to the simple people. "The Christian gnosis of Clement or Origen unequivocally explains itself as an attempt to satisfy the gnostic appetites of their contemporaries in a legitimate fashion."[8] The elite Gnostics possessed an esoteric knowledge of the mysteries *(alētheia)* while the pistics had a lower exoteric experience *(doxa)*. But the Christian gnosis was the only true mystery which superceded all the false mysteries of the pagans.

Jaeger warns against identifying Origen too strongly with any one philosopher.

If we ask where we can grasp the intrinsic unity of Origen's diffused and vast theological thought, we see that it is to be found not in his adherence to any single philosophical system such as Platonism or Stoicism or in an eclectic mixture of these, but in the basic view of history emerging from the constellation of an age that saw classical Greek culture and the Christian church undergo a process of mutual adaptation.[9]

7. Ibid., p. 53.
8. Ibid., p. 54.
9. Ibid., p. 62.

In the cultural osmosis of the time the people saw that the two traditions had something in common especially when looked on as paideia. Thus Christianity became the new paideia of the Word of God.

As Plato insisted that man should be trained to choose the real good over the apparent, the true over the false, so Origen built his paideia to help the Christian mold himself on his master, Jesus Christ, the divine Logos.

But it is not enough to declare Christianity as the new paideia and Christ as the new pedagogue. No, Christianity had to produce a literature comparable to that of the Greek paideia, but based on the Christian Bible. "Christians had to show the formative power of their spirit in works of superior intellectual and artistic caliber and to carry the contemporary mind along in their enthusiasm."[10]

Thus far we have seen something of the teaching tradition of second and third century Alexandria. Origen is of particular importance for he is at the watershed. Starting out as an independent lay *didaskolos,* he was chosen by Demetrius to run the catechetical school in Alexandria where he developed his Greek-Christian paideia. But he soon saw that he would have to be ordained in order to continue, for the doctor's *cathedra* was being taken over by the hierarchy.

Is Origen, then, the last of the independent, non-clerical *didaskoloi* in the church? Not by any means, for their heritage continues in the glorious tradition of the monk-teachers carrying on into the Middle Ages. But more and more, the bishops would be drawn from the ranks of the *didaskoloi,* especially as the paideia grew more sophisticated for the educated classes who were converting to Christianity.

Origen's student, Gregory the Wonderworker, was a bridge between his master and the Cappadocian *didaskoloi* monk-bishops, Basil, Gregory of Nazianzus and Gregory of Nyssa. But whereas Origen's paideia was a theology based largely on Greek philosophy and the gospels, the Cappadocian paideia included a whole literature and way of life.

10. Ibid., p. 73.

4

6

RAISE UP AN ATHLETE OF CHRIST (John Chrysostom, *On Vainglory and the Right Way for Parents to Bring Up Their Children* 19)

THE CHURCH of the monks was to continue the paideia of the *didaskoloi*. Basically it was a book religion with the reading of Scriptures and the reciting of office, requiring a minimum of literacy. So we see the early Egyptian monasteries teaching reading and writing to the unlettered fellahin novices. Also the monks taught the people from the neighborhood, opening up the monasteries once a week to heal the sick, feed the hungry, and give spiritual conferences.

Let us turn now to the monastic education in Asia Minor, Cappadocia and Pontus, for here Christian paideia developed both in the monasteries and in the catecheses of the Cappadocian monk-bishops. First of all there are Basil and Gregory of Nazianzus, two friends and fellow rhetors, who started a monastery at Annesi.

A. BASIL OF CAESAREA

Basil came from Caesarea, capital of Cappadocia, and center of industry, trade and learning. He came to a love of learning naturally since his father, Basil senior, was a lawyer and rhetor in Caesarea. Both Basil's father and his mother Macrina were from illustrious families.

Sent to live with his grandmother at Annesi, Basil learned from her the Origenist teachings of Gregory the Wonderworker. It seems at the time he also studied the liberal arts under his father who was teaching then at Neo-Caesarea nearby. Next Basil went to Caesarea to study philosophy and rhetoric. Here he probably first met his friend and fellow student, Gregory

4. Hippo Regius, presbyterium of Augustine's cathedral. Augustine taught the people from his cathedra in the rear of the apse.

of Nazianzus. Then he proceeded to Constantinople to study
rhetoric under Libanius.

In 351 he traveled to Athens where he again met Gregory.
Basil, who was of a serious scholarly bent, was irritated at the
fun and games of the Athenian students, and the rivalries between
the various national student groups. However, this was a small
price to pay for studying under the top scholars of the day. Basil
and Gregory divided their time between studies and religious
duties.

> Two ways were known to us, the first of great value, the second of
> smaller consequence: the one leading to our sacred buildings, the
> other to secular instructors. All others we left to those who would
> pursue them—to feasts, theatres, meetings, banquets, for nothing
> is in my opinion of value, save that which leads to virtue and to the
> improvement of its devotees. (Gregory of Nazianzus, Oration 43:21)
> (NPNF)

They were soon surrounded by a group of like-minded students,
an early example of the colleges of pious scholars that always
would be found on the university campuses right up to modern
times.

In his eulogy (Oration 43:23) Gregory magnifies Basil's
proficiency in rhetoric, grammar, languages, philosophy, dia-
letic, astronomy, geometry and mathematics. However, "Excessive application to them he despised as useless to those whose
desire is godliness." What are all these studies when compared
with the moral discipline of man?

Basil returned to Caesarea as a famed teacher of rhetoric
(356). The citizens of Neo-Caesarea, where his father had
taught, also sought his services. But probably at his sister
Macrina's urging, he left off the flattering of his pupils and
patrons and converted to Christ. "Much time had I spent in
vanity, and had wasted nearly all my youth in the vain labor
which I underwent in acquiring the wisdom made foolish by
God" (L 223). Gregory implies that about this time they had
indulged in the theater (Oration 43:25).

At his conversion, Basil prayed "that I might find some one
of the brethren who had chosen this way of life, that with him
I might cross life's short and troubled straight" (L 223). And
he discovered others of like bent living nearby, including Eusta-

thius of Sebaste. On Eustathius' advice, he visited the monks of Egypt and Palestine and on his return was baptized by Dianius bishop of Caesarea and ordained a reader. Returning to Annesi, he founded a monastery across the river from his sister's place.

Though he gave up his rhetor's *cathedra*, Basil still taught the monks. Moreover, some children of the neighborhood were educated there, though Basil did it with reluctance. The paideia offered in his monastery was not the same as that offered in the secular schools, which does not please God, and is not compatible with the monastic profession (Short Rule, SR 292).

The boys should live apart from the monks, lest too much familiarity breed lack of respect. Also their noisy clamor might disturb monastic peace and tranquillity. Although the boys eat and sleep separately, they can join the monks in prayer. "The young, on the one hand, are generally stimulated by the example of the more perfect, and, on the other, their elders are in no small measure assisted in their prayer by the children" (Long Rule LR 15).

An older monk, patient and experienced, should be put in charge of the children.

> Thus he will correct the faults of the young with fatherly kindness and give wise instruction, applying remedies proper to each fault, so that, while the penalty for the fault is being exacted, the soul may be exercised in interior tranquillity. (LR 15)

Anger is counteracted by kindness, gluttony by fasting, insults by silence. In their studies they should take a spiritual outlook based on Scripture and historical accounts, rather than drawing from the pagan myths. Learning the maxims from Proverbs, they should commit to memory facts and names. Thus under the teacher's guidance, habits of attention and concentration can be developed. "A child of tender age, simple, candid, and un-skilled in deceit, readily reveals the secrets of his soul" (LR 15). "While the mind is still easy to mold and pliable as wax, taking the form of what is impressed upon it, it should be exercised from the beginning in every good discipline" (LR 15), reflecting the formative nature of Greek paideia. Then when they reach the age of reason, these early habits will form a foundation for reasonable choices.

Once the age of discretion was reached, Basil allowed his students to take the vow of virginity, witnessed by ecclesiastical officials. It would seem that Basil's school was principally for those seeking the monastic state. But not all his pupils entered the monastery, some returning home, bolstered by the monastic paideia.

But what about the study of the pagan classics? Basil himself was well schooled in them. Did he feel that they were harmful or helpful? He explains his position in his *Exhortation to Youths As to How They Shall Best Profit by the Writings of Pagan Authors* which may have been written in the later days of his bishopric to some young cleric students of his.

> I come immediately after your parents in natural relationship to you, so that I myself entertain for you no less good-will than do your fathers; and I am sure, unless I am somewhat wrong in my judgment of you, that you do not long for your parents when your eyes rest upon me. (LCL) (1)

Basil takes the road of moderation we have seen before in Clement and Origen. Though the classics are far below Scriptures, much good can be found in them and they can pave the way to Scripture, if used prudently.

> This it is, and naught else, that I have come to offer you as my counsel—that you should not surrender to these men once for all the rudders of your mind, as if of a ship, and follow them whithersoever they lead; rather, accepting from them only that which is useful, you should know that which ought to be overlooked. (1)

How can the two types of education, pagan and Christian be made compatible?

> Now if there is some affinity between the two bodies of teachings, knowledge of them should be useful to us; but if not, at least the fact that by setting them side by side we can discover the difference between them, is of no small importance for strengthening the position of the better. (3)

Basil uses the example of a tree which has both fruit and leaves. The fruit is the holy truth as found in Scriptures, but it is surrounded and enhanced by the leaves of literature. However, pagan works which can be harmful should be avoided. In plucking the rose, watch out for the thorns. But examples of virtue can be found hidden in the pagan works.

As an educator, Basil tried to begin from the viewpoint of his audience, attempting to reconcile divergent views. But he was challenged for his doxology "Glory be to the Father with the Son together with the Holy Spirit" which some thought de-emphasized the divinity of the Holy Spirit. He responded in his *On the Holy Spirit* (375) where he does not hesitate to become involved in semantics, discussing the use of "through whom," "of whom," and "with whom."

Often theologians and teachers have been accused of Indulging in semantic games. But Basil defends it, at least in the beginning.

> The beginning of teaching is speech, and syllables and words are parts of speech. It follows then that to investigate syllables is not to shoot wide of the mark. Nor, because the questions raised are what might seem to some insignificant, are they on that account to be held unworthy of heed. Truth is always a quarry hard to hunt, and, therefore, we must look everywhere for its tracks. The acquisition of true religion is just like that of the crafts. Both grow bit by bit. Apprentices must despise nothing. If a man despises the first elements as small and insignificant, he will never reach the perfection of wisdom. (Ch.1, N.2) (NPNF)

Basil then proceeds to show that though pagan philosophers distinguish between syllables, e.g. "through whom" "of whom" etc., the Scriptures do not in regard to the Father, Son and Holy Spirit.

Basil bemoans the present state of the church split up into factions and schools. Sometimes he thinks it is better to keep silent, but he wrote the treatise to help one Amphilochius, a serious and taciturn friend. "A guarantee that you would not publish what I was about to say to all the world,—not because it would not be worth making known, but to avoid casting pearls before pigs" (Mt 7:6) (Ch. 30, N. 79) (NPNF).

Yet Basil was attacked by the pneumatic and conservative monks for not coming right out and saying that the Holy Spirit is God. But he was defended by Athanasius (LL 62, 63) and Gregory of Nazianzus (Panegyric, 68).

He postponed for a time the exact term, begging as a favor from the

Spirit Himself and His earnest champions, that they would not be annoyed at his **oikonomia** (i.e. not saying that he is God). Nor by clinging to a single expression, ruin the whole cause, from an uncompromising temper, at a crisis when religion was in peril. He assured them that they would suffer no injury from a slight change in their expressions, and from teaching the same truth in other terms, for our salvation is not so much a matter of words as of actions. (NPNF)

Basil was doing what any good teacher would do, namely, seeking a common language between himself and his hearers, trying to pass on the sacred message by the use of weak secular words. Actually this is the history of the church's teaching whether the words be *"hypostasis," "homoousios," "filioque"* or *"transubstantio."* And Basil's teaching on the Spirit helped lay the groundwork for the Council of Constantinople in 381, when the theology of the Holy Spirit was worked out in a more definitive manner.

B. GREGORY OF NAZIANZUS

Gregory of Nazianzus, as his friend and fellow monk-for-a-time Basil, was a product of the *egkyklios paideia,* yet we find him critical of the pagan culture that surrounded him. Initially the Christian apologists had presented Christianity as the true moral religion, whereas pagan culture was false and corrupt, In the beginning Christianity gloried in the simple unsophisticated teachings of the gospel and so it appealed to the lower classes. But once it became an approved religion and the rich and cultured found it expedient to join up, Christianity found itself in a dilemma, for the upper classes, trained in the classical paideia, looked down on the simple Christian *alogia.*

Christianity still considered the pagan world to be the work of the devil, and yet, unless it was to remain an illiterate proletarian religion, it could do nothing else but adopt the culture of this world, since it was the only culture that it knew.[1]

Gregory compares the simple language of the gospels with

1. R. Ruether, **Gregory of Nazianzus,** Oxford, 1969, p. 158.

the flowery rhetoric of pagan literature. "Be it mine to speak five words with my understanding of the church, rather than ten thousand words in a tongue" (1 Cor 14:19) (Oration 16:2). He felt that the flowery pagan rhetoric of some Christian preachers degraded the gospels (Oration 21:12). In fact, as Basil, he feels that the rhetor's *cathedra* and Christian teaching are incompatible. Thus he abrades Gregory of Nyssa, Basil's brother, for ascending the rhetor's chair.

> What happened to you, O wisest of men, and for what do you condemn yourself, that you have cast away the sacred and delightful books which you used to read once to the people . . . or have hung them up over the chimney, as men do in winter with rudders and hoes, and have applied yourself to salt and bitterness and preferred to be called a professor of rhetoric rather than of Christianity. (L 1) (NP NF)

Yet, despite his protests, Gregory of Nazianzus was not above using rhetoric himself and was asked to stay on at Athens in this capacity. "A cultivated Christian like Gregory was caught between two value systems, belonging to both and yet feeling that the two were fundamentally incompatible."[2]

This attitude of the Christians vis a vis the classical tradition probably was a factor in Julian's Law (362) forbidding them to teach in the public schools. Since Greek culture and religion overlapped, no one could teach them adequately who did not believe in the Greek gods. Dr. Ruether observes:

> By his educational edicts Julian apparently intended to push the Christians back into the cultureless ghetto from which they had come and, by depriving them of the skills of persuasive language, prevent them from communicating effectively with the secular world.[3]

Gregory rose to the occasion, writing two invectives against Julian's decrees. Praising rhetoric and protesting the bias against Christian education, he rates the value of literature as second only to the joys of eternal life. Fortunately Julian died in 363 and his decrees were soon abrogated.

2. R Ruether, op cit., p. 162.
3. Ibid., p. 163.

In his *Poems to Seleucus* Gregory takes a moderate view of classical culture similar to Basil's approach. Thus one should take from the classics what is useful and shun the rest. Though philosophy and rhetoric should never be used as ends in themselves, they can be studied within the Christian paideia as aids to Christian teaching for it is fitting that man's *logos* be used to explain God's Logos.

Gregory held the same ambivalence towards Greek philosophy as he had towards rhetoric (Oration 27:8; 32:25). But the Christians had something in common with the philosophers, both rejecting the anthropomorphisms of Greek mythology.

> In the last analysis, the answer of the Christian "philosopher" to the problem of rhetoric and literary culture, in general, was strikingly similar to that of Plato. Both advocated plucking literature from its native value system and transferring it to the value system of philosophy. Both would envisage a **paideia** in which literature "purged" of its indecency, could be used to buttress morality and introduce the student to the higher life.[4]

With all of this comes a certain amount of censorship, necessary to expurge the pagan literature of its immorality. But can a viable synthesis be worked out between philosophy and culture or between Christianity and culture without turning philosophy into rhetoric or literature into a sterile piety? Certainly on the personal level men like Basil and Gregory of Nazianzus made the synthesis in their own lives. And maybe that is where the solution lies in a personal rather than institutional paideia.

C. GREGORY OF NYSSA

Let us now see another famous rhetor of the period, Gregory of Nyssa, Basil's brother and friend of Gregory of Nazianzus! The second Gregory has a deep understanding of the methodology and purpose of Greek paideia, finding his rhetor's chair not incompatible with his Christianity, though at the importunities of

4. Ibid., p. 174.

Basil and Gregory of Nazianzus, he forsook it for the clerical life.

> He understood paideia as the formative process of the human personality, which the great educators of Greece had sharply distinguished from the substance that is the **sine qua non** of the educational process.[5]

The essence of Greek paideia is *morphosis*. The growth of one's personality is analogous to his physical growth and indeed paideia included both. However, spiritual growth is not spontaneous as that of the body and so needs guidance.

In his *Christian Institute,* written to monks who wanted guidance in contemplation and aid to attaining the Spirit, Gregory of Nyssa tries to harmonize Christian teaching of divine grace with the Hellenist tradition of virtue *(aretē).*

The Greeks, too, felt that they needed divine assistance to reach *aretē.* And this was the point where Gregory saw the meeting of Greek paideia and Christian teaching, man and the Holy Spirit cooperating, with the divine assistance increasing with man's efforts. With Plato, Gregory feels that the will is aimed at the good, and any falling back is due to ignorance and self delusion.[6]

The solution lies in paideutic catharsis of the soul and alienation from evil.

> Christian paideia is conceived by this theological thinker in metaphysical terms that project its continuation into cosmic dimensions. But it reaches its conclusion in the final restoration of the perfect status of God's original creation.[7]

The Christian paideia of Christ, teacher and healer, is essentially a restoration of the world to its natural good state.

True fulfillment of Christian paideia is found in a lifelong struggle to reach perfection and assimilation to God. As the Greek philosopher's paideia was through his philosophical ascetics, so the Christian's is based on *theōria,* contemplation

---

5. W. Jaeger, **Early Christianity and Greek Paideia**, pp. 86-87.
6. **Ibid.**, p. 89.
7. **Ibid.**,

of God and union with him. We can easily see how Basil and his companions looked upon the monastic way as a philosophy and called themselves philosophers.

Greek paideia differed from all other forms of education insofar as it was determined by its object. "If we regard education as a process of shaping or forming, the object of learning plays the part of the mold by which the subject is shaped."[8] At first Greek paideia was shaped by Homer, later by other poets, and finally by all of Greek literature. Only later did other branches of learning such as rhetoric and philosophy come into Greek paideia. The arts (propaideia) were related to philosophy the height of paideia.

As we have seen, Basil and Gregory of Nazianzus were trained in this egkyklios paideia. Gregory of Nyssa received much of his training from his brother. He saw that as the Greek paideia included all of Greek literature, the Christian paideia was built upon the Bible, presenting the ideal man in Jesus of Nazareth. Following the Greek idea of paideia as morphosis, one reading the Bible, models himself on Christ. As Jaeger points out,[9] when Gregory of Nyssa quotes the Bible, he doesn't say "As the Apostle says," but "As the Apostle educates (paideuei)." For the Christian Bible is not so much Law as education, paideia of the Holy Spirit.

This teaching of the Holy Spirit is found in the scriptural senses of Origen, namely, literal, historical and spiritual. And the Spirit not only teaches through the Bible, but also through the generations of interpreters, the didaskoloi. Especially in the Psalms, both Gregory and Basil found a paideia suited to whatever needs or stages of life one might be in.

What in the Greek paideia had been the formation or morphosis of the human personality now becomes for the Christian the metamorphosis of which Paul had spoken when he wrote to the Romans (12:2), asking them to undergo a process of radical metamorphosis through a renewal of their spirit.[10]

8. Ibid., p. 91.
9. Ibid., p. 93.
10. Ibid., pp. 97-98.

Modeling himself on Christ, the Christian studies the paideia of the gospels under the guidance of the Holy Spirit, his metamorphosis making him more like God in Christ.

A practical example of Gregory's paideia is his *Great Catechism*, a defense of Catholicism against its enemies. His purpose was to help teachers of catechetics with their large variety of catechumens, with different educational and environmental backgrounds, some affected by one heresy, others by another. The *didaskolos* must seek a common language with his students, using the more human psychological approach rather than the more abstract and noetic philosophical approach to teach the basic truths of the faith: The Trinity, Incarnation, Redemption, Baptism and the Eucharist.

Gregory writes in his prologue:

> The presiding ministers of the "mystery of godliness" (1 Tim 3:16) have need of a system in their instructions, in order that the church may be replenished by the accession of such as should be saved through the teaching of the word of faith being brought home by the hearing of the unbelievers. Not that the same method of instruction will be suitable in the case of all who approach the word. The catechism must be adapted to the diversities of their religious worship, with an eye, indeed, to the one aim and end of the system, but not using the same method of preparation in each individual case. (NPNF)

In other words, the mode of instruction must be tailored to the listeners.

Gregory of Nyssa uses the forms of Greek paideia to build a Christian culture, a Christian variant of the original classical mold. His paideia is basically man's return to his original nature which was made to God's image and likeness and so brings man in closer union with God. The monastic life is the ultimate in Christian paideia. Gregory's paideia would influence both East and West and even Islamic mystics of a later age.

D. JOHN CHRYSOSTOM

Let us now look at another eastern rhetor called "The Great Teacher of the Earth" and see how he attacked the problem of pagan education. This is John Chrysostom of Antioch. From a wealthy family, he studied philosophy under Andragathius and rhetoric under Libanius. But at the age of 18 he tired of the pagan studies and turned to theology under Diodore of Tarsus, and was baptized and appointed reader by bishop Meletius of Antioch. In those days the reader sometimes performed much the same as the *didaskolos* of earlier times.

Advancing up the *cursus honorum*, he was chosen bishop of Constantinople in 397. Immediately he set about reforming the monks, the clergy and the lay people, even challenging bishops and the empress herself. All of which earned him an exile in 404.

John Chrysostom writes on the education of his time, contrasting the solid spiritual teaching of the monks with pagan learning. Generally the young lad was conducted to school by a pedagogue, usually a slave, who had authority to discipline the child, though by no means able to teach. Usually by the age of 18 the youth was free of his pedagogue.[11] But John maintains that despite the pedagogue, faithful though he may be, without a good, solid Christian education, the young man is not ready to face the dangers and immorality of life.[12]

The solution is a good Christian training under the monks. John begs the laity of Antioch to let their sons enter the monasteries, or at least to go there for a time. The age of ten is crucial for here the youth must render an account of his faults.[13] At this age he should be taken to the monastery where he would remain under the guidance of the monks for ten or twenty years. Then he can safely go on to study secular literature.[14] In sum, John's Book Three of his work *Against the Opposers of the Monks* underlines the monastic training as the sole safeguard of the virtue of the youth of pagan Antioch.

One of the dangers of the pagan schools pointed out by Festugiere[15] is pederasty. In many ways pederasty, the mutual love between master and student, is the very basis of Hellenistic

11. A. J. Festugiere, **Antioche païenne et Chrétienne**, Paris, Editions DeBoccard, 1959, pp. 187ff.
12. **Against the Opposers of the Monks.**
13. **Ibid.**, 3:17.
14. **Ibid.**, 3:11.
15. A. J. Festugiere, **op. cit.**, pp. 195ff.

education.[16] But particularly in the nudity of the gymnasia aberrations grew up which were abhorrent to both Jews and Christians. Certainly wherever men shut themselves away from women this danger arises whether in the army, academy or monastery. For example, early Christian abbots frequently warned against it.

But, as Marrou comments[17] "Greek love" gave classical education both its material conditions and its method. And this love is essentially educative. The differences in the ages of the two lovers made an inequality as exists between older and younger brother.

> The lover's desire to gain the boy's affection and shine before him roused feelings of ardent and active admiration in the latter. The older man was his hero, the higher type who was to be his model and to whose level he would try gradually to rise.[18]
> The love relationship entailed for the older man, the labor of teaching which grew naturally out of his fatherly attitude; for the younger, an attitude of docility and veneration, which led to a growth in maturity. The relationship was maintained openly by daily association, personal contact and example, conversation, a sharing in the common life, and the gradual initiation of the younger into the social activities of the elder—the club, the gymnasium and the banquet.[19]

In a word, for the Greeks *paideia* found its realization in *paiderasteia*. Thus *paideia* is the personal relationship between the *pais* and his *didaskolos*, his model, guide, initiator, a warm personal relationship. Basically the rapport between master and pupil is that of lover and loved. Of course this sometimes led to out and out homosexuality. This was one of the things John Chrysostom feared and prompted him to recommend monastic training for the youth of Antioch.

But the number of parents who followed John's advice was probably small. Certainly few boys would want to spend ten or more years of their young active lives behind monastic walls. Moreover, they would receive little practical education to help them earn a living when they returned to the world.

16. H. Marrou, op. cit., pp. 27ff.
17. Ibid., p. 29f.
18. Ibid., p. 30.
19. Ibid., pp. 30-31.

In his *On Vain Glory and on the Education of Children*
(393) John takes a similar tack, though stressing more the
parents' educational responsibility. Thus the first part outlines the
loose living and vanity of Antioch and the second part tells the
parents how to instill proper moral training in their children to
overcome contemporary immorality. Putting the emphasis on
moral discipline rather than intellectual achievement, it covers
the same ground as Clement of Alexandria's *Pedagogue*.

Education begins in the home. John points out the danger
of spoiling the young boy with wealth, long hair, effeminacy.

> What will become of boys when from earliest youth they are without
> teachers? If grown men, after being nurtured from the womb and
> continuing their education to old age, still do not live righteously,
> what wrong will not children, accustomed from the threshhold of
> life to empty words, commit? In our own day every man takes the
> greatest pains to train his boy in the arts and in literature and speech.
> But to exercise this child's soul in virtue, to that no man any long-
> er pays heed. (18)[20]

John pleads for discipline, not that the lads be raised up as
monks, but rather as athletes of Christ. "Raise up an athlete of
Christ and teach him though he is living in the world to be rever-
ent from his earliest youth"(19). When they are young, they are
as formable as wax and easy to teach. "Like the creators of
statues do you give all your leisure to fashioning these wondrous
statues for God" (22).

A child's soul is a city, writes John (23-25) and so needs laws
to regulate it. The body is the city wall and the four senses gates
which must be guarded from the enemy starting with the tongue
so that nothing flippant or foolish is spoken. Moreover, he should
not hear foolish tales. For example: "This youth kissed that
maiden. The king's son and daughter have done that"(38).
"Make your stories agreeable that they may give the child pleasure
and his soul may not grow weary"(39).

John also underlines the mother's role in the education of the
child. Thus when a biblical story is read, the mother should be

there corroborating, praising. Moreover, these stories make the church readings more meaningful. As the child grows, more fearful stories may be related. For example, the flood, Sodom, hell and damnation.

His eyes and whole body must be guarded and his appearance carefully watched.

> We must remove the chief part of his physical charm by clipping the locks on his head all round to attain severe simplicity. If the boy complains because he is being deprived of this charm, let him learn first of all that the greatest charm is simplicity. (57)

His spirit, too, must be trained and tested. And the home is the best place for this.

> Just as athletes in the wrestling school train with their friends before the contest, so that when they have succeeded against these they may be invincible against their opponents, even so, the boy must be trained at home. (68)

Of course, the father can hardly be a good teacher unless he has discipline himself (70). By all means keep the boy away from spectacles.

> "My child, spectacles such as those, the sight of naked women uttering shameful words, are for slaves. Promise me not to listen to or speak any unseemly word and go thy way. There it is impossible not to hear what is base. What goes on is unworthy of thy eyes." As we speak to him, let us kiss him and put our arms about him and press him to us to show our affection. By all these means let us mold him. (78)

John further suggests that the father take his son to the theater in the evening at the end of the spectacle to make fun of the dirty old men sulking out and the young men inflamed with desire. "What have all these people gained? Nothing but shame, reproach and damnation."

Train the boy in prayer, fasting and virtue. Introduce him to a proper bride and prepare him for politics and the military. And let the mother train her daughter in virtue.

> Young men are troubled by desire, women by love of finery and excitement. Let us, therefore, repress all these tendencies. Thus we shall be able to please God by rearing such athletes for him. (90)

But there is a difference between this Christian morality as outlined by John Chrysostom and Greek paideia. Of course, no one would deny that the Greek paideia can lead to virtue *(aretē)* including moderation, decency, honesty, appreciation of beauty—what are sometimes called the pagan virtues and are based on reason. Since man is reasonable, he must act reasonably, decorously, in his own eyes and in the eyes of his fellow men. But Christian morality is more God-centered with sin an offense against God, and to be punished by him. Of course, Greek paideia can be a help toward Christian morality; on the other hand, reading of the immoral myths and legends and cults of the pagan gods can be harmful. And, as we have seen, both the philosophers and the Christian teachers opposed them.

E.   JEROME OF STRIDON

Let us now turn to a great Latin educator of the period, Jerome of Stridon. In a way he links the Greek and Latin traditions. He was one of the few Latins of his time knowledgeable in Greek and, at least in his earlier days, a great fan of Origen's. At the age of twelve, he went to study grammar in Rome (359). Under the famous master Donatus, he read Virgil, Sallust, Terence, Plautus, Lucretius, Horace, etc. along with commentaries by Asper, Vulcantius and Donatus. Virgil and Cicero were his favorites. Using Cicero as a model, he practiced his writing and built up his library by hand-copying works of Plautus, Virgil and Cicero.

Next he proceeded to the rhetor where he learned to make those articifial speeches and grew in his knowledge of philosophy, science and law. He also attended the Athenaeum, a university founded by Hadrian to teach public speaking, science and literature. Jerome, as Basil, Gregory of Nazianzus, Gregory of Nyssa, not to mention Clement, Origen and Augustine, owed his success as a writer to his fine training in the classical grammar and rhetor schools.

And he never found his studies incompatible with his Christianity, deciding for Baptism in 366 at the age of 18. For Rome was not only a center of learning, but also a hub of Christianity with basilicas and tombs of the martyrs.

After a brief sojourn in Gaul, Jerome settled down in Aquileia near his home town of Stridon, founding an oratory there with his fellow students Bonosius, Rufinus, Heliodorus, and Paul who had a fine library of the Fathers. Here Jerome began an educational apostolate that he would pursue the rest of his life, namely, instructing groups of Christian women. These were likely from the upper classes for they were well educated and possessed a good library.

Forced to leave Aquileia, perhaps because of his abrasive personality or because of false rumors, he set sail for Athens and Cilicia. At Antioch he met Evagrios, the translator of Antony's life, and he spent some time in study at Evagrios' villa. While there, he fell sick and experienced a dream (L 22), in which he was accused by the Judges, "You are a Ciceronian, not a Christian. Where your treasure is, your heart is." Ordered flogged, he vowed, "Lord, if ever I own profane books again, or if I read them, it will mean I have denied you." Does the dream represent his conversion from the classics to the monastic way? Soon after, he repaired to the desert of Chalcis. But later when he was teaching classics to the boys of Bethlehem, Rufinus challenged him for going against his vow. But Jerome dismissed the dream as of little import *(Apology Against Rufinus, 1:30).*

Jerome tried the monastic way for a while in the desert, but was driven out, he claimed, because of his loyalty to orthodoxy. He was ordained a presbyter by the bishop of Antioch.

Returning to Rome (382), he served as a secretary to Pope Damasus. There once again he took up the instruction of women: Paula with her daughters Blesilla, Paulina, Eustochium and Rufina and her son Toxotius; and also Marcella and her friends in her palace on the Aventine hill. Both groups were living in religious communes under Jerome's guidance. Besides their prayer life and charity, Jerome encouraged the study of Scripture, even to the learning of Hebrew. As Steinmann notes,[21] Jerome by his

---

21. J. Steinmann, **St. Jerome and His Times,** Notre Dame, Fides, 1959, pp. 125f.

Scriptural teachings to the Roman women, tried to overcome anti-biblical traditions of men like Symmachus and Praetextatus who thought that the Bible was filled with non-sensical Eastern fables. Both had come under the influence of men like Celsus and Julian. Jerome felt that the lack of knowledge of the ancient languages of the Bible, particularly Hebrew and Greek, was part of the problem. Also at the time the monks of the desert were anti-intellectual and uninterested in exegesis. And the clergy, as the Roman flamina, were more like government officials.

But Jerome found a receptive audience in his women. They were his inspiration, some even following him to Bethlehem. Perhaps we have underrated the position that women have held in the education of the church. Drawn to religion more so than men, both by temperament and inclination, they gave Jerome a rousing reception.

Jerome absorbed some of Origen's love of Scriptures, translating 70 of his works into Latin, though later in his controversies with the Origenists, John of Jerusalem, Rufinus, Melania and Evagrius, he would criticize Origen's Platonism especially his pre-existent souls *(Against John of Jerusalem)*.

Pope Damasus used Jerome's talents in rhetoric and translation to revise the current Latin translation of the Bible. Since the third century Latin had been used in the Roman liturgy, replacing the original Greek. Now the Greek originals of the New Testament were virtually unknown for few could read them any more since Greek was dying out in the Roman schools.

A number of Latin versions of the New Testament arose; often expanded with various agrapha and glosses. Jerome set to work to achieve a more critical text. Here translating can be seen as an attempt to make the ancient truths more relevant by expressing them correctly in the language of the day, whether this be the lingua franca or the philosophical jargon of the era. Jerome used the Italian and African Latin versions and Greek MSS in his translations.

But he was a realist enough to know that his modern translation would not be accepted by the old timers who were used to the ancient faulty versions.

> Any one who picks this volume up and notices what he is reading, whether he is a scholar or an ignoramous, will not even give himself time to swallow, he will immediately start screaming that I am guilty of falsification and sacrilege. I have dared to add to, to alter or to correct the old books. (**Introduction to the Gospels**)

Two things consoled Jerome, namely, the Pope's command and the fact that present texts often contradicted themselves, so the only choice was to go back to the original.

> In this way we shall be able to correct what has been badly rendered by incompetent translators, or corrupted in bad faith by presumptuous incompetents, or added or changed by transcribers who were half asleep. (**Introduction to the Gospels**)

But he limited himself to correcting only the most flagrant errors and glosses. In his satirical manner he tossed a barb at his detractors. "You do not play a lyre before an ass" (L27:1).

But his conservative and ignorant enemies wanted him out of Rome and they attacked him before the presbytery for his relations with Paula and Marcella. Though acquitted, he had to leave Rome for the East.

Paula followed and together they traveled to Palestine, visiting the shrines there, whence they set out for Egypt to see the monasteries, settling down ultimately in Bethlehem. There the wealthy Paula built a double monastery; she was in charge of the women, whereas Jerome presided over the monks. Jerome settled down once more to his exegesis and was drawn towards hagiography including the lives of Paul the Hermit, Malchus and Hilarion.

Paula, Eustochium and their fellow nuns continued their Scripture study under Jerome's guidance. The New Testament was naturally their main interest, and to help them Jerome wrote some commentaries on Paul's epistles. He spent the rest of his days finishing his translation of the Old Testament, writing a voluminous correspondence, other commentaries, translations, hagiographies and polemics against his many enemies.

But what were Jerome's views on education? We have seen his classical training. Was this entirely abandoned after his conversion to the monastic way? It seems that he did not recommend pagan works to the monks and nuns, if we can gauge his view by his letter to Laeta about the education of her daughter Paula who was destined to be a consecrated virgin (L 107). He recommended an education centered around the Bible and the Fathers.

> Thus must a soul be educated which is to be a temple of God. It must learn to hear nothing and to say nothing but what belongs to the fear of God. It must have no understanding of unclean words, and no knowledge of the world's songs. Its tongue must be steeped while still tender in the sweetness of the psalms. Boys with their wanton thoughts must be kept from Paula: even her maids and female attendants must be separated from worldly associates. (L 107:4) (NP NF)

Jerome goes on to explain how Paula should have letters made of boxwood or ivory and a stylus and wax tablet for writing. Small rewards should be given for good spelling and emulation should be encouraged with her fellow students. Excellent educational psychology is displayed in Jerome's advice.

> You should not scold her if she is slow to learn, but must employ praise to excite her mind so that she may be glad when she excels others and sorry when she is excelled by them. Above all you must take care not to make her lessons distasteful to her lest a dislike for them conceived in childhood may continue into her maturer years. (4)

He places great emphasis on the memory, especially learning the names of the patriarchs, prophets and apostles. Moreover, her instruction should be under a male teacher, a well-educated man of culture. "Early impressions are hard to eradicate from the mind. When once wool has been dyed purple, who can restore it to its previous whiteness?" (4).

But Scripture is to be her main stay.

> Let it be her task daily to bring to you the flowers which she has culled from Scripture. Let her learn by heart so many verses in the Greek, but let her be instructed in the Latin also. (9)

As a perfect virgin let her model herself on her mother, Laeta, learning to pray, study Scripture, spin wool, etc. In her study of Scripture she should progress gradually through the Proverbs, Solomon, Preacher, Job, Acts of the Apostles, Epistles, then the Prophets, Heptateuch, Kings, Chronicles, Ezra and

Esther. Finally she is ready for the Song of Songs. But she should avoid the apocrypha. Besides Scripture, she should read the Fathers, including Cyprian, Athanasius and Hilary.

Besides Jerome's teaching of the virgins in Scripture and asceticism, he seems to have had a small school for Latin boys-perhaps some were orphans-teaching them the Classics, grammar, poetry and history.

Despite his earlier dream-vow against the Classics and his view that they were incompatible with the monastic way, he saw their usefulness in Christian teaching. For example, in 397 he wrote to Magnus, a Roman official (L 70), who had accused him of polluting Christianity with pagan examples. He quotes Deuteronomy (21:10-13), which allows Hebrews to marry beautiful Gentile captives provided that first the girls' nails are clipped and their hair shaved, and putting off their native garb they mourn their parents for a full month. In like manner, all the Fathers have used the wisdom and erudition of the pagans while clipping away their idolatry and debauchery. Jerome feels that the challenge really came from Rufinus. "Please beg of him not to envy eaters their teeth because he is toothless himself, and not to make light of the eyes of gazelles because he is himself a mole" (L 70, 6).

Jerome's attitude towards the Classics, namely, that they contained some of God's truths and so can be used with discretion, would serve as a basis of Christian humanism in future ages.

Earlier in a letter to Damasus (L 21, 13) (383) he had applied the same Deuteronomic analogy. But at the same time he warns against the dangers of paganism which can make a slave of the Gentile maiden instead of having her serve us as a handmaid. Perhaps Jerome's ambivalence of usefulness/danger in pagan literature is the very tension of Christian life in the world, acceptance/rejection, living in the world, but not of it. His opinion reflects the attitude of many of his contemporary rhetor-Fathers and gave precedent for future syncretism such as Augustine's with Neo-Platonism and Thomas Aquinas' with Aristotle. In a word, the Christian paideia would meet and osmose with zeitgeist philosophies through an endless chain of syncretisms which can never cease unless Christianity itself ceases. And it is the job of the Christian *didaskolos*, knowledgeable in both Christian tradition and contemporary philosophy, to translate the ancient truths into a language which speaks to the people of the day. Otherwise the Christian tradition itself becomes dead and sterile. And, as Jerome, the Christian teacher must be condemned by both sides for his trouble, by the old-timers for changing the changeless truths, and by the philosophers for misusing their wisdom.

7

THE TEACHER MUST BEGIN WITH WHAT THE STUDENT ALREADY KNOWS AND GIVE HIM A GLIMPSE OF WHAT THERE IS STILL TO BE KNOWN (Augustine, *Trinity*, 10, 1)

A. AUGUSTINE, EARLY LIFE

AUGUSTINE, contemporary and correspondent of Jerome, exemplifies the syncretism necessary for a successful teacher. He translated the ancient Christian traditions into the popular Neo-Platonism of his day, and his Christian Neo-Platonic school or heresy would dominate western thought right up through the Middle Ages and into Reformation theology.

Augustine was one of the last great Roman teachers, flourishing just before the barbarian invasions. Safe in Africa, he was able to pursue his teaching, study and writing in his episcopal school at Hippo. His library of treatises, letters, sermons, etc., edited by himself, has been preserved practically intact. He was one of the few teachers of all time who had the opportunity at the end of his life to get his notes in order, editing, commenting, giving reasons for and against former opinions in his *Retractations* (426-427).

Augustine was one of the last of the great rhetor-monk-bishops which include such giants as Basil, the two Gregories, and John Chrysostom. And as they were the beacons of Greek Christianity, Augustine's heresy or school would dominate the West.

Augustine was, of course, many things—rhetor, philosopher, monk, bishop. But, first of all, he was a teacher, instructing in the African and Italian schools from 373-386. As so many of his Christian predecessors and contemporaries, he quit the rhetor's chair at his conversion; nevertheless, as they, he did

not quit teaching, but rather switched from the paideia of Cicero
to that of Jesus Christ, at the same time taking along his rhetorical methodology.

Born in Tagaste, North Africa of a pagan father, Patricius,
and a Christian mother, Monica (354), Augustine studied in
nearby Madaura (365-69), then pursued the rhetorical course at
Carthage (370-73). While there he discovered Cicero's philosophy in his *Hortensius,* "I did not use the book to sharpen my
tongue, nor did it impress me by its way of speaking, but rather
by what it spoke" (*Confessions* 3, 4, 7). Whereas rhetoric stresses
method of expression and elocution, philosophy points more
to what is spoken.

While at Carthage he took a wife in a second class marriage, sometimes called an unequal marriage. She was probably
a slave girl. According to Roman law this arrangement could be
terminated at any time for a more permanent marriage usually
with a girl of the upper classes, who could only be won once
one's career was well established. When Augustine finally a-
bandoned her after 15 years, it was because Monica had a rich
young girl lined up for him in Milan.

After teaching grammar for a year at Tagaste, Augustine
returned to Carthage as a rhetor. Although in the beginning he
had been attracted to the Manichees, he was soon disillusioned
especially at the ignorance of their leader, bishop Faustus.

In 374, Augustine sailed for Rome, a more attractive educational center.

> The greatest and almost the sole reason was because I had heard
> that young men studied there in a more peaceful way and were kept
> by the restraints of a better order and discipline. They were not
> allowed to rush insolently and at random into the classroom of a
> teacher with whom they were not enrolled, nor were they let in
> at all unless he gave permission. (**Confessions** 5, 8, 14)

Recent Roman laws insured the proper conduct of the students.
For example, when they arrived in Rome, they had to go immediately to the tax assessor, with birth certificate and recom-
mendation, and indicate what profession they wished to study.

> In the third place, the office of tax assessment shall carefully in-
> vestigate the life of the students at their lodging places, to see that

they actually do bestow their time on the studies which they assert
that they are pursuing. These same officials of tax assessment shall
warn the students that they shall severally conduct themselves in
their assemblies as persons should who consider it their duty to
avoid a disgraceful and scandalous reputation and bad associations,
all of which We consider as the next worst thing to actual criminality.
Nor shall the students attend shows too frequently nor commonly
take part in unseasonable carousals. We further grant you as prefect
the authority that, if any student in the City should fail to conduct
himself as the dignity of a liberal education demands, he shall be
publicly flogged, immediately put on board a boat, expelled from the
City and returned home. (C.Th 14, 9, 1) (March 12, 370)[1]

The perpetual student was a problem in those days as he is today.
So if they were not finished by their twentieth year, they were
to be shipped back home.

Augustine was glad to get rid of his Carthaginian students
with their impudent license, wandering in and out of classrooms.
Like madmen, they rushed in to disrupt classroom discipline.
At Rome Augustine set up his rhetorical school in his home,
gathering students with whom he hoped to gain a reputation.
But the Roman students, though more orderly, were also more
slippery, transferring from one teacher to another in order to
avoid paying.

When a rhetor's chair was vacated in Milan, Augustine applied for the job and was tested by a public discourse. Accepted,
he traveled to Milan, where he met Bishop Ambrose, through
whom he was introduced to the joys of Neo-Platonism. Exper-
iencing a conversion to Christianity (386), Augustine abandoned his rhetor's chair to seek the peace and contemplation of a
friend's villa at Cassiciacum.

> some of your servants, my brothers, may say that I sinned in this
> matter, in that, with a heart now completely in your service, I
> allowed myself to sit for even a single hour in that chair of lies.
> (Confessions, 9, 2, 4)

His ill health was another factor in his resignation.

We have seen numerous examples of converts leaving their
rhetor's chairs. Reborn in Baptism, they left their past lives

1. **The Theodosian Code**, tr.. C. Pharr, Princeton Press, 1952, p. 414.

entirely behind. Relinquishing their former profession, their
new paideia was that of Christ. But Augustine did not give up
teaching. He never could. To his dying day he would be a
magister. So when he retired to Cassiciacum for a few months'
rest, he continued a philosophical school there, teaching in the
popular dialogue form, going back to the early Greek philosophers. Besides his mother Monica, his son Adeodatus, his brother
Navigius, friends Alypius and Evodius, there were two young
boys sent to him for instruction.

These halcyon scholastic days Augustine called, "Christianae vitae otium" (*Retractations*, 1, 1). The Cassiciacum dialogues may be found in *Against the Academics, On the Happy
Life, On Order*, and *Soliloquies*. Augustine's view of these dialogues in which teacher and students learn together may be
found in *On the Happy Life*. Whether the dialogues are real or
literary forms, they probably have some basis in his teaching
methodology. And the exchanges were appreciated by both
teacher and students. "You have truly contributed so much to our
discussion that I cannot deny that I have been sated by my own
guests" (*On the Happy Life*, 36).

Augustine always had the heart of a teacher. He never
talked down to students or lectured to them, but respected their
persons, loved them—the essence of Greek *paiderastia*. The Cassiciacum dialogues brings this out. Augustine's enthusiasm and
expectancy constantly pop up with both students and teacher
learning from each other. A certain amount of camaraderie and
light hearted kidding were the order of the day. As an experienced
teacher, Augustine did not rush through the matter, but let the
dialogue follow the students' pace, repeating the matter whenever
a slower one required it.

As Howie points out[2] the Cassiciacum dialogues illustrate
well Augustine's active teaching method. Thus rather than lectures, they are explorations into a problem whether it be the
happy life, or the principle of order. By and large they were
what moderns would call group learning experiences. Any one

---

2. G. Howie, **Educational Theory and Practice in Augustine,** London,
Routledge and Kegan Paul, 1969, pp. 164.

who hopes for orderly progress and fixed conclusions will be disappointed. Later dialogues as *On Music, Greatness of the Soul* and *The Teacher* are more stilted.

Although at times the discussion may seem to be directionless, Augustine would intervene when it got too far off the track (*Against the Academics* 2, 22). After a long prelude by their mentor, the students take over the discussion. Then when he feels that they have gone far enough, Augustine gives a concluding exposition. Having wandered hither and yon, his pupils are now willing to listen to directions.

In promoting the dialogues, Augustine recognizes a basic pedagogical principle, namely, one really teaches himself with God's help. He used the Socratic question and answer method to bring out the best in his proteges, at the same time taking care not to embarrass them.

> Since, on the one hand, truth cannot be better pursued than by question and answer, and since, on the other hand, hardly any one can be found who is not ashamed to be defeated in an argument, with the result that it almost always happens that a subject for discussion which is well begun is driven out of mind by the unruly noise of self-opinion, accompanied also by wounded feelings which are usually concealed but at times evident—for these reasons, it was my pleasure to seek the truth with God's help in peace and propriety by questioning and answering myself. (Soliloquies 2, 7, 14)

Augustine prided himself on the progress of his students, writing their parents when they had made some advance (*Against the Academics*, 1, 4).

As we have seen, in Augustine's Cassiciacum seminar spontaneity was of the essence. He seemed to sense when his companions were eager to tackle some relevant problem of the day. And sometimes the question they started out with they did not end with. For example, they might begin with an inquiry into the meaning of happiness. But happiness consists of searching for the truth. But what is truth?

Augustine's Cassiciacum school did not have regular classes, but rather lively discussions after meals or after the farm chores had been done. In fair weather they went out into the meadow and sat under a large tree; when it rained, they repaired to the baths. Often they talked on into the night, and on at least one occasion in the dormitory (*On Order* 1, 8).

Augustine had an insatiable inquiring mind, never resting till he found the cause of anything. And he instilled this same curiosity in his students. He was a father to them, delighting at their growth towards maturity.

> I could not restrain my joy in seeing this young man (Trygetius), the son of a very dear friend, becoming my son also; and still more in seeing him growing and developing into a friend, when I had despaired of being able to cultivate in him a taste even for the ordinary study of literature. (**On Order** 1, 6, 16)

After his conversion, Augustine took his little group of Servants of God back to his family place at Tagaste, where he continued the enthusiastic discussions.

Let us now glance at several works that Augustine wrote specifically about Christian education including *The Teacher* (389), *First Catechetical Instruction* (405), and *Christian Education* (397/426).

In *The Teacher*, probably dedicated to Adeodatus who had just died at the early age of 16, the central theme repeats the basic educational message of both Jewish and Christian revelation—here with Platonic overtones—namely, that God alone is man's teacher. Here, of course, he teaches through his Son, Jesus Christ, who throughout all of Christian tradition has been *The* Teacher, with all subsequent instructors subordinate to the Master.

The Teacher is a dialogue between Augustine and Adeodatus, starting out to find the purpose of speaking—to teach or to remind (1, 1). Then Augustine makes the important distinction between realities and words. The Supreme Teacher taught the apostles realities by means of words or signs (1, 2) And, of course, the realities are more important than the signs. "For whatever exists for the sake of something else must be inferior to that for whose sake it exists" (9, 25). Of course, signs are an essential part of teaching, though not necessarily verbal signs. Thus one can teach also by action. And, indeed, Jesus taught in both ways, by word and example.

However, the signs themselves do not teach, but lead the way to learning the truth.

> For when a sign is presented to me, if it finds me ignorant of the reality of which it is a sign, it cannot teach me anything; but if it finds me knowing the reality, what do I learn by means of the sign. (10, 33) (ACW)

Not by external words do we learn, but by the Internal Teacher, Christ. The internal light here is a popular Platonic theme in Augustine, the divine light illuminating the unchangeable truths. Just as the sun aids the human eye to see by illuminating its object, so the interior light brightens the object of the mind, the eye of the soul (*Trinity* 12, 15). Of course, John, also Greek influenced, had called Jesus the light (1:4-5).

> Regarding, however, all those things which we understand, it is not a speaker who utters sounds exteriorly whom we consult, but it is truth that presides within, over the mind itself; though it may have been words that prompted us to make such consultation (11, 38).

But if Christ, The Teacher, instructs man internally, does not this make the external teacher superfluous? Augustine Platonically explains teaching as primarily reminding. Most teachers do not give their own thoughts to their students, but rather transmit branches of learning, rhetoric, mathematics, etc.

> When the teachers have explained, by means of words, all those subjects which they profess to teach, and even the science of virtue and of wisdom, then those who are called pupils consider within themselves whether what has been said is true. This they do by gazing attentively at that interior truth, so far as they are able. (14, 45)

Are pupils, then, self-taught? Not really, for they are taught internally by the divine light. But why do they call their external prompter, teacher? Because there is such a short interval between the external and internal teaching. "He himself will teach us, who has also counseled us through the instrumentality of human beings—by means of signs, and externally—to turn to him internally and be instructed" (14, 46).

B. TEACHER-BISHOP

It was Augustine's teaching and writing ability, along with

his piety, which attracted the people of Hippo to choose him first as presbyter, then as bishop. As a teacher-bishop, Augustine was concerned primarily with the instruction of catechumens. Since Christianity is basically paideia, from the beginning it had been necessary to teach the newcomers the new way. And since it is a book religion, as its mother Judaism, the sacred books had to be explained. Often the former religions of the catechumens whether pagan or Jewish were shown in the apologetic manner to be inferior. Next the convert was shown his existential place in the world by a brief sketch of salvation history from Adam up to Christ who initiated the final stage in which the new Christian is now entering.

We have seen early catechisms in Jewish and Christian literature including the Essene *Scroll of the Rule,* Paul's letters, *Didache,* Barnabas, *Didaskalia Apostolorum,* etc. Usually they showed the two ways: light/dark, good/bad, God/man, etc.

There were four classes of people on the way to Christianity: *accedentes,* candidates for admission to the catechumenate; Catechumens; *competentes,* catechumens approved for Baptism on the Easter vigil; *neophyti,* the newly baptized, whose instruction continued through the Easter octave. The great episcopal catecheses of Gregory, Cyril, Ambrose, Theodore of Mopsuestia are addressed to the last two classes, while the deacons instructed the beginners.

In fact, it is to a deacon Deogratias of Carthage that Augustine sends his instructions on catechizing the *accedentes* (405). Augustine limits this to one instruction including a brief narration of salvation history and an exhortation to the Christian moral life based on the two great commandments.

Besides two sample catecheses, Augustine gives some practical hints for successful instruction. This work, along with its companion volume on *Christian Education* (397/426), a textbook of homiletics, would serve as a basis of monastic education including men like Cassiodorus, Isadore, Bede, Alcuin and Rabanus Maurus.

The catechesis itself should sketch briefly an outline of salvation history, including the Old Testament, the coming of Christ as a manifestation of God's love down to the present stage of church history. At the same time, the candidate should

5. Ruins of Bede's monastery in Jarrow, England, eighth century Anglo-Saxon educational center.

be questioned concerning his motives for joining Christianity (ch. 3-6), followed by the moral exhortation underlining certain temptations open to the catechumens. For example, they should avoid non-believers and sinners such as drunkards, adulterers, etc. (7).

All students should not be treated alike, but according to their educational background. Since some came already prepared in Scripture, they should not be bored by repetition. Do not be afraid to build on their classical backgrounds, at the same time weaning them away from any heretical teachings they may have read.

Students from the grammar and rhetoric schools should be' trained in humility and shown that the simple doctrines of Scriptures are not to be taken literally but rather explored for their hidden spiritual meanings.

> For it is most useful for these men to know that the meaning is to be regarded as superior to words, just as the spirit is to be preferred to the body. And from this, too, it follows that they ought to prefer to hear true rather than eloquent discourses, just as they ought to prefer to have wise rather than handsome friends. (9, 13) (ACW)

Also these wise fellows should not make fun of the imperfect diction of often poorly educated ministers of the church, a common problem in the days of Augustine.

Augustine goes on to bolster up Deogratias who is discouraged and bored at his thankless task. Catechists suffer from the occupational hazard of accidie, which often leaves them down in the dumps and weary of mind. Augustine outlines one cause.

> Just because the subjects that the candidates have to be taught are now so thoroughly familiar to us and no longer necessary for our progress, it irks us to return to them so often. And our own mind, as having outgrown them, no longer moves with any pleasure in such well-trodden and, as it were, childish paths. Moreover, a hearer who remains unmoved makes the speaker weary. (10, 14)

Sometimes the catechist is speaking over the pupil's head and must slow down, lowering his sights till he reaches the level of intelligence of his listeners (10, 15). Language is a problem for

often the words of the catechist do not adequately express the
the ineffable mysteries and sometimes mistakes are made. At
other times the listener thinks the Christian doctrine harsh.
In all of these clarification should be made from both reason
and authority (11, 16).

The boredom which settles over both pupils and teacher
may be helped by a sympathetic love for the students and a
sincere attempt to see the ancient and repetitious truths anew
through the fresh eyes of the pupil.

> Again, if it is distasteful to us to be repeating over and over
> things that are familiar and suitable for little children, let us suit
> ourselves to them with a brother's, a father's and a mother's love,
> and when we are linked to them thus in heart these things will
> seem new even to us. For so great is the power of sympathy, that
> when people are affected by us as we speak and we by them as they
> learn, we dwell each in the other and thus both they, as it were,
> speak in us what they hear, while we, after a fashion, learn in them
> what we teach. (12, 17)

The interpenetration of teacher and student in the learning
process has rarely been better expressed.

There are other causes of apathy among the students. One
is shyness. "We must drive out by gentle encouragement his
excessive timidity, which hinders him from expressing his opinion. We must temper his shyness by introducing the idea of
brotherly fellowship" (13, 18). Judicious questioning may bolster
his confidence.

But what if the student is just plain dull? Bear with him
in charity and patience, trying to impress upon him in capsula-
ted form, the unity of the church, the nature of temptations and
the Christian manner of living pointing towards the last judge-
ment (13, 18).

Sometimes the candidate is just physically tired out from
the day's work or from the previous night's outing, or just from
standing and listening to a droning catechist, yearning for the
end of the class. Wake him up by saying something personal.
Offer him a seat, make him comfortable (13, 19).

A final word of advice concerns the type of audience, whether in private or in public, few or many, learned or unlearned,
city slickers or country bumpkins, or mixed. Of course, the well-

educated upper classes are more pleasing to teach. In general, the candidates should be grouped according to their abilities.

Augustine concluded his work with a model discourse, both in long and short form with its brief narrative of salvation history and its moral exhortation based on the decalogue and the two great commandments.

The companion volume to Augustine's *First Catechetical Instruction* is his *Christian Education* (397/426). In books One and Two he writes of sacred and profane subjects necessary as preparation for reading and interpreting the Bible including: God, the Trinity, Wisdom, Christ, church, resurrection, brotherly love, the relationship between God and man, Scripture and its interpretation; the nature of signs and writing, steps to wisdom, the canon of Scriptures, the languages of Scripture and their translations.

Augustine's attitude towards pagan writers mirrors his contemporaries. Use what is useful, discard what is not. "Every good and true Christian should understand that wherever he discovers truth, it is the Lord's" (2, 18, 28) (FOC). Some sciences are dangerous and superstitous, e.g. astrology. On the other hand, many branches of secular learning aid us in our study of Sacred Scripture. For example: history, the science of animals, plants and the stars, mechanical arts (2, 30, 47). Dialectics (including conclusions, definitions and divisions) and rhetoric are also useful, not to mention mathematics. But all should be studied in moderation (2, 39, 58).

God's truth may be found also among the pagans.

> If those who are called philosophers, especially the Platonists, have said things by chance that are truthful and comfortable to our faith we must not only have no fear of them, but even appropriate them for our own use from those who are, in a sense, their illegal possessors (2, 40, 60).

But pagan knowledge, no matter how high, is always inferior to Scriptures (2, 42, 63).

Book Three of *Christian Education* is devoted to hermeneutics, explaining the various senses of Scripture and including the seven rules of Tyconius for unlocking the secrets of the Bible. Book Four is a manual of homiletics, giving practical suggestions to the Christian teacher, based on Cicero and Quintilian's rhetorical principles.

Certainly the Christian teacher should make use of eloquence. "Why, then, do not the good zealously procure it (eloquence) that it may serve truth, if the wicked, in order to gain unjustifiable and groundless errors apply it to the advantage of injustice and error?" (4, 2, 3).

If his listeners are ignorant, the Christian teacher must instruct them. If, on the other hand, they are already instructed, but indifferent—he must rouse them. "In that case, entreaty and reproof, exhortation and rebuke, and all other means designed to rouse hearts, are indispensable" (4, 4, 6). However, both wisdom and eloquence are needed, for it is not enough to be an expert orator if one has nothing to say.

For the sake of clarity, difficult passages of Scripture should be avoided in public. The teacher should, as far as possible, speak in the language of his students, though his usage be colloquial and even incorrect. This is a fascinating pedagogical insight.

> Good teachers have, or ought to have, such great care in teaching that, where a word cannot be pure Latin without being obscure, they should use it according to idiomatic usage, if it avoids ambiguity and obscurity. They should employ it not as it is used by the learned, but rather as the unlearned usually express it. (4, 10, 24)

Augustine gives the example of *os* which can mean either mouth or bone, confusing the simple people. Why not use *ossum* for bone whose plural is *ossa*? Here we have the very basis of good teaching, communication and relevance. Both teacher and student must speak the same language.

> What benefit is a purity of speech which the understanding of the hearer does not follow, since there is no reason at all for speaking, if those for whose enlightenment we are speaking do not understand what we are saying (4, 10, 24).

Augustine especially warns against silence either in a class or during a sermon in church. A crowd that wants to learn shows this by its movement and Augustine encouraged applause and other reactions to his teachings. If some one has his speech memorized, he cannot go over matters again to call attention to this or that point. Room must be left for spontaneity.

Quoting Cicero (*On Oratory* 2, 27 & 28), Augustine maintains that it is not enough to teach, but one must also please and persuade. The first depends on what we say, while the second and third on how we say it. "Just as he is pleased if you speak attractively, so he is moved if he finds pleasure in what you promise, dreads what you threaten, hates what you condemn, etc." (4, 12, 27). The three styles of eloquence: subdued, moderate and grand, relate to teaching, pleasing and persuading. Augustine gives examples of all three styles from Scripture and the Fathers.

Moreover, the teacher should vary his style. For example, if the grand style is pursued too long, it will make people edgy. It is best to alternate the grand and subdued styles as the waves of the ocean. The introduction should always be moderate, while knotty problems are discussed in a subdued style. In a word, the moderate style pleases, while the grand manner persuades (4, 23, 52).

But no matter what style the teacher uses, his life should mirror his words. It is possible to benefit some by preaching alone, but if one practices what he says, there will be a much greater effect.

We have seen several of Augustine's works on education, but some of his keenest hints may be found in other treatises. For example, *The Trinity* (399-416). To try to bring this deep mystery home to his listeners, he illustrates it with human triads, for man is made to the image of the Triune God. Some examples: lover, loved, love (8, 10); mind, knowledge, love (9, 4), memory, intellect, will (14).

As Plato, Augustine places the stress on love and memory in his theory of knowledge. Some slight knowledge is required first to stimulate a love of learning. But the more a thing is known, but not fully known, the more the mind desires to know the rest (10, 1). The scholar is driven on in his desire for the splendor of knowledge. "The splendor of such knowledge is already seen in his thoughts, and is loved by him as something known. And it is so seen and so arouses the zeal of learners that they are spurred into activity on account of it" (10, 1). Something that they know only in theory such as a foreign language, they desire to master also in practice.

Despair is the bane of all learning for it crushes desire.

> Subjects are studied more eagerly when people do not despair of being able to grasp them. When a man has not the hope of being able to attain his end, he either loves the object in a lukewarm manner or does not love it at all, however, valuable he may see it to be. (10, 1)

The implications for a teacher are clear. He must start with what the student already knows and instill in him a desire to know what he does not yet know, the euthusiasm of the teacher carrying the students over discouragement and despair and urging them on to greater heights.

In conclusion, then, we have seen something of Augustine the teacher. Though called reluctantly to administer the church of Hippo, Augustine was first, last and always a teacher. Trained in the rhetoric of Cicero and Quintilian, he taught first at Carthage, then at Rome and Milan.

At Cassiciacum he began his career as a Christian teacher, beginning with philosophical dialogues here and at Tagaste and continuing through his catecheses and homilies at Hippo. Truly after Jesus and Paul, Augustine is *The* teacher of the West and his educational thories, especially as seen in his *First Catechetical Instruction* and his *Christian Education,* were foundations of western monastic education and indirectly influenced the medieval universities.

8

I STROVE WITH THE MOST HOLY AGAPETUS,
BISHOP OF THE CITY OF ROME, TO COLLECT
SUBSCRIPTIONS AND TO HAVE CHRISTIAN
RATHER THAN SECULAR SCHOOLS RECEIVE
PROFESSORS IN THE CITY OF ROME (Cassiodorus,
An *Introduction to Divine and Human Readings*, 1, 1)

LET US NOW look at Europe, Ireland and Britain to see the
advance of Christian education there. In the face of the barbarian
invasions, not only did the Roman empire collapse, but its school
system as well. In Britain the Anglo-Saxons broke the system,
while on the continent other Germanic invaders laid it waste.
Cities were devastated and the schools disintegrated. As Marrou
astutely observes:[1]

> Again, as they (the schools), and with them the whole system of
> classical education, had gradually passed out of private hands and
> into the sphere of public service, they had come to depend more and
> more on the state and the local authorities for money and organiza-
> tion. Their fate was bound up with the political structure of the
> Empire.

This keen observation has been repeated through history to this
day. Thus public education is bound inexorably with politics
which in the end invariably destroys the paideia by using it
for its own ends.

Ausonius was one of the last great teachers of Gaul under
the old system. Born in Bordeaux, an early cultural center with
Celtic and Greek classical heritage, he studied grammar and
rhetoric and in 334 began his professional career as a grammarian
in Bordeaux, then succeeding to the rhetor's chair. Here he had

---

1. R. Marrou, **op. cit.**, p. 344.

many famous students including Paulinus of Nola. In 364 he was summoned to Treves to teach the youth Gratian, emperor-to-be. When Gratian acceded to the throne, Ausonius helped him draft laws adding to the prestige of the Roman teachers (CTh 13, 3, 11; 15, 1, 19). His *cursus honorum* ended with the consulship in 379, but his star waned after the revolt of Maximus (383).

Ausonius has given us some colorful insights into the professors at Bordeaux.

> I will sing of Ammonius also—for, indeed, it is a solemn duty to commemorate a grammarian of my own native place—who used to teach raw lads their alphabet. He had scant learning and was of an ungentle nature, and, therefore,—as was his due—was held in slight repute. (10, 35-40) (LCL)

To his nephew Herculanus, a grammarian at Bordeaux,

> Herculanus, though you came from my bosom and my class, you have repaid your uncle with promise rather than fruit. You shared in the work of my class, and might have succeeded to my chair, had not the swerving steps of slippery youth caused you to fall headlong, through not keeping to the right path, traced out by Pythagorus. (11)

To Nepotian, grammarian and rhetor,

> Witty and cheerful, an old man with a heart of a youth, whose soul, steeped in honey with no drop of gall, never throughout all your life instilled aught of bitterness, balm of my heart, Nepotian. . . . Honorable, pure, sparing, frugal, temperate, eloquent, you were second to no orator in style, while in argument you were the equal of Cleanthes the Stoic. . . . You were my comrade, companion, and my guest continually; and not my guest alone, but the awakener of my mind. None gave advice of a heart more sincere, or concealed it, when given, with deeper secrecy. (15)

A final glimpse of a scholarly assistant teacher, a *proscholus* or *subdoctor*.

> Scholarly Victor, gifted with memory and a quick brain, how patiently you used to pore over books which no one read, and study only abstract lore! You liked better to unroll worm-eaten and outlandish scrolls than to give yourself to more familiar pursuits. (22)

Here was a real bookworm grammarian who died an untimely death before his renown had spread far.

Ausonius gives us a good cross-section of the Bordeaux scholars the harsh grammarian, the youth of high but unfulfilled promise, the elderly, witty and virtuous counselor, and the studious assistant professor. As today, the faculty was a mixture of the good and bad, successful and failures. But these are pagan schools at the tail end of their golden era. Though Ausonius was a Christian and knew something of Scriptures, he was by no means the Christian teacher as Augustine, Jerome or Ambrose.

A. MONASTIC SCHOOLS

We first find Christian education in Gaul with the monasteries and the clerks and almost always with a view to educating towards the clergy or monastic life. So Christian schools did not arise to educate the laity at the demise of the Roman system. And only the wealthy in their embattled villas could afford to hire a grammarian or a rhetor to teach their children.

But how about the monastic schools? Since Christianity and its elite monasticism were both book religions, at minimum the monks and nuns had to learn to read the Scriptures and to learn to write to facilitate the copying of manuscripts. On the island of Lérins Honoratus founded a monastery (400-410) to be a school of bishops, saints, missionaries and scholars.

The great literary heritage of Lérins succeeds that of southern Gaul, including Bordeaux and Marseilles with their Celtic and Greek classical background. For 100 years the principal bishops and thinkers of Gaul came from Lérins, including Hilary of Arles, Eucherius of Lyons, Lupus of Troyes, Faustus of Riez, Vincent of Lérins, Caesarius of Arles. Lérinsian missionaries traveled through Gaul and Britain and British monks came to live at Lérins. Fifth century invasions helped increase the number of monks as intellectuals and aristocrats fled to the islands. Other monks, the Massilians, including John Cassian, engaged Augustine in scholarly debate over predestination and original sin.

The monks taught, and in many ways they were the heirs

of the lay *didaskoloi* of the early church. But what about the clerical teachers? As Moignt points out,[2] increasing sacerdotalism in the fourth and fifth centuries saw more stress on liturgical gestures overshadowing the ministry of the word, which had formerly distinguished the clerical teacher and the lay *didaskolos*. More and more the Christian cleric resembles the Jewish or pagan priest offering at his local shrine. Along with the liturgical stress and its analogies with ancient rites and symbols, there is a gradual decrease in catechetical instructions as infant baptism replaces adult conversions. Moreover, the necessity of doctrinal homilies diminishes after the age of the great heresies. Thus the Christian priest becomes more of a cultic functionary in his local sanctuary and less of a teacher, judge and minister of the word, so that precious little learning was needed for the job.

Of course, there was teaching in the cathedral schools as Augustine held at Hippo, but this was largely for the training of clerks. And in 529 the Council of Vaison instructed local priests to take young lectors into their homes for training in the psalms, *lectio divina,* and the law of the Lord. Those who did not proceed to orders, returned to the world. This custom was also observed in Italy.

In Italy the Ostrogoth Theodoric (493-526) with the aid of Boethius and Cassiodorus, encouraged classical education, raising teachers' salaries, etc. Thus in Rome the old school system was preserved on into the sixth century with professors of grammar, rhetoric, law, and medicine teaching in their auditoriums ranged around Trajan's Forum. Other Italian educational centers were at Milan and Ravenna.

But the Lombards would shatter Roman education (568).

Barbarism spread over the whole of the country. And for nearly 100 years, from the end of the sixth century to the end of the seventh, the land which had been for so long the guardian of classical tradition, was forced to watch its intellectual standard decline to Merovingian level. This period was kind of a watershed,

---

2. "Caractère et ministère sacerdotal," **RSR** 56 (1968), p. 572.

beyond which the only education that remained was almost entirely religious.[3]

Up till this time there had been a dualism of the Christian paideia and the state classical schools. We have seen the clash before, the rhetor converts leaving behind their pagan authors. Yet, on the other hand, they knew that the pagan classics were not all bad since they contained some of God's truth albeit hidden among the pagan myths and legends.

Cassiodorus, who had been Theodoric's chief of the chancellery, earnestly promoting the classical education, wanted also to start a Christian school in Rome like those in Alexandria and Nisibis.

> Perceiving that the schools were swarming with students because of a great longing for secular letters (A great part of mankind believed that through these schools is attained worldly wisdom), I was, I confess, extremely sorry that the Divine Scriptures had no public teachers, since worldly authors were rich in instruction beyond doubt most distinguished. I strove with the most holy Agapetus, bishop of the city of Rome, to collect subscriptions and to have Christian rather than secular schools receive professors in the city of Rome.[4]

Cassiodorus' plan was never fulfilled because of the turmoil of the times. But he was able to found a double monastery with a fine library at his family estate, the Vivarium, in Calabria. There he employed translators and copyists, making it a center of biblical studies. At the same time he experimented in Christian humanism synthesizing the Bible and Christian tradition with the best of classical learning.

> I was driven by divine charity to this device, namely, in the place of a teacher to prepare for you under the Lord's guidance these introductory books, through which, in my opinion, the unbroken line of the Divine Scriptures and the compendious knowledge of secular letters might with the Lord's beneficence be related . . . They are extremely useful, since through them one learns the indicated origin of both the salvation of the soul and secular knowledge.[5]

3. H. Marrou, ou. cit., p. 347.
4. Preface of Book I, **An Introduction to Divine and Human Readings,** tr., L. W. Jones, New York, Columbia, 1946, p. 67.
5. **Ibid.**

These quotes are taken from his *Introduction to Divine and Human Readings* (551) which was written for the instruction of the monks. In the first treatise he writes of the Bible, describing its contents and naming its chief commentators and cautions his scribes and editors to use care in transcribing. He also urges the monks to cultivate learning as a means to better understand the Scriptures. Cassiodorus was a collector of manuscripts, revising the Vulgate on his own. He also discussed orthography, bookbinding and mechanical aids to copying.

Book Two is a brief discussion of the liberal arts (grammar, rhetoric, dialectic, arithmetic, music, geometry, astronomy). Cassiodorus was consistent in his praise of the liberal arts, and, as many of his predecessors, saw them as aids to the study of theology and Scripture. All literary culture and science are ultimately contained in Scriptures and so are somehow derived from them. God's truth is also found in pagan authors, but in a more indirect way.

Cassiodorus' great contribution is not only in organizing religious and secular learning, but also in transforming the monastery into a theological school and scriptorium. How much Cassiodorus influenced other monastic strains such as the Irish and Benedictine we are uncertain, but his *Introduction* was used as a bibliography for future libraries and Book Two was an important textbook of the early Ages.

B. CELTIC & ANGLO-SAXON LEARNING

Let us now look for a moment at the British and Irish monastic educational tradition. Roman education in Britain was all but destroyed by the Anglo-Saxon invasions of the fifth century. But, though driven to the rims of Wales and Scotland, the British church kept in contact with Gaul. And the monasteries there were influenced by Gaulic learning which they brought along on their emigration to Ireland.

Two educational forces preceded the monks in Ireland, namely, the Druids and the bards. The Druids were known throughout the Celtic centers of Europe. In fact, some of the

Gaulic educational centers had previously been Druidic hubs. The Druids were sort of a priesthood, specialized in prophecy, sacrifice and magic. They seemed to be an educated class, training the young men in their profession.

Their prestige seems to have been succeeded by the bards, poets who were sometimes of the aristocrat or warrior class. By the fifth century they formed colleges of education and music. Trusted keepers of the annals, they also were public relations men for the king.

Much of the honor given to the bards was transferred to the learned monks. By the sixth century the Irish church was largely monastic, with teachers, scholars and missionaries trained in the monasteries of Wales, whence they returned to build their own retreats on Irish soil. For example, Finnian of Clonard (d. 549), founder of the second order of Irish saints, studied in Wales in the schools that produced the great Welsh scholars Gildas and David. Cadoc was his teacher at Llancarvan.

Finnian started a monastery and school at Clonard where he taught the twelve apostles of Ireland, including: Ciaran of Saigher, Ciaran of Clonmacnois, Columba of Iona, Brendan of Clonfert, Brendan of Birr and others. Other schools were built by Ciaran at Clonmacnois (544) and by Brendan at Clonfert (556), and by Comgall at Bangor where Columban, Dungall and Gall studied. Still other schools were located at Moville, Iniscaltra, etc.

Who studied in the Irish monastic schools? Mostly boys who intended to join the monastery, although the sons of chiefs were also educated. They studied Scripture, especially as translated and interpreted by Jerome, though the Gaulic fathers were also read, especially Hilary of Arles. Other studies were: grammar, arithmetic, chronology, astronomy and other branches of the natural sciences. The bardic love of poetry was practiced in Irish and Latin songs. In the liberal arts Martianus Capella's *De Nuptiis Philologiae et Mercurii* served as a foundation. Both classical and patristic authors were read. And perhaps the Provence Greek traditions were transferred to the Celtic foundations. Calligraphy, an important contribution of the Irish monks, was a speciality.

While learning was at a low ebb on the continent and in Anglo-Saxon Britain, Irish monasteries, free from barbarian invasions, kept the ancient classical and religious traditions alive. How many boys came from the continent or from Britain to study in the Irish monasteries is uncertain. Bede writes of those who went from Northumbria after its conversion by the Celtic monks.

> There were in that same place at that time many nobles as well as common sort of English race, who in the time of the bishops Finan and Colman had left their native island and departed aside thither either to read sacred writings or to live more strictly. And certain of them bound themselves faithfully to the monastic life, while others wandering rather about the cells of such as taught gladly, gave good heed to reading; all of whom the Scots entertained cheerfully and were forward to give them daily sustenance free, also books for reading and teaching without payment. (Bede, **History**, 3, 27) (LCL)

One gets the impression from Bede that these boys went to Ireland with religious studies in mind, or at least some type of conversion. Many famous church leaders and not a few kings were trained in the Irish monastic schools, for example: Agilbert, bishop of Dorchester; Dagobert, Frankish king; Aldfrith, king of Northumbria.

Irish missionaries spread the faith and learning: Columba to the Picts and Scots, Gall in Switzerland and Alemannia, Kilian and Virgil in Thuringia and Carinthia. These great teachers were to be the guardians of theological and classical tradition, scribes of biblical manuscripts, balladeers, and fore-runners of medieval learning.

Columban had a school at Luxeuil and later at Bobbio. Most of his pupils were young boys seeking to be monks, learning first the alphabet, then reading and writing and some arithmetic. Then they were ready for the liberal arts, starting with the treatises on grammar of Donatus and Priscian. His monastic companion would be the psalter, so he began by reading it. Also the Latin classics were read including Virgil, Horace, and Livy. Columban loved the classics and encouraged his monks to make copies of them. His monastic libraries included: sacramentaries, antiphonaries, lives of the saints, passionals, commentaries on Scriptures, works of Augustine, Jerome, Gregory the Great, Ambrose, Prosper, Bede, Isaidore, Priscian,

Donatus, Virgil, Horace, Boethius, Cicero, Terence.

The study of grammar led to rhetoric and the practice of writing and dialectics. Those inclined to mathematics took up the quadrivium. The Celts naturally put a high priority on music, especially the singing of the psalms. Here perfection was required, any lapses punished by blows.

So both at home and abroad the Irish monks were leading educators, with a classical Christian humanism with roots going back to Lérins. Scriptures were the main stay, although the Fathers also were read. Profane literature was an aid in getting a mastery of the Latin tongue.

What Columba, Aidan, Columban, and Gall planted, was brought to maturity by Cuthbert, Chad, Wilfred, Bede, Willibrord, Boniface and Alcuin.

The Celts had established Christian monastic camps throughout Britain and the continent, but they would be supplanted by the diocesan system under Canterbury, founded by Augustine. The Synod of Whitby (597) settled the matter of jurisdiction in favor of Rome and Canterbury over the Celts, but both systems would endure, Celtic and Roman, Lindisfarne and Canterbury, their dualism reflected in the English church and in English learning. Thus there were Celtic teachers in Northumbria in the seventh and eighth centuries, and Rome-oriented students sailed to study in the monasteries of Ireland.

When the Romans came to Britain under the leadership of Augustine, they were not noted for their learning. But when Theodore of Tarsus, a well-known scholar, succeeded to the chair of Canterbury, education became the order of the day. He was accompanied by Hadrian, abbot of a monastery near Naples and Benedict Biscop, a Northumbrian, who had been a monk at Lérins.

They soon attracted Anglo-Saxon students to Canterbury.

Why should Ireland, whither troops of students are carried in fleets from this country, enjoy any such supreme distinction. As if here on the fertile soil of England Greek and Roman masters were not to be found to solve the hard problems of the heavenly library for all who seek to learn of them? (Aldhelm, **Letters to Eahfridus**) (PL 89, 94)

At Canterbury the Anglo-Saxon boys learned Greek and Latin, Scripture, church music, geometry and some medicine. Many famous leaders studied there including Aldhelm, abbot of Malmesbury, John of Beverly, bishop of Hexham, etc.

As Gaskoin comments[6] the history of letters for the next 100 years is divided into three great schools under Aldhelm of Malmesbury, Bede of Jarrow, and Alcuin of York. Aldhelm studied under the Irish monk, Maidulf, till 670 when he went to Canterbury to study under Hadrian, but he soon returned to Maidulf's school which grew in reputation. Gaskoin[7] points out the superficiality of monastic learning at this time.

> The bombastic manner which he (Aldhelm) affected, the childlike naivete with which he paraded all his learning and strewed his pages with Graecisms as meaningless as they are disconcerting, doubtless impressed the ignorance of his contemporaries.

The Anglo-Saxons delighted in jumbling together Greek, Latin and Anglo-Saxon syllables, striving for alliterations. Aldhelm always remained a staunch defender of the Roman position vs. the Celtic customs such as tonsure and Easter date. And in 705 he was rewarded with the bishopric of Sherborne.

While Hadrian held forth at Canterbury, Benedict Biscop brought learning to Northumbria where first Jarrow and then York became centers of literary promise. Returning from a journey to Rome, laden with books, Benedict built the monastery of St. Peter near the mouth of the Wear River (674). Another trip to Rome brought more books, pictures and relics. He built another monastery dedicated to St. Paul on the South bank of the Tyne and one of the first aspirants was the young lad Bede, destined to be the star of the school of Jarrow.

Benedict died in 689.

> His labors had inaugurated a new era in Northumbrian an era in which a new type of religious house, increasingly self-centered, and

6. Gaskoin, **Alcuin,** New York, Russell and Russell, 1966, p. 19.
7. **Ibid.,** pp. 21-22.

pursuing knowledge as an end in itself, to a large extent superceded the mere missionary center of an earlier date.[8]

As he died Benedict asked the monks to preserve the fine library he had brought from Rome.

Among the scholars of Northumbria at this period are: Wilfrid of Ripon, Cuthbert of Lindisfarne, Adomnan, biographer of Columba, John of Beverley, bishop of Hexham and then of York. But Biscop and Ceolfrid had been their forerunners in bringing the learning of Canterbury to Northumbria. Collecting libraries of books and manuscripts, they built their monasteries on the Roman plan with a view to training scholars.

> The most convincing proof of the excellence of any school is to be found in the achievements of its pupils, and it is thus that the worth of Biscop's twin foundations must be measured. Of Coelfrid there are but the most meagre literary remains, of Biscop, none. But they have their memorial in more than one great personality. For Wearmouth and Jarrow produced Bede, and through him, the school of York, Alcuin and the Carolingian School, on which the culture of the Middle Ages was based.[9]

Bede (b. 673) entered Wearmouth at the age of seven, transferring the next year to the new foundation at Jarrow, where he studied under Trumbert, Cuthbert, Eath and possibly John of Beverley. For 54 years he studied, taught and wrote, culling the fruits of both Roman and Irish learning from the monastic library. His masterpiece is his *Church History of the English People* (731). Besides his history, Bede's astronomy, paschal tables, martyrology, etc. were read and consulted in monasteries throughout Europe.

As leadership in Northumbria passed to the church of York, it became the intellectual center. Egbert, favorite pupil of Bede's became archbishop there in 735, establishing a school which would outshadow its predecessors at Canterbury and Jarrow. For 50 years it maintained its position as the educational leader of Europe till Alcuin left to spread English learning

8. **Ibid.**, pp. 25-26.
9. **Ibid.**, p. 28.

among the Franks. But as Gaskoin comments,[10] York not only possessed great individual teachers and an excellent library, like the other centers of the time, but had a certain spirit and personality all its own. Its motto was "Disce ut doceas" (Alcuin L19, L31). The student is the father of the teacher.

At York the school was highly organized, differing from the one-on-one tutorials of the monastic tradition. They had special classes for reading, singing and writing. Of course, the trivium and quadrivium were the foundation of the program; to this were added Scripture and moral training, with the seven liberal arts as subordinate to Scripture and theology. They studied Boethius, Cassiodorus and Isidore of Seville, by-passing Martianus Capella so popular in the Irish schools. York was a center of Roman learning, bent on the task of Romanizing all of England, which had been begun by Augustine and continued by Wilfrid and his successors.

C. ALCUIN

As a boy Alcuin came to York to study under Aelbert and Egbert. Like his predecessors, Alcuin was Roman to the core, Gregorian and Orthodox, following the Roman rite. He preferred Isidore and Bede to Boethius and Cassiodorus, and studied secular as well as sacred writers, quoting frequently from Ovid, Horace and Terence. Though Alcuin was not the scholar Bede was, he excelled as a master and organizer. And his reputation as a teacher, his enthusiasm, patience, and skill at stimulating students drew pupils from all over England and abroad. Alcuin is a good example of a mediocre scholar making a good teacher, perhaps because he appreciates the struggle that the mediocre student has to go through, and having suffered from the dullness of study, he knows how much enthusiasm is necessary to stimulate his students.

As abbot of York, Alcuin continued to build up the library. On his journies to France he met many scholars either in po-

10. Ibid., p. 34.

sitions of administration in the Frankish church or in the royal
court at Aachen. Charles the Great urged him to join his royal
stable of scholars. Whereas England was in a state of decline,
soon to be devastated by the Danes, France seemed to be on
the way up. Everything was favorable to Alcuin's move, for
Aachen was a great intellectual center boasting Frankish, Italian and Anglo-Saxon scholars.

In 782 Alcuin set sail for France where he took over the
headship of Charles' palace school, teaching the royal children
along with those of the nobles and including some adult men
and women. Even Charles himself sat in on some lectures, for he
felt deeply his lack of education. Following Anglo-Saxon custom,
Alcuin gave his pupils either biblical or classical names. Thus
Charles became "David", Pippin "Julius", and Alcuin himself
was called "Flaccus Albinus". In true monastic tradition the
seven liberal arts were introduced to aid the understanding of
Scriptures. To ease the boredom of learning, Alcuin introduced
mathematical puzzles or whimsical definitions, plus the writing
of verse, epigrams or riddles.

A good example of Alcuin's banter with his students is
found among his works (PL 101, 975-980).

Pippinus: Quid est littera?
Albinus: *Custos historiae.*
P: Quid est verbum?
A: *Proditor Animi.*
P: Quid est lingua?
A: *Flagellum Aeris.*
P: Quid est aer?
A: *Custodia vitae.*
P: Quid est vita?
A: *Beatorum laetitiae, miserorum moestia, expectatio mortis.*
P: Quid est mors?
A: *Inevitabilis eventus, incerta peregrinatio, lacrymae viv-
entium ,testamenti firmamentum, latro hominis.*
P: Quid est homo?
A: *Mancipium mortis, transiens viator, loci hospes.*

Alcuin did much to restore the intellectual life of France,
for under the Merovingian kings in the seventh and eighth cen-

turies it had slipped to nothing. Though learning was preserved in a measure in the church and monastery, even they were in decadence at the accession of Charles Martel. Some feel that the church's negative or at best tolerant attitude towards the classics was one reason for their decline. The replacing of or at least the subordination of classical learning to the ecclesiastical led to a mediocrity in education for precious little of the three "R's" was necessary to be an ecclesiastical functionary. In all the schools, either episcopal, monastic, or parish, the training was largely for ecclesiastics.

The new literary low coupled with the Saxon and Saracen invasions of the eighth century met their match in Charles Martel. He and Boniface laid the groundwork on which Alcuin and Charles the Great would build. "Before the intellectual life could be resuscitated, it was necessary, on the one hand, to deliver the kingdom from danger without and discord within, and, on the other, to teach bishops and abbots that they must do something more than hunt, fight and drink."[11] As peace settled, ecclesiastical education began to develop at Utrecht, Metz, Salzburg, and S. Gall and in Boniface's foundations. Moreover, the Palace School began to improve under Pippin.

When Charles the Great ascended the throne, he had the ambition to make France the intellectual leader of the world, attracting the top teachers of the era: Peter of Tuscany, Paulus Diaconus, and Alcuin. When Alcuin arrived at Aachen, he had his work cut out for him, namely, the supervision of the Palace School, helping the king improve his weak educational background, upgrading the clerical training and revising the liturgy and biblical manuscripts.

First of all, Charles insisted upon a learned clergy, ordering the suspension and even the deprivation of clergy who were ignorant. Writing to the hierarchy of France around 789, he decrees:

> Be it known to your Devotion pleasing to God that we and our faithful have judged it well that, in the bishoprics and monasteries

11. Ibid., p. 172.

committed by Christ's favor to our charge, besides the due observance of a regular and holy life, care shall be had for the study of letters, that those to whom God has given the ability to learn may receive instruction, each according to his several capacities, and this, that, just as obedience to the rule gives order and beauty to your acts, so zeal in teaching and learning may impart the like graces to your words, and thus those who seek to please God by living aright may not fail to please him also by right speaking.[12]

The danger is clear. Even though a monk, priest or bishop be a holy man, if he has not the learning to comprehend Sacred Scriptures, he soon falls into error and drags others along. The clergy should at least be able to recite the office, chant the Psalms and know the ecclesiastical formularies, teach catechism and give homilies to the faithful. Needless to say, many of these directives reflected the influence of Alcuin and the school of York. Once Charles made it certain that there would be no advancement of the clerks without learning, the cathedral and monastic schools grew apace.

But was Charles' educational reform limited to clergy and monks? A capitulary (802) instructs that every one should send his son to school to study letters and he should stay there until well instructed in learning (*Capitula Examinationis Generalis,* 17). How many sent their sons to these schools can only be conjectured.

In the Diocese of Orleans bishop Theodulf, Alcuin's pupil, encouraged the presbyters to erect elementary schools in their parishes.

Let the presbyters have schools in villages and country places, and if some of the faithful want to send their small boys to them to learn letters, let them not refuse to accept and teach them. But let them teach them with greatest love, remembering what Scripture says: "They that are learned shall shine as the brightness of the firmament, and they shall instruct many to justice, as stars for all eternity." And when they teach them, let them charge nothing, nor accept anything from them, except what parents voluntarily offer. (PL 105, 196)

At the time the children of the wealthy were favored and many

12. **Ibid.**, p. 182.

monasteries charged tuition. Alcuin himself had written in favor of free education. "Discere si cupias, gratis; quod quaeris, habebis" (Carmen 119 *De Via Duplici ad Scholam et Cauponam*) (PL 101, 737).

One gets the feeling that, in general, the education of non-clerics or non-oblates was reluctantly carried out, at best. The dangers to the monks of training externs was recognized in 817 by the Assembly of the Benedictine abbots at Aschen who instructed that thenceforth the monks should limit their instructions to their oblates, that is, those seeking entrance into the monastery. The episcopal schools followed suite (Council of Aachen, 816). And the Council of Attigny (822) provided for the education of those seeking to be secular priests.

To return to Alcuin, when he retired from the Palace School, he established a monastic school at Tours where he taught many famous students including Wadilcoz from Richenau and Hatto and Rabanus Maurus from Fulda.

Alcuin's writings are not the most erudite, but homely attempts to abridge the works of earlier scholars for the use of rude students. Though his notes were rough, his classroom manner was excellent, with enthusiasm and patience, drawing out the best from all.

Though the Carolingian revival in learning was brief, it carried on in Rheims and Fulda. With John the Scot and Peter Abelard came a new trend, giving rise to scholasticism and the medieval universities. Abelard tended to ignore the ancient traditions, and instead of blanketing his works with patristic quotes, he was well aware of their fallibility. But Alcuin, by helping to preserve the past, had laid the groundwork for the medieval *paideia*.

9

NO ONE SHALL BE A SCHOLAR AT PARIS WHO HAS NO DEFINITE MASTER (Rules of the University of Paris, 1215)

A.   MIDDLE AGES

IN DISCUSSING the medieval universities, we should first take a brief look at what is meant by the Middle Ages. As Pieper points out,[1] originally Middle Ages was a term of opprobrium cast on the sterile period between the death of the Greek philosophical schools in the sixth century and the glories of the Renaissance. So the term "Middle Ages" takes on many of the prejorative connotations, attached to middle aged people on the part of the younger set, namely, stereotyped, stodgy, set in their ways, "over the hill," intellectually sterile, etc.

Simultaneous with the closing of the Greek philosophical schools by Justinian in 529, arose Benedictine monasticism, a new life of the church which through the centuries would develop an intellectual life of its own, although more oriented towards sacred literature and theology than philosophy. Boethius was a bridge. Trained in the schools of Greece, he was a contemporary and probably a relative of Benedict. And he introduced the invading Goths to the classical tradition.

As Pieper comments,[2] the intellectual center switched from Athens, Alexandria, Antioch and Carthage to the courts of Theodoric and Charlemagne and the cities of Canterbury, Paris, Oxford, Cologne and Rome. Pieper, following the lead of Hegel, sees the Middle Ages as formed by a marriage of the Germanic

---

1. J. Pieper, **Scholasticism**, London, Faber and Faber, 1960, p. 15.
2. J. Pieper, **op. cit.**, p. 21.

peoples with the classical tradition. "Scholastic philosophy is this utter confusion of the barren understanding in the rugged North German nature."[3]

Pieper remarks:[4]

> The incorporation of something not sprung from native soil, the acquisition of both a foreign vocabulary and a different mode of thinking, the assimilation of a tremendous body of existing thought— all that was in fact the problem which confronted medieval philosophy at its beginnings, and which it had to master. In the very act of mastering it, medieval philosophy acquired its own character.

To begin to understand scholasticism, one should see it as primarily scholarship and learning, covering several centuries and incorporating and organizing both pagan and Christian systems of knowledge. Naturally this process of organizing, summarizing, synthesizing seems impersonal and abstract, with little originality displayed on the part of the authors. Yet the summists required a certain genius of their own. And once the *summae* were written with previous traditions well organized, the stage was set for new breakthroughs in knowledge.

Let us now look at the institution which brought about this synthesis of ancient learning, namely, the medieval university.[5] Two ecclesiastical schools preceded the universities, as we have seen, the monastic and the cathedral or bishop's school. Certainly the withdrawal of the monasteries from external schools in the ninth century under the reforms of Benedict of Aniane was a vital factor in the ultimate rise of the universities. The monastic schools had always stressed sacred literature, and even read the classics as a means to bettering their knowledge of letters. But they spent little time on philosophy or theological speculation. In fact, when new theological theories made incursions into the monasteries, they often caused consternation, as Augustine's ideas on predestination had shaken up the simple monks at Hadrumetum.

3. G. Hegel, **Lectures on the History of Philosophy,** New York, Humanities Press, 1955, vol. 3, p. 95.

4. J. Pieper, op. cit., p. 22.

5. L. Daly, **The Medieval University,** New York, Sheed and Ward, 1961, pp. 6ff.

The bishop's school or cathedral school was really a diocesan seminary to which the young lectors came after their preliminary training in the parishes. These schools reached their greatest heights in the eleventh and twelfth centuries and often were training centers for the cathedral canons, stressing philosophy and theology.

The Third Lateran Council (1179) voiced the need of cathedral, parish or monastic schools for the poor, for all should equally share in the learning of the ages

> Since the church of God as a kindly mother is held to provide for those needs which pertain to physical welfare and those which contribute to the progress of souls, lest the opportunity of reading and education be denied poor children who cannot be aided by the resources of their parents, let some sufficient benefice be set aside in every cathedral church for a master who shall teach the clergy of the same church and poor scholars gratis, whereby the need for a teacher shall be met and the way to knowledge opened to learners.[6]

Other schools of increasing importance were the guild schools. Besides their apprenticeship programs, the guilds sponsored Latin schools for boys aiming at the professions. City schools also were growing in Germany by the thirteenth century and rivaled the church schools especially in the teaching of Latin.

By the twelfth century dialectic was applied to theology which heretofore had been largely a repetition of scriptural and patristic positions. However, it was not attempted without the resistance of the pious who felt that the new probings into ancient mysteries were leading to dangerous new schools of thought. Two opposing schools in the twelfth century were those of Bernard and Abelard. Abelard taught that man should use his reason to probe the mysteries of faith, since so many of the opinions of the Fathers contradicted themselves (*Sic et Non*). Reason and revelation cannot contradict each other since both are from God.

Abelard's question and answer dialectic reached perfection

6. L. Thorndike, **University Records and Life in the Middle Ages,** New York, Columbia, 1944, p. 10.

6. Chartres cathedral, right (South) portal on West. At bottom left above capitals is represented Aristotle writing. At bottom right Pythagoras and Donatus.

in men like Peter Lombard and Thomas Aquinas. But the use of reason in matters of faith was questioned by the schools of Bernard, John of Salisbury, certain condemnations (e.g. Paris, 1277), and the later school of Martin Luther.

Two great educational heritages of the Middle Ages are the cathedral and the university. The towering cathedral, built by the contributions and labor of rich and poor alike, is an education in glass and stone for both the simple and the learned, covering the life of Christ, Old Testament Heroes, the saints and mysteries of the faith. Millions of pilgrims over the centuries have enjoyed the stained glass windows and been edified by the soaring naves and transepts.

B. THE UNIVERSITY

The universities were more for the learned elite aiming at the professions, first at Paris and Bologna, then elsewhere. Whereas earlier ecclesiastical education had stressed grammar and rhetoric, the universities were centers of dialectic controversy with grammar and literature in subordinate positions.

Daly[7]lists some factors contributing to the rise of the medieval universities: the rediscovery of Aristotle, Roman and church law, and Greek medical writing, the Moslem culture, the growth of the cities, guilds, and the whole educational tradition going back to Alcuin and Charlemagne. Aristotle came through the Spanish Arab schools and the Italian translators and was important to the advancement of scholasticism as Galen was to medicine, and Justinian's code to the study of law. The growing medieval towns not only gave birth to the trade guilds and their schools, but also city schools for the three "R's", classical Latin schools and finally the universities.

Paris rapidly became the intellectual hub of France. As Rome, Alexandria and Byzantium before, it drew teachers and scholars of every sort. As in earlier times, the teacher was the founder of the school, for example, William of Champeaux and

7. L. Daly, op. cit,, p. 17.

Peter Abelard. Abelard was young, controversial, iconoclastic, enthusiastic, and, as today, young scholars were drawn to his dynamism.

Theology was the speciality at Paris and there were three main schools: the cathedral school of William of Champeaux, the school of the church of Ste Genevieve on the left bank where Abelard taught, and the school of St. Victor.

By this time there was an established educational tradition, a teachers' guild, a *universitas*. A *universitas* could be an association of merchants, craftsmen, tailors, masters or scholars. Only later did the term designate the place or the buildings where education was carried on. The common term for what we call the university today was *studium generale* for it had more than one faculty and drew students from many nations. Sometimes, as at Paris, it had the right of conferring the *ius ubique docendi*.

In order to become a master, and member of the *universitas* one had to go through an apprenticeship and receive the approval of the masters. Only then could he begin teaching. Rules regulated official dress, order of lectures etc. Moreover, the *universitas* itself was a corporation, a legal body which could sue or be sued.

Very early there was a struggle for power between the bishops and the university. In a sense, it was a struggle over the teacher's cathedra which had a long history. Is the bishop the official teacher of the diocese? Are the university clerks under the bishop, or if not, under whom? The rise of the regular clerks at the universities and their clashes with the seculars and the bishops is related to this problem. Especially when new fangled doctrines were taught, such as Aristotelianism, tensions arose between teachers and episcopals. It seems that the diocesan chancellor felt that he had the power to grant or not to grant the right to teach. The chancellor was the bishop's appointment, whereas the rector was usually elected from and by the masters or proctors for a short term. At Oxford and Cambridge chancellor and rector were the same, but at Paris they were not, inevitably leading to jurisdictional clashes. More and more the *universitas* sought papal protection from episcopal and local government interference. In this the universities resemble more the cosmopolitan monasteries than the cathedral schools for the training of local canons.

A cardinal legate exercised jurisdiction over the University of Paris as is reflected in the rules (1215).[8] Thus, Robert, the cardinal legate, describes the method in arts and in theology, indicating what books the masters of arts should not read, drawing up disciplinary rules for the scholars and for the whole school. To lecture in arts at Paris one had to be 21 years of age. "And he shall have heard lectures for at least six years before he begins to lecture, and he shall promise to lecture for at least two years, unless a reasonable cause prevents, which he ought to prove publically or before examiners." He must be morally upright. He will lecture on Aristotle, but not on his metaphysics or natural philosophy. He will teach both Priscians and avoid the doctrines of David of Dinant and Mauritius of Spain.

Ground rules were laid for conduct: "In the principia and meetings of the masters and in the responsions or oppositions of the boys and youths there shall be no drinking." "No one shall wear the round cape, shoes that are ornamented or with elongated pointed toes." "Each master shall have jurisdiction over his scholar." "No one shall receive the licentiate from the chancellor or another for money given or promise made or other condition agreed upon." "No one shall be admitted at Paris to formal lectures or to preachings unless he shall be of approved life and science. No one shall be a scholar at Paris who has no definite master." Theologians could not teach until they were 35 years old, had studied for eight years and attended lectures for five years.

The universitites were cosmopolitan with masters and students from many nations. So it was natural at Paris for the arts masters to gather into national guilds, but the faculties of medicine law and theology did not do so. At Bologna the guilds were of scholars. There were four nations at Paris: French, including: Paris, S. France, Spain, Italy, Greece and the East; Norman, including the Low Countries and N. France; English including the British Isles, Holland, the Germanies, Sweden,

8. L. Thorndike, op. cit., pp. 27-30.

Denmark, Norway, Hungary and the Slavs; and the Picard nation.

During the thirteenth and fourteenth centuries the nations became, in effect, semi-independent colleges within the university, with their own officers, masters, students, buildings, chapels, funds, etc. Each nation had its own proctor or rector. And by 1249 the four proctors are electing the rector of the university. The policies of the faculty of arts were determined at weekly assemblies which only regent masters could attend. Between the meetings the university rector and four proctors served as an executive council. The nations also oversaw the examinations of the scholars.

The officers had extremely limited terms. At Paris the national proctors served one month and the university rector a month or six weeks. After 1266 he served three months. The real power lay in the university assembly. Teaching and learning were the name of the game in the medieval university. And the rectors and proctors were elected only to insure that this went on in the best possible manner. At Paris these officials were "Teachers, elected by a body of teachers to supervise a place where teaching was going on."[9] Many, if not most of the evils of modern universities can be traced to a neglect of this principle. Some scholars served as college chaplains, minor clergy conducting services in the college church, and at least at Oxford, waiting table for the fellows.

The University of Bologna, rather than run by national guilds of masters, was controlled by nations of students. Actually there were two universities, one for the ultra-montanists and the other for the cis-montanists. In the beginning the students banded together for mutual protection, leaving the academics to the professors' guilds. Moreover, they received the protection of Pope Honorius III (1216-27) against the commune of Bologna which was trying to dissolve them and against Frederick II who attempted to break up the Bologna universities. But eventually the student guilds were encouraged and given privileges of draft and tax exemptions by the town fathers.

9. Ibid., pp. 122-23.

In the thirteenth century the two law universities were sub-divided into 14 ultra-montane nations: French, Spanish, Provencal, English, etc., whereas the cis-alpine had four divisions: Rome, Campania, Tuscany and Lombardy with further sub-divisions. Each nation had a consiliarius, or representative on the university council, except Rome and Sicily which had two.

A university of arts and medicine was also formed in the latter part of the 13th century, electing their own rector, alternating among the four nations of the university: ultra-montane, Lombard, Tuscan, Roman for a one year term.

Daly comments:[10]

> The formation of these universities had been unsuccessfully opposed by both the professors and the commune. The professors were excluded from the nations. And the commune, not unnaturally probably feared the possible abuse of power by irresponsible student rectors. By repeated threatened or actual migrations, however, and more especially through the constant defense and help of various popes, the student universities gradually won out. By the second half of the 13th century they were sharing, through their nations and elected representatives, not only the election of their own rector, but also in the general administration and direction of the studium generale itself.

Since the medieval universities drew students from many nations, some sort of lodging had to be provided. Often benefactors erected hostels for poor students such as the Sorbonne at Paris (1257) and Balliol (1263) and Merton (1264) at Oxford. Gradually these quarters evolved into full colleges with regulations, elected officials, etc. The Oxford colleges remained independent, whereas those at Paris came under the control of the university.

Let us now take a closer look at the medieval university students. Who were they? How did they conduct themselves? From the Jewish rabbinical schools down through the Roman and Carolingian systems, most students were trained so that they could teach, granted that not all actually became teachers. *Disce ut doceas.* Thus the medieval student aimed at professorship, and

10. Daly, op. cit., p. 34.

at a certain point in his career he both studied and lectured as a teaching fellow. But, as in ancient times, not all the students joined the teaching profession, some going into church or government service, etc.

When the new student arrived at Bologna, he joined a student nation with all of its rights and privileges. Next he set about finding a master. This was almost always a buyers' market, so the student could shop around, attending various lectures until he found a master of his liking. As today, the less demanding teachers probably attracted the most students. As a *beanus,* an initiate, he was subject to a certain amount of hazing on the part of the upper classmen. This increased in vigor so that by 1340 the University of Paris legislated against the undue indignities.

> The said university bids the said freshmen, under penalty of deprivation of any honors from the said university, that if any one does wrong to them by word or deed on account of their class, they shall straightway secretly reveal this to the proctors and deans of the faculties who in general congregation shall be required to reveal the names of the offenders by their oaths.[11]

As might be expected, not all of the students were ideal. Many were shiftless, running from school to school, and master to master, enjoying life. Alvarus Pelagius, appropriately named grand penitentiary under John XXII at Avignon (d. 1352), lists some of the faults of the scholars.[12]

> 1. Sometimes they wish to be above their masters, impugning their statements more with a certain wrong-headedness than with reason . . .
> 3. They attend classes, but make no effort to learn anything . . .
> 4. They frequently learn what they would better ignore . . . such things as forbidden sciences, amatory discourses, and superstitions.
> 6. They defraud their masters of their due salaries, although they are able to pay . . .
> 7. They have among themselves evil and disgraceful societies, associating together for ill. And while in residence they sometimes are guilty of vices, against which their masters ought to provide and take action so far as they can . . .

11. H. Denifle, ed., **Cartularium Universitatis Parisiensis II** Brussels, 1964, p. 496. Thorndike, **op. cit.,** p. 193.
12. Thorndike, **ibid.,** pp. 173-74.

8. They are disobedient to the masters and rectors of the universities and sometimes transgress the statutes which they have sworn to observe . . . (punishable by rods).

9. On feast days they do not go to church to hear divine service and sermons and above all the full mass which all Christians are supposed to attend, but gad about town with their fellows or attend lectures or write up their notes at home. Or, if they go to church, it is not to worship, but to see the girls or to swap stories.

12. The expense money which they have from their parents or churches they spend in taverns, conviviality, games and other superfluities, and so they return home empty, without knowedge, conscience, or money.

Any one familiar with modern colleges, realizes that times have not changed, though the majority seriously pursue their studies. And, of course, students are not the only ones with faults. Alvarus Pelagius has a few comments to make about the professors, who are unprepared, envious. "They scorn to admit well-prepared subordinates to professorial chairs." They are arrogant, teaching useless and even false doctrines, and are respectors of persons rather than truth.

Town and gown was another problem. The university was really an international enclave outside the town jurisdiction. But inevitable clashes occurred between the two. As today, most trouble started in the taverns in which the students found fresh courage in alcohol and in numbers. And as in recent times the result was sometimes tragic. For example, in Paris, April 1229 (spring has always been the riot season at universities) several students were killed by the provost's guards, supported by Queen Blanche of Castille. In protest the masters voted to close the university for six years. Some masters returned in 1231, armed with Pope Gregory IX's Magna Carta, insuring their right to strike and limiting the powers of the chancellor of Paris. Similar skirmishes occurred at Bologna, Oxford, Cambridge and elsewhere.

The lingua franca of the medieval universities was Latin and most students came from the parish or cathedral schools with an acceptable knowledge of the language. The *beanus* came from the grammar school at the age of 15-16, enrolling in his national college. He began as an artist studying the liberal arts for four or five years, attending lectures, disputations, working under a regent master, who would give him the go-ahead for his qualifying exams. The nation oversaw the preliminary exam before the student could apply for permission "to determine."

To qualify for the determination, besides the approval of the masters of his nation, the artist had to swear that he had studied arts four or five years at Paris or elsewhere, that he had his own master under whom he could determine, and that he would use the schools of a regent master. He was examined on works by Aristotle, Gilbert of Poree, Boethius and Donatus.

The determination disputations were held during Lent. And once the artist was determined, he became a bachelor or beginner. The bachelor's degree was sufficient to teach in the grammar schools, but some went on for the master's. At Oxford this entailed further readings in Aristotle, Boethius, Cicero, Ovid, Euclid, Vitellio and Ptolemy.

Between the bachelor's and the master's a teaching licentiate was required from the church authorities. Originally this came only from the chancellor of Paris, but later it was also given at Ste. Genevieve. The formula was read by the vice-chancellor.

> I, by the authority invested in me by the apostles, Peter and Paul, give you the license for lecturing, reading, disputing, and determining and for exercising other scholastic and magisterial acts both in the faculty of arts at Paris and elsewhere in the name of the Father and of the Son and of the Holy Ghost. Amen.[13]

But the licentiate was only given after all kinds of oaths and promises, including: not accepting or giving bribes, the promise to teach for two years, to give honest information about the students. Moreover, he must not be married or a member of a religious order and promise to keep the peace between the artists and theologians, the regular and the secular clergy.

One can easily see that we have here a church school through and through perhaps and evolution of the cathedral school taught by and for clerks. And one can also see why trouble ensued when the regular clerks came on the scene to start their own colleges.

Between the licentiate and the master's or doctor's degree was the inception ceremony. Sometimes more books were required to

13. **op. cit.**, p. 135.

be read such as Aristotle's ethics and meteorology. After the student promised loyalty to his nation, there were two disputations. At the formal inauguration disputation after receiving his magisterial biretta, a book and a kiss of fellowship and the right to wear the professorial cape, he sat on the magisterial chair, the cathedra, with traditions going back to the early didaskoloi of the Greco-Roman paideia. After the disputation the new master gave a banquet for the masters and other guests. The regent masters taught in the arts colleges and the universities, while others went into ecclesiastical and civil life, in both of which the degree was a distinct advantage. Still others went on to professional studies in law, medicine or theology.

The lectures of the regent masters were supposed to be hasty rather than slow, evidently to discourage note-taking.[14]

> Two methods of lecturing on books in the liberal arts having been tried, the former masters of philosophy uttering their words rapidly so that the mind of the hearer can take them in, but the hand cannot keep up with them, the latter speaking slowly until their listeners can catch up with them with the pen. Having compared these by diligent examination, the former method is found better. Wherefore, the consensus of opinion warns us that we imitate it in our lectures.

The slow lecturer was removed from the classroom for a year, and the penalty doubled for future offenses.

The students did not appreciate having their shortcut to learning removed and they let everybody know it. The university responded.

> Moreover, listeners who oppress the execution of this our statute by clamor, hissing, noise, the throwing of stones by themselves or by their servants and accomplices, or in any other way, we deprive of and cut off from our society for a year, and for each relapse we increase the penalty double and quadruple above.

Beyond lecturing, the masters had to participate in the disputations which were formal discussions of problems, between two or more scholars, one defending his thesis and the other

14. H. Denifle, op. cit. III, pp. 39-40. Thorndike, op. cit., p. 237.

objecting. Besides the formal disputations had at bachelor's and master's ceremonies and on other special occasions (De Quolibet), there were informal ones in the classroom. Also there were ordinary public disputations with a student defending and objecting and the master summing up. The give and take of the disputation, although it tended to become wooden and stereotyped, has something in common with the dialogues of learning going back to the ancient philosophers and rabbis.

We mentioned earlier that the medieval universities were under clerical control with clerical offices, masters and students. But it was easy for a student to become a clerk and so have ecclesiastical protection. It seems that all he had to do was receive tonsure and use the clerical dress. "The adoption of the clerical tonsure and dress conferred, as long as the wearer continued celibate, the immunities and privileges of the clerical order-exemption from the secular courts, personal inviolability and the like.[15]

Besides the tonsured, large numbers of students had major or minor orders and so were eligible for benefices. Only in the theological faculty were orders required for the masters, but gradually more ordered clerics were found in the chairs, especially when they were endowed with prebendal stalls.

Celibacy was required to retain the clerical status and the master who married, lost his regency. It was not until the 15th century that the University of Paris allowed married professors to teach in the faculty of medicine. And it seems that some unmarried scholars were at Oxford in the same period, but it also seems that they were not eligible to receive degrees. In the less ecclesiastical universities of southern Europe, married professors and students had to pay a special tax (charivari), under pain of harassment.[16]

Disputes between the clerical scholars and local chancellors and governments led to papal intervention, as we have seen. Of the 79 medieval universities in Europe, 53 were either founded or

15. H. Rashdall, The Universities of Europe in the Middle Ages, Oxford, 1936, vol. 3, p. 394.
16. H. Rashdall, op. cit., p. 395ff.

confirmed by papal documents. A papal prize was the *ius ubique docendi* given by the pope to the professors of Toulouse, Paris and Bologna in the 13th Century. Also the popes allowed clerics to study at the university while still drawing benefices, provided they had a good replacement.

The medieval universities were the favorites of the popes, as the monasteries had been favored in earlier times and perhaps for the same reasons. Both were international, and, therefore, in a sense, churches above or outside the local churches. Both were persecuted by local bishops and civil authorities. Both were dedicated to education. In many ways the medieval universities succeeded the monasteries with their tutorials, libraries, scholars and scriptoria. As the monk was the pope's man, so is the university scholar and master. But as the monarchies grew in strength, the universities lost power and independence. For example, the University of Paris, weakened by the Hundred Years War and the withdrawal of the English scholars, the Western Schism and a feeble papacy and the Black Death, was deprived of its independence by Charles IV in 1446, placing it under the jurisdiction of Parliament and leading the way to governmental domination of education which has reached its nadir in modern times.

Another ecclesiastical event which influenced the universities was the rise of the friars and regular clerks. Perhaps, in a way they were the natural outgrowth of the papal universities and their papal sponsored scholars. But friction would soon develop between them and the seculars.

Dominic Guzman educated his friar clerks to combat the devastating Albigenses, modeling his conventual schools and studia generalia on the university plan, establishing the latter near universities as at Paris in 1228. But his philosophy students attended the order schools rather than the liberal arts college of the university, proceeding to theology without the benefit of a master's degree, a further cause of friction especially at Oxford.

In the university strike and dispersion of 1229 the Dominicans did not join in, but continued to teach in their own school. Not only were some of the secular doctors such as John of St. Giles and Alexander of Hales attracted to the friars, but also friars began to occupy vacant university chairs. This the seculars opposed when they returned in 1231, bringing on papal intervention on behalf of the friars.

C. THOMAS AQUINAS

One of the most famous of the friar masters was Thomas Aquinas. Trained by Benedictine monks at Monte Cassino, he then studied at the University of Naples and at Dominican conventual schools at Cologne and Paris. His first stint as theology professor at Paris was 1256-1259. But at the time there was still ill-feeling against the friars and he and Bonaventure were only admitted to the faculty in compliance with the papal bull *Quasi Lignum Vitae* of Alexander IV in 1255. In his *Contra Impugnantes Dei Cultum et Religionem,* Thomas replied to the charges of the seculars that it is improper for a religious to teach, asserting that although as a monk a religious must pray and do penance, as a clerk he must teach.

Another product of the period is his *Truth* (1256-1259), Question 11 of which discusses the teacher whose prime function is to communicate truth. In this public disputation involving both students and professor we find some of Thomas' keen educational psychology with Augustinian and Aristotelian nuances. Following the accepted procedure, a bachelor examined the problem and offered his solution. Then the professor and the other students spoke out their objections. That evening the professor looked over the day's discussion and the next day gave his solution in the form of an Article, including the difficulties proposed, arguments to the contrary from authorities, the professor's reply and answers to the difficulties.

Aquinas follows the traditional line of Jewish and Christian antiquity, namely, that God is *the* teacher and that education is basically a dialogue between God and the human mind. But, then, is the human teacher needed?

Therefore, just as the doctor is said to heal a patient through the activity of nature, so a man is said to cause knowledge in another through the activity of the learner's own natural reason and this is

teaching. (Question 11, Article 1, Response)[17]
But man's reason is a gift of God, the divine teacher.

Now, the light of reason by which such principles are evident to us
is implanted in us by God as a kind of likeness in us of the un-
created truth. So, since all human teaching can be effective only
in virtue of that light, it is obvious that God alone teaches interiorly
and principally, just as nature alone heals interiorly and principally.
Nevertheless, both to heal and to teach can still be used in a proper
sense in the way we have explained. (Article 1, Response)

Teaching and healing are similar, for the teacher heals the ignorance of his pupils, but only with the aid of the Interior Teacher.
Christ exemplified the teacher-healer. Both teacher and healer
are called doctor.

Since all teaching comes from pre-existing knowledge (Aristotle, *Posterior Analytics*) what good are the sensible signs
offered by the teacher?

Our intellect derives intelligible likeness from sensible signs which
are received in the sensitive faculty, and it uses these intelligible
forms to produce in itself scientific knowledge. For the signs are not
the proximate efficient cause of knowledge, but reason is, in its
passage from principles to conclusions, as has been said. (Art. 1,
Answer 4)

Is the knowledge communicated by the teacher numerically
the same as that arising in the student? No, but it is similar.
And the students knowledge is raised from potency to act by
the teacher's stimulation (Answer 6). Aquinas' Aristotelian epis-
temology is evident not only in his act and potency, but also in
his stress on the agent intellect. Thus he says, "In the pupil the
intelligible forms, of which knowledge received through teaching
is constituted, are caused directly by the agent intellect and
mediately by the one who teaches" (Answer 11). The words of
the teacher heard and seen in writing have the same effectivity as
other objects. "Although the words of the teacher are more
proximately posed to cause knowledge than things outside the
soul, insofar as they are signs of intelligible forms" (Answer 11).

---

17. Quotes from **Thomas Aquinas, The Teacher, The Mind, QQ 10, 11,**
J. McGlynn, tr., Chicago Regnery, 1965.

Although the student may possess the principles of knowledge, he needs help to reach the conclusions.

Before the teacher speaks, the pupil would, if asked, answer about the principles through which he is taught, but not about the conclusions which some one is teaching him. Hence, he does not learn the principles from the teacher, but only the conclusions. (Answer 18)

Though the student can acquire knowledge by the light of reason unaided by a teacher, he is not his own teacher for "The teacher or master must have the knowledge which he causes in another explicitly and perfectly as it is received in the one who is learning through instruction" (Article 2). The student only has this knowledge seminally or potentially and so has not the perfect mastery of it required in the teacher.

In Article 4 Aquinas asks whether teaching belongs to the active or contemplative life. Perhaps he had in mind some of his arguments with the seculars who claimed that teaching was incompatible with the religious life. Thomas responds.

In the act of teaching we find a two-fold subject matter, and as an indication of this, two accusatives are used as objects of the verb which expresses the act of teaching. This is so because the subject which one teaches is one kind of subject matter of teaching, and the one to whom the knowledge is communicated is another type of subject of teaching.

The former stresses the contemplative life, while the latter the active. But teaching as a whole pertains more properly to the active life.

Among all the works of Aquinas including his commentary on the Sentences, commentaries on Aristotle and Boethius, disputed questions, questions de quolibet, treatises on various subjects, commentaries on Scriptures, most outstanding is his *Summa Theologiae* (1265-72).

This was the age of summists: Alexander of Hales, Gaufried of Poitiers, Peter of Capua, Philip the Chancellor, Praepositus of Cremona, Stephen Langton, William of Auxerre, to name a few. Largely the *summas* were textbooks of theology written to aid students and encompassing the long traditions of Scriptures and the Fathers and including the philosophies of the Greeks, Jews and Arabs, plus medieval syntheses of philosophy and theology in a more or less orderly manner, covering the central topics of God, man, Christ and church. Certainly the summists had no intention of finalizing all Christian thought, but rather presented the status quo of their particular school at the time. Of course, there was a great deal of borrowing back and forth as might be expected.

Aquinas had written an earlier *summa* (*Contra Gentiles*) (1259-64), a manual for the use of Christian missionaries in Spain. Also called *On the Truth of the Catholic Faith*, it is in part a Christian reaction to Arabian Aristotelianism. In his later *Summa Theologiae* Thomas makes sure in the prologue that all know that his work treating of God, man, Christ and sacraments, is for beginners.

> For we have observed that beginners in this doctrine have been considerably hampered by what various authors have written. They have been hampered partly because of the multiplication of useless questions, articles and arguments. Partly, too, they have been hampered because those things that are needful for them to know are not taught according to the order of discipline, but rather according as the order of exposition in books demands, or according as the occasion for disputation arises. And partly they have been hampered because frequent repetition brought about weariness and confusion in the minds of the readers.[18]

Perhaps much of Aquinas' genius is that he saw the difficulties of the disputations and treatises of the time, which he sought to correct. And this explains the popularity of his *Summa* over against the previous efforts.

He starts out his *Summa* with a question on sacred teaching which is really what the *Summa* is all about. Sacred teaching is a science,

> Because it proceeds from principles made known by the light of a higher science, namely, the science of God and the blessed. Hence just as music accepts on authority the principles taught by the arithmetician, so sacred doctrine accepts the principles revealed by God. (ST Q.1, A.3)

18. Quotes from the Summa from **Basic Writings of S. Thomas Aquinas,** A. Pegis, ed., New York Random House, 1945.

Moreover, it is both a speculative and practical science since it studies both God and his works (A. 4). And it is the highest of the sciences because of its higher certitude based on the inerring light of divine science, its transcendent object and its end which is more final, namely, eternal beatitude (A. 5). Of course, Christ is *The* Teacher of this sacred doctrine (ST 3, Q.7, 7c).

One of the principal problems in sacred teaching is the changing propositions. As his medieval predecessors, Aquinas taught that though the articles of faith might multiply and the enunciables change, faith itself remains the same (Truth Q.14, A.12). The unity of faith is based on its formal object, First Truth, while the complexity of the articles of faith is caused by man's inability to see the divine object. The propositions of faith, then, are not ends in themselves, but means to the end, namely, to attain First Truth.

> Now the act of the believer does not terminate in a proposition, but in a reality, for we do not form propositions, except in order to have knowledge about realities through their means. And this is true of faith as well as science (ST 2-2, Q.1, A.2, Ad 2).

Of course, changing propositions have been the meat of sacred science since the beginning with teachers and students seeking a common language to express the realities under discussion. We run across it in the various schools represented in the New Testament itself.

Another related problem is the confrontation of Christianity with *zeitgeist* philosophies, which had been a matter of concern from the beginning. Thomas followed the moderate view going back to men like Clement of Alexandria and Origen, who saw some of God's truth in the pagan philosophers.

> Just as sacred teaching is founded on the light of faith, so philosophy is founded on the natural light of reason. It is therefore impossible that what belongs to philosophy be contrary to what belongs to faith; it rather falls short of it. It contains, however, certain likenesses of what belongs to faith, and certain preambles to it, as nature is a preamble to grace. (**Commentary on Boethius' Trinity**, Q.2, A.3)

To be sure there are errors in philosophy, but they are due to the defects in man's reason; and philosophy is useful to faith.

But the enemies of Aristotle at the University of Paris achieved a condemnation in 1277 of certain propositions some of which seem to have been taught by Aquinas. Many see this condemnation on the part of Etienne Tempier, Bishop of Paris and a traditionalist, as a landmark in the history of religious teaching. Some feel that the theological faculty of Paris were panicked by the popularity of Aristotle among the artists. At any rate, the decree froze the intellectual atmosphere at Paris for many years. Sixteen days after the Paris decree, Robert Kilwardby, Archbishop of Canterbury, with the backing of the Oxford masters, condemned among other tenets, the Thomist doctrine of the unity of the form of man. Conservative Augustinianism of the Oxford Franciscan school was at the bottom of the antagonism against the Thomist views on individuation and unity of form. Yet as Rashdall comments.[19]

> In the long run the Franciscan spirit proved more fruitful in new ideas, both philosophical and theological, than Thomism with its new-fangled but immovable Aristotelianism in philosophy and its conservative orthodoxy in theology which reigned at Paris.

In the 14th century Oxford took the lead from Paris in scholasticism with Oxonians like Duns Scotus and William of Ockham leading the way.

Some feel that from the condemnations of 1277 Christian thought—which earlier had attempted to reconcile faith and reason, theology and philosophy—became more opposed to secular knowledge, leading to the mutual distrust between religion and reason and science reaching right down to modern times. But as we have seen, there always had been an ambivalence towards secular learning. More immediately the split dated back to Abelard and reason's questioning of tradition and his application of dialectics to theology, the popularity of Aristotle and an accompanying rationalistic trend. Thus the condemnations of 1277, anticipated by the ban on Aristotle in 1210, rather finalized

19. Medieval Universities, Oxford, 1936, vol. 3, p. 253.

than caused the ultimate split between philosophy and theology, reason and faith.[20]

Thus far we have seen the rise of the cosmopolitan medieval universities with their teacher and student nations and their relationships with each other and with town and church. By the end of the 13th century, there were universities all over. Italy: Bologna, Salerno, Padua, Naples, Pisa, Curia Romana. Iberia: Valencia, Valladolid, Salamanca, Lisbon-Coimbra. France: Paris, Montpelier, Orleans, Toulouse, Angers. England: Oxford and Cambridge. Soon they would also be found in Germany, Austria, Bohemia, Netherlands, Poland, Scotland and America.

What effect did these schools have on the future of education? First of all, they trained the leaders of the time: popes, theologians, bishops, civil rulers, lawyers, physicians, etc. Faculty and students were drawn from all nations, an intellectual melting pot. Also the classical revival of medieval scholasticism helped pave the way for the classical Renaissance in Italy in the 14th to 16th centuries. It was not until the 15th century rise of nationalism that the strength and autonomy of the medieval university would be challenged.

Our modern universities are direct descendents of their medieval ancestors. Methodology has changed. The old liberal arts curriculum is either gone or evolved into scarcely recognizable form. But in many ways the modern university is still an arena of thought, a fomenter of ideas, although perhaps less so in politically dominated state schools. Basically the university is still a combination of professors and students, dialoguing over the realities of life and continuing to produce new advances in science, religion, philosophy, politics, etc.

Still today the universities are the great producers of the professional classes, law, medicine, education, etc. And most recently the theologians have returned to the campus after their long cessatio and withdrawal to the seminaries. This may indicate a healing of the old philosophy-theology dichotomy. New phi-

20. J. Pieper, op. cit., pp. 126ff; E. Gilson, **History of Christian Philosophy in the Middle Ages**, New York, Random House, 1954, pp. 385ff.

losophies: existentialism, phenomenology, language analysis and process have replaced the medieval dialectics, with new syntheses and condemnations in order.

Modern student power has roots going back to the Bologna student nations and rectors, and the student selection of teachers. But one modern abuse, which the medieval universities had sense enough to avoid, is the entrenchment of certain ruling juntas, thus centering the power in the administration rather than in teachers and students where it belongs. As we have seen the proctors and rectors at the University of Paris were elected from and by the teachers for limited terms of only a few months. However the modern university with its long term presidents and deans came into being, it is long overdue for revision.

The medieval universities were centers of religious renewal as well as intellectual, as we have seen. Both students and teachers were clerks. The new friars flocked there. Later many other religious flowers would blossom there including the Reformation, Jesuits and the Counter-Reformation, Pietism, Methodism, Oxford Movement and modern Pentecostals, Jesus movement, transcendental meditation and various Eastern religions. In the following chapter we hope to see several Renaissance developments in which the universities played an important part.

10

IT IS OUR INTENTION THAT YOUNG PERSONS SHOULD BE INSTRUCTED AND TRAINED IN OUR COLLEGES AND THE SCHOOLS BELONGING TO THEM IN LEARNING AND VIRTUE. (Ignatius of Loyola, Letter to the Rectors of the Colleges, Rome, March 3, 1554)

A. RENAISSANCE EDUCATION

THE ITALIAN Renaissance (14-15c) was a natural outgrowth of medieval culture, with a renewed hope of reviving the glorious Roman past. Italy as the focal point of East and West was the logical point for the Renaissance to arise, just as her dominant position in the Mediterranean aided her success in ancient times. The recovery of ancient monuments and sculpture added to the excitement. Under the patronage of popes, princes and rich merchants, libraries, museums, scholarship and art grew. The Renaissance man was a humanist, a universal man, versatile as Dante, Da Vinci and Raphael or radical individualist as Michiavelli, Cellini, Botticelli or Nicholas V.

Renaissance humanism has been described by Dupuis[1] as "A specific reaction against the theocentric concerns of medieval studies and a return to the classical ideal of man as portrayed in the masterpieces of pagan Greek and Roman literature and art." Man is the center with his intellectual, social, physical and at least in the beginning, his spiritual and moral development of prime concern. Christian humanism was the very foundation of Renaissance education.

The Italian Renaissance supplanted the medieval trivium

---

1. "Education I, Renaissance and Humanism," NCE 5, p. 119.

of grammar, rhetoric and dialectic, with a greater variety of Latin and Greek authors. Language and literature were the Renaissance fortes. Cicero was a favorite, also Quintilian, Salust, Virgil, Horace, Homer, Xenophon, Demosthenes and others, with more time spent on the Latin authors.

Vernacular studies were omitted for the early humanists were interested in the education of the upper classes, nobles, and wealthy merchants, and not the masses. The printing press made textbooks available. New schools sprang up: court schools in Italy, colleges and lycees in France, gymnasia in Germany, new grammar schools in England.

The classical revival came to the north countries about a century after Italy. By 1500 the Brothers of the Common Schools were encouraging Renaissance classical education in Holland. Though the University of Paris opposed the growth of humanism in France, King Francis I encouraged it. Erasmus, Vives, and Ramus were leading humanists with a renewed study of the Greek Bible and translations into the vernacular. Moreover, some began to ask questions about the present day church and its lack of correspondence with the early Christian community of the New Testament.

Whereas earlier Renaissance education saw the value of Christian piety, integrating religion and pagan learning, later trends glorified the human mind to the exclusion of church dogma and revelation, leading the way to 18th and 19th century rationalism with its apotheosis of the intellect. This rationalistic humanism seems to have been an important factor in bringing about both the Protestant and Catholic Reformations. Dupuis comments: "The Christian reaction, both Protestant and Catholic, sought the educational integration of theological doctrine with classical learning. The resultant Christian humanism was to remain the central focus of education until the late nineteenth century.[2]

Let us now look at German educational developments during the Reformation. Before the Renaissance, German schools were of several types, namely, monastic, cathedral and chantry schools

2. **Ibid.**, p. 119.

taught by an endowed priest, and guild schools for the education of the guildsmen's children. As urbanization increased, local governments took a more active role in directing these burgher schools. And although most of the instructors were clerks, lay teachers were on the increase.

By the time of the Reformation there were some radical changes in German education. First of all, besides the rational humanism mentioned before, the speedy increase in commerce was accompanied by a certain spirit of materialism. Why spend a lot of time in school learning useless ancient languages, if one is to spend his life as a tradesman or merchant? *Gelehrte sind verkehrte.* Another adverse factor was the mass exodus of the monks and nuns and the subsequent collapse of their schools.

In the past, education had been largely confined to the clerks and other professionals. But for the new low-key Protestant ministerial office many felt that learning was not required. Also many parents kept their children home because they felt that false doctrines were being taught in the schools. Even university enrollment fell off. Some blamed the anti-intellectual spirit of the Reformation and the fostering of the vernacular Bible. At any rate, there was a great decrease in educational opportunities, except for the few boys destined for the professions.

Concerned about the situation, Martin Luther encouraged the burghers to establish schools for the children and the basis of their religious instruction was to be the vernacular Bible.

> Above all, the foremost reading for everybody, both in the universities and in the schools, should be Holy Scripture—and for the younger boys, the gospels. And would to God that every town had a girls' school as well, where the girls would be taught the gospel for an hour every day, either in German or in Latin. (**To the Christian Nobility,** 1520)[3]

The situation had grown so bad that even some of the prelates and bishops did not know the gospel.

Although Luther agreed with his confreres that the old

---

3. T. Tappert, **Selected Writings of Martin Luther,** (SWL), Philadelphia, Fortress, 1967, vol. 1, pp. 341-42.

classical education was outmoded, this did not mean the abandonment of all education.

> My idea is to have the boys attend such a school for one or two hours during the day. And spend the remainder of the time working at home, learning a trade or doing whatever is expected of them. In this way study and work will go hand in hand while the boys are young and able to do both. Otherwise they spend at least ten times as much time anyway with their peashooters, ball playing,racing and tussling. (To the Councilmen of Germany, 1524) (SWL 3, p. 62)

And in 1529 he wrote to Margrave George of Brandenburg.

> It is well that in all towns and villages good primary schools should be established out of which could be picked and chosen those who were fit for the universities out of which the men can then be taken who are to serve your land and people.[4]

If the town cannot afford a school, they should support a couple of bright boys to study in an abandoned monastery. And when these become pastors or hold other offices, the townspeople will begin to see the value of education towards earning a living.

And Luther was by no means of the opinion that preachers and ministers did not need any training.

> We must certainly have men to administer God's word and sacraments, and to be shepherds of souls. But where shall we get them if we let our schools go by the board, and fail to replace them with others that are Christian. (To the Councilmen of Germany, 1524) (SWL 3, p. 63)

And again in 1530 in his *Sermon on the Duty of Sending Children to School.*[5]

> I should like to know where in three years we are to get pastors, teachers and sextons? If we remain idle, and if the princes in particular do not see to it that both preparatory schools and universities are properly maintained, there will be such a want of educated persons, that three or four cities will have to be assigned to

---

4. F. Eby, **Early Protestant Educators**, New York, McGraw-Hill, 1931, p. 99.
5. **Ibid.**, p. 124.

one pastor, and ten villages to one chaplain, if perchance ministers can be found at all.

Luther followed Christian tradition in stressing the necessity of catechetics, even writing two catechisms himself in 1529. Whereas in his earlier years he felt that the Bible was enough, his later experiences with the Peasants' Revolt and the Anabaptists, showed him that Scriptures, not properly interpreted, could lead to trouble. So he began stressing the catechetical side of Christian doctrine. In the preface to his short catechism he writes:

> In setting forth this catechism or Christian doctrine in such simple, concise and easy form, I have been compelled and driven by the wretched and lamentable state of affairs which I discovered lately, when I acted as inspector. Merciful God, what misery I have seen, the common people knowing nothing at all of Christian doctrine, especially in the villages! And unfortunately many pastors are well-nigh unskilled and incapable of teaching; and though all are Christians and partake of the Holy Sacrament, they know neither the Lord's Prayer, nor the Creed, nor the Ten Commandments, but live like the poor cattle and senseless swine, though, now that the gospel is come, they have learnt well enough how they may abuse their liberty.[6]

Luther's Small Catechism covered the basics: ten comandments, creed, Our Father, Baptism and Eucharist, and prayers.

The catechists should use uniform texts and prayers to keep from confusing the people. And when they know the little catechism, move on to the larger one for a deeper understanding. Also no force should be used to bring them to the sacraments as the Papists do. "But we ought to preach so that they come without our laws and, as it were, force us, their pastors, to give them the sacrament."

Schools were established under Luther's direction and the sponsorship of the princes. For example, Duke Christopher of Württemberg in 1559 set aside the endowments of the monasteries for religious education, thus, in a way, continuing the monastic

6. Ibid., pp. 88ff.

educational tradition. He advocated three levels of education to train boys for the offices of church and state: the lower particular schools, the middle pedagogia leading to the university, and cloister schools for the poor. Over all was the University of Tübingen. Also they had elementary German schools for the larger towns and catechetical instructions for the villages.

Both church and state cooperated in the German schools with men like Bugenhagen, Melanchthon and Sturm leading the way. The Reformation marks the beginning of the transfer of education from the church to the state, which would be completed in the 19th century.

Calvin paralleled Luther's interest in religious education. In his catechism (1536) he writes: "It has ever been the practice of the church, and one carefully attended to, to see that children should be duly instructed in the Christian religion."[7] To further this, schools were started and catechisms written. Calvin wanted the instructions to be based on early Christian doctrine before corruption had crept in. Both education and moral conduct were overseen by the elders in his tradition. The institute founded at Geneva combined humanism and religion in its gymnasium (classical preparatory) and academy (theological seminary). It was to serve as a model for future Calvinist foundations including Leyden, Edinburgh, Emmanuel College, Oxford, and perhaps Harvard. Prayers, sermons and catechism were essential parts of the curriculum.

B. INIGO OF LOYOLA

Let us now look at another great Renaissance educator, the founding father of the Counter Reformation, Dom Inigo of Loyola. He arrived at the University of Paris, February 2, 1528, at the age of 37, after a career as a soldier, wounded at Pamplona, conversion, pilgrimage to the Holy Land and studies at Barcelona, Alcala and Salamanca. He had spent much of his time giving spiritual exercises, helping others to experience the conversion

7. Ibid., p. 247.

as he had and teaching Christian doctrine. But the church authorities challenged his right as a lay man to teach and guide others in spiritual matters. So he proceeded to Paris, the mother of Universities, to get the education necessary for what he wanted to do.

Though the University of Paris did not have the power and autonomy that it had enjoyed in medieval times, yet it was still a vast enterprise with a world-wide fame. Occupying the left bank of the Seine, it was a city in itself. The four nations still dominated the scene, namely the French (including Spain), Picards, Norman, and German (formerly English).

Arriving at Paris, Inigo lodged with other Spanish students. He knew his educational background was weak, so he enrolled in a grammar school, College Montaigu. At Paris he hoped to settle down and acquire some solid learning with the help of benefactors in Barcelona. As in medieval times, most students at the university were underwritten either by benefactors or church benefices.

After lending what little money he had to a friend, Inigo found himself destitute and had to beg, finally finding lodging in the distant Spanish hospital of S. Jacques de Compostella. Each summer vacation Inigo went to Flanders to collect alms from the Spanish merchants to subsidize his schooling.

At Paris Inigo continued the life of conversion he had practiced in Spain—though without the rigorous fasts he had pursued at Manresa—daily Mass, weekly confession and communion, examination of conscience.

Another interesting conversion occurred at Paris about the same time, namely, that of John Calvin. Calvin received his Masters of Arts in 1528 the year Inigo arrived at Paris. Both were alumni of College de Montaigu and Ste Barbe. After a try at law to please his father at Orleans and Bourges, Calvin returned to Paris in 1531 to study the classics. Then he experienced his conversion, surrendering his clerical benefice. One conversion was from classics to theology, another from the clerical church as he knew it to a life of spirituality.

Calvin's conversion in the spring of millennial year 1534 anticipates by a few months the first vows of Inigo and his companions on Montmartre. Inigo and his Society's loyalty to the pope and church was, perhaps, more consonant with the papal traditions of the Paris University. After association with other students of similar bent at Paris, Poitiers, Angouleme and Orleans, Calvin traveled to Basel to study Scripture and the Fathers, writing the first edition of his *Institutes* in 1536, dedicated to the French king, Francis I.

Back to Inigo. As all converts, he was zealous to tell his experience to others, so that they could share in it. And the university environment was ideal with its atmosphere of exploration and an abundance of eager young minds. Inigo, because of his advanced age and experience could easily play the part of a master. His first three disciples were a bachelor DeCastro from Toledo and a member of the Sorbonne; Peralta, a student; and Amador, a student from Biscayan at the College of Ste Barbe. Inigo led them through his Spiritual Exercises, concentrating on the ultimate realities of life. They also experienced his conversion, giving up their studies for the service of God and retiring to the hospital of S. Jacques. But these spiritual dropouts caused consternation among the faculty. Accusations multiplied, namely, that Inigo was corrupting youth, teaching false doctrine, etc.

Returning from a journey of charity, Inigo faced the charges with Matteo Ori, Dominican theologian and Grand Inquisitor of Paris, who gave him the permission to pursue his studies in peace. But Inigo's first three dropouts were forced by their friends to return to their studies, putting off any conversion till they had completed their work. Perhaps Inigo learned a lesson for he always insisted that his future disciples finish their studies.

After Inigo had completed his elementary studies at the College Montaigu with the help of Flemish benefactors, he entered the College Ste Barbe October 1, 1529, to begin his study of philosophy. Gouvea, the rector, was a Portuguese scholar and had placed the college under the Portuguese sovereign, Don Juan, who endowed it. Both Spaniards and Portuguese were in attendance.

Inigo's roommate and study partner, Peter Favre, coached him in philosophy, trying to keep his mind on the books for Inigo was so filled with spiritual zeal that he found philosophy dry and abstract by comparison.

Meanwhile, despite his earlier experiences, he could not

help but teach his companions the joys of his spiritual conversion. The result was that the students began to neglect their studies and missed the Sunday disputations in favor of mass and prayer. The rector of the college along with Professor Pena resolved to have Inigo striped to the waist and beaten before the students in the refectory, a punishment reserved for serious infractions of the university rules. But the rector relented, begging Inigo's pardon before all. Later he was instrumental in having the Jesuits serve the Portuguese missions.

Inigo's prestige soared and many scholars and masters flocked to hear him. One Martial, a professor of divinity, impressed by the profundity of his discourses, wanted Inigo to take a degree in theology, bypassing the philosophy degree. But Inigo refused.

Inigo thought highly of his University. Writing to his brother, Don Martin in 1532, he advised him to send his son there to study theology.

> To further this end, I believe that you will not find in all Christendom, such helps as there are in this University. . . . In my opinion, if you look at the cost (50 ducats) in this University you will be the gainer, for he will get greater good here in four years than he would in any other that I know in six, and were I to say even more, I think I should not be far from the truth.[8]

Inigo took his licentiate March 13, 1533, after passing a rigorous examination, plus paying a golden crown and minor fees. He never would have been able to pursue his degree at all without the help of the Flemish merchants and Spanish benefactresses such as Dona Ines Pascual and Dona Isabel Roser. March 14, he took his Master's degree after his examination before the faculty of arts. His diploma read in part:

> Wherefore, we, desiring herein to render witness to the truth, do, by the tenor of these presents, make known to all and every whom it concerns, that our well-beloved and discreet Dom Ignatius de Loyola, of the diocese of Pamplona, Master of Arts, hath laudably and honorably obtained the degree of Master of Arts at Paris, after

8. S. Rose, **St. Ignatius of Loyola and the Early Jesuits,** New York, Catholic Publication Society, 1891, p. 157.

rigorous examinations duly passed, according to the statute and customs of the aforesaid Faculty of Arts and with the usual formalities, in the year of our Lord, 1534, after Easter. In witness thereof we have ordered our great seal to be affixed to these presents.[9]

Inigo was a late bloomer, but conversion often comes late in life, when the passions of youth are calmed down. Receiving his Master's at the age of 43, what he lacked in memory and sharpness of intellect he more than made up by his wisdom and experience. After his conversion he had much to say, but he knew that without a university education no one would listen.

We have seen his zeal for souls which he exercised at every possible opportunity in and around the university, persuading many to follow his way of conversion one of his first converts was his roommate at Ste Barbe, Peter Favre, to whom he ceaselessly outlined his high hopes to follow in the footsteps of the Master in the Holy Land, teaching where he taught, and suffering where he suffered. Favre made the Spiritual Exercises under Ignatius' guidance and was ordained a priest in 1534.

Francis Xavier came to Paris from Navarre in 1526 and after four years of study began to lecture on Aristotle in the College de Beavais. Ignatius sent scholars to hear him, meanwhile instructing him when the opportunity arose. Two young men from Alcala, Diego Lainez and Alfonso Salmeron, hearing of Ignatius, came to Paris to study under him. Another scholar from Valladolid who came to Paris to study theology was Nicholas Alfonso Bobadilla. Still another student was Simon Rodriguez who talked with Ignatius about his plans for the Holy Land.

After his Master of Arts degree in 1534 Ignatius took up the study of theology with the Dominicans on St. Jacques St. And no doubt would have obtained a doctorate had not health problems intervened. Meanwhile he gathered his eager young disciples about him: Favre, Xavier, Lainez, Salmeron, Bobadilla and Rodrigues telling them about his vision of work in the Holy Land, consecrating himself to the service of God by vows of celibacy, poverty and service in the Holy Land.

9. **Ibid.,** p. 162.

All agreed to go to Venice and if they could not find passage there, to offer their services to the pope. But Ignatius prudently insisted that they finish their theological studies first. The little group took their vows August 15, 1534, in the chapel of St. Denis on Montmartyre. Favre celebrated the mass, holding up the Eucharist while the vows were being recited. They also promised never to take money for their services.

Under Ignatius' guidance their spiritual lives were balanced with meditation, examination of conscience, Holy Communion and reading the Bible and the Imitation of Christ. Though they did not live in a commune, they tried to meet as often as possible to talk and recreate together.

Of course there were other schools among the students at Paris. We have already seen John Calvin who was even influencing the rector Kopp with his teachings. Moreover, German professors at the university spread the teachings of Luther and Zwingli. Other Paris scholars would be attracted to Ignatius' school including Codure, Claude Le Jay from Geneva and Pas chase Bruet.

But Ignatius' initial successes would soon be challenged out of fear of heresy. Truly his society was a school or heresy in the root meaning of the word, that is, a way of life, choice or option. And as all new ways of life, it was looked upon with suspicion. Reported to the Inquisitor, Ignatius took a notary and some of the University doctors with him to get an official approval of his doctrine.

> We also know the said De Loyola and M. Peter Favre, and some of his friends, and we have seen them live in a Catholic and virtuous manner, and have observed nothing in them but what becomes Christian and virtuous men. The "Exercises" also, which the said Loyola teaches seem to us, so far as we have looked into them, to be Catholic. (January 23, 1535)

After a trip to Spain to recover his health and carry out some business, Ignatius proceeded to Venice according to plan to await passage to Palestine. While there, he taught his exercises, making more converts to his way.

By mid Lent 1537 the group had gathered and set out for Rome for Holy Week, except for Ignatius. There they requested permission of Paul III to go to Jerusalem and to be ordained, for they had the required theological training and had vowed poverty. This was the absolute ordination which had made the friars so effective and perhaps not unrelated to the *Ius Ubique Docendi* of the papal medieval universities.

When war broke out with the Turks, they abandoned their pilgrimage, setting out in pairs to preach the word of God in Vicenza, Monselice, Bassano, Verona, Treviso, living in hermitages or abandoned buildings. The whole group assembled at an abandoned convent near Vicenza where Ignatius had been living with Favre and Lainez. There they said their first mass except for Simon Rodriguez and Ignatius who put theirs off till the following year. Then Ignatius, Favre and Lainez went to Rome, the rest being sent to university towns to work with the students. This is the earliest evidence of Ignatius' educational apostolate. Basically Ignatius, as so many religious founders back to Jesus himself, was a teacher. And he recognized the university campus with its ferment and open young inquiring minds as fertile ground for his Spiritual Exercises.

Xavier and Bobadilla went to Bologna; Rodriguez and Le Jay to Ferrara; Salmeron and Broet to Siena; Codure and Hozes to Padua. They were to live on alms and stay in hospitals along the way. Each took a turn as superior for a week, preaching in the town square and instructing children.

Paul III received Ignatius cordially in Rome and requested that Favre teach Scripture and Lainez theology in the University of the Sapienza. Meanwhile Ignatius taught the Spiritual Exercises. In 1538 Ignatius summoned the companions he had left behind to meet him in Rome where they preached in a number of churches, rousing the people for their spiritual indifference. And, at the pope's request, they taught catechism to the boys of the city. In 1540, after much prayer and discernment, they decided on a vow of obedience, especially to the pope, to teach catechism to children, and to go through the Spiritual Exercises. Paul III approved their Constitutions in his bull *Regimini Militantis Ecclesiae.*

It seems that Lainez first proposed the idea of founding colleges in 1539. And though some saw a problem with poverty, Lainez satisfactorily answered their objections. Initially the

7. Closeup of 6. Pythagorus writing (below MUSIC, with bells) and Donatus with book (below Grammar, with pupils, rod).

colleges, according to *Regimini Militantis Ecclesiae*, were to be for students of the order. Actually up to 1546 *collegium* meant only this in the Jesuit documents. Afterwards it could also mean schools for externs or mixed schools. The very first colleges were residences for Jesuit students at Lisbon, Coimbra, Padua, Valencia, and Venice, or sometimes they were lecture halls where Jesuit professors taught scholastics humanities, philosophy and theology.

Farrell[10] lists several reasons why Ignatius decided to open colleges for non-Jesuit students. First of all, was the success of Xavier at the College of Goa, where as early as 1543 Jesuits taught Indian and Portuguese boys humanities and Christian doctrine. Also the success of the College of Gandia founded by Francis Borgia, the Duke of Gandia in 1545. Although initially the college was for Jesuit scholastics, by the next year secular students were invited to join the lectures.

In 1548 the citizens of Messina along with the Spanish viceroy invited the Jesuits to open a college in their city.

> Our request is that you send us five masters to teach theology, arts, rhetoric and grammar, and another five to pursue their studies and give assistance in works of Christian zeal. The city will supply them with food, clothing, and a residence suitably furnished. And in order to execute our will in proper form, the citizens have considered it in council and given it their unanimous sanction, to which is added that of His Excellency the Viceroy.[11]

In 1549 a similar request came from Palermo.

The system followed at Messina and Palermo was basically Parisian since many of the professors had been trained in Paris. Grammar, humanities, and rhetoric were taught in that order with a special emphasis on Latin eloquence. Daily exercises, weekly repetitions, written compositions and public disputations were the form. The spiritual life of the students including daily mass, catechism once a week, monthly confession, daily examin-

---

10. A Farrell, **The Jesuit Code of Liberal Education**, Milwaukee, Bruce, 1938, p. 16.

1. Farrell, op. cit., p. 26.

ation of conscience, Sunday sermon, prayers in private and in public.

In 1549 Ignatius summoned Canisius and Salmeron from the College of Messina and sent them along with Le Jay to Bologna to get doctors' degrees and then preceed to the University of Ingolstadt to teach theology there at the request of Wilhelm, Duke of Bavaria through Paul III. There Salmeron lectured on Paul, while Canisius concentrated on Thomas Aquinas. Canisius was made rector the next year. Recalling Salmeron for service elsewhere, Ignatius replaced him with two others.

But when conditions at the Ingolstadt school failed to improve, the Jesuits requested to leave. When the bishop objected, Polanco responded that Jesuits were not supposed to be attached to one school, but free to move wherever needed. Moreover, they preferred not to teach in a college where only secular clergy studied.

Meanwhile many other Catholic princes requested the Jesuits to teach in their kingdoms. For example, King Ferdinand asked them to begin a university that he had planned for Vienna. Ignatius answered (April, 1551):

> Among other remedies which it is proper to use against the widespread disease which afflicts Germany, that one should be sought which is to be found in the presence at the universities of men who, because of the example of their religious life and the soundness of their catholic teaching, will endeavor to help others and to lead them to what is good. This seems to be not only a prudent and very practical thought, but one that is necessary and even inspired by God. Would that this could be in part realized, with the help of the divine clemency, by means of the college of our society, which your majesty writes he is going to establish in Vienna.[12]

Ignatius promised to send two theologians, Le Jay and Schorich, and some scholastics to Vienna.

At the time of the Reformation, the education of the clergy was at a low ebb as we have seen. And bishops and princes hoped to upgrade it by bringing in some top theologians. The Council of Trent stressed the need for seminaries. But there was a prac-

12. **Letters of St. Ignatius of Loyola,** tr. W. J. Young, Chicago, Loyola University Press. 1959. pp. 232-33.

tical problem, namely many of the students who came to the universities from the provinces were ill-prepared. What good were top teachers, if the students are mediocre? Ignatius wrote his plan to Duke Albert (September 22, 1551).

> For the languages we choose masters capable of teaching the classics verbally and by the usual exercises, and also of leading them in a pious and pure life, by preaching, by the sacraments, and by good example. When they have made sufficient progress, and are numerous enough, we give them a professor of dialectics, and in the following strive to light a spark of love for religious doctrine in these young hearts so that they may have a desire, as the term of all, to learn theology, before they are allowed to commence its study. Then, but not sooner, they will begin with good-will, and if possible in large numbers, their theological course. And we shall take care to procure them masters who will help them to make considerable progress.[31]

Thus over the years a number of good theologians would be built up to confront heresy and preach to the people. Ignatius had learned much about teaching in his years of studies and was ideally equipped to institute a new religious education which would culminate in the *Ratio Studiorum*.

Ignatius loaned Canisius and Goudanus to Vienna with a promise that they would be restored to Ingolstadt when the Vienna college had been established. A college was opened in Ferrara the summer of 1551 by the help of the Duke Ercole D'Este II at the request of Francis Borgia his kinsman. Bruet and Le Pelletier were chosen to go there. Another college was founded at Coimbra in Portugal.

In 1550 Ignatius started the Roman College, but not without some opposition. He hoped it would be a center, like Paris, to which men would come from many nations. On February 16, 1550, Fr. Le Pelletier and 13 scholastics moved to a small house at the foot of the Capitol. Then with the help of Francis Borgia's 6000 gold crowns they moved to a larger house near the Minerva. Since they taught free, they drew scholars from other schools, causing jealousy. But Ignatius forbade the fathers to accept any students without their parents' permission (January 23, 1552).

13. S. Rose, op. cit., p. 452.

Beginning with philosophy and the humanities, in three years they also had a chair of scholastic theology. Most of the professors were trained in Paris. Ignatius' system of education was not unique, but modeled on other schools of the time particularly Paris, with literature, philosophy and theology.

When an inquiry came asking Ignatius how the day pupils should be handled, he replied:

1. Every one, whether rich or poor, is admitted to the lessons or exercises in classics and literature, out of pure charity, without any remuneration being accepted.

2. Those who are under guardians are received from their hands; and if the youths are judged fit to continue their studies, they must be examined as to whether they will be obedient to their masters, in matters pertaining to learning, and observe due decorum in everything. Then if they agree to this, their names are inscribed in a book, and are seen to that they may be carefully taught and become good, as if they were members of the household.

3. It is customary, as much as possible, to make them hear Mass every day and the Catechism; and a sermon, when there is one, every Sunday and festival; also to confess every month; and they are trained to recommend themselves to God; and finally, they have a careful education in classics and religion.

4. For the little ones who cannot be ruled by words only, a corrector is to be kept at the expense of the College, on the spot, to keep the young ones in awe. And if the master orders it, punishes them, though they are to be beaten only when nothing alse will do. And if this does not suffice, the incorrigible are dismissed.

5. As for the teaching in the classes or various schools, according to their capacity, they are taught literature, Latin, Greek, and even Hebrew, if they have the ability. And when there is a suitable number of persons already advanced in these studies, and that it is not more convenient to send them elsewhere, they learn also logic and philosophy, and the Society provides lecturers, who go through the course of arts, and finally that of theology, as they do at Paris. And these not only give lectures, but exercise all the scholars in composition and disputes, and various conferences, which perhaps are more useful than lectures.[14]

Ignatius used the educational system at hand, but with a difference, placing stress on the moral and religious training to which the intellectual is subordinate. Notice the concern for the poor students in accordance with the long tradition of religious edu-

---

14. Ibid., pp. 512-13.

cation and the insistence on frequent, even daily mass, confession and commendation to God.

Ignatius, as many Christian educators before him, was concerned about the pagan classics—on the one hand, realizing their necessity for solid learning, and on the other, worried about injurious passages. Since the Society was becoming heavily involved in the running of schools, it was thought opportune to get to work on the texts. Terence, in particular, was expurgated for the sake of the innocent young scholars, which was done largely by substituting conjugal for profane love.

In Rome in 1552 Ignatius founded the German College to train badly needed secular priests for Germany, backed by the pope and the cardinals. He hoped that English and Irish students would also attend as at Paris. They attended lectures in the Roman College, which now also taught philosophy and theology.

> For scholastic theology and the sacred scriptures we shall this October appoint several lecturers, and these, like the others, are the best we have been able to find in all our Society, robbing the other colleges, because we judge this to be the greatest and most universal good, for the glory of God, our Lord. (Ignatius to Morone, February 25, 1553)[15]

The Roman College was, in a sense, to be the mother college of Jesuit education. Under Nadal's genius for organization it grew to 1000 pupils in three faculties by 1565, and Ledesma continued the leadership till 1575.

Meanwhile petitions came in for other colleges and Ignatius filled as many as he could. Venice, Ferrara, Bologna, Florence (1551); Naples, Perugia, Padua, Modena, Gubbio (1552); Tivoli (1553); Argenta and Genoa (1554); Loretto (1555); Siena (1556). These Italian schools put in the Messina Plan, now called the Roman Plan, but not without difficulties. Some of the problems encountered were: the low state of Italian secondary education, intractable boys, too strict discipline, lack of proper accommodations for school and teachers, too fast turnover of

---

15. Ibid., p. 522.

staff, insufficient training for teachers, boys entering the order without their parents' permission.[16]

Writing of Gubbio, Polanco's *Chronicon* graphically describes the situation there.[17]

> The youth of Gubbio, who are devoted to war-like pursuits rather than to literary and spiritual advancement, have shown almost no interest either in study or in their religious duties. Besides, since the Society had no house or church of its own, and no stable income, Ignatius did not think it wise to continue the expenditure of so much effort where the fruit was so small. Hence measures were taken to close the college, so that the teachers could be sent where they would be of more use in the service of God.

Two problems that plagued the College of Brescia were, first, the students, instead of applying themselves to grammar and humanities, spent their time on logic, law and music which were more to their liking. Secondly, they were fond of vacations, as Father Negone bemoaned to students and parents:

> The pupils make rules for themselves. Some come on alternate days, allowing one day for study and the next for bodily relaxation. Others take a vacation of two, three or eight days; and these would be tolerable when compared, if we allowed any comparison, with those who absent themselves for a month, two or even three months at a time. Some who went into the country last summer to seek a respite from the heat, have returned to us only at this moment, in the spring.[18]

Though some Italian colleges as Gubbio and Modena had to be closed, others thrived and many more were added.

Meanwhile colleges were built also in Spain and Portugal. We have already seen Gambia. Also there were houses of study for Jesuit scholastics in Lisbon, Evora and Coimbra in Portugal; and in Burgos, Medina del Campo and elsewhere in Spain. Some of these were turned into classical colleges for youth. For example; Lisbon, Evora and Cordova (1553); the University of Coimbra (1555); Murcia, Burgos, Medina del Campo, Plas-

---

16. Farrell, **op. cit.**, p. 99.
17. **Ibid.**, p. 103.
18. **Ibid.**, p. 106.

cencia (1555); Monterey (1556). Ignatius sent Nadal to install the Roman Plan in these colleges. Important lessons had been learned in the Italian colleges so the Spanish and Portuguese foundations went more smoothly. Two contributions of the Iberian schools to the *Ratio Studiorum* were the *decuriones*, students who acted as teachers' aids and were each in charge of ten students, and the stress on drama.

Besides their work in the colleges, the Jesuits also preached, gave the Spiritual Exercises and taught on the missions all of which were extensions of their apostolate in Christian education.

C. RATIO STUDIORUM

The core of Jesuit education is contained in the famous *Ratio Studiorum*, with roots going back to the *Constitutions*. Initially, as we have seen, Jesuit colleges were for the training of their own men, as the *Constitutions* clearly spell out.

> The aim which the Society of Jesus directly seeks is to aid its own members and their fellow men to attain the ultimate end for which they were created. To achieve this purpose, in addition to the example of one's life, learning and a method of expounding it are also necessary. . . . Toward achieving this purpose the Society takes charge of the colleges and also of some universities, that in them those who prove themselves worthy in the houses but have entered the Society unequipped with the necessary learning may receive instruction in it and in other means of helping souls. (307)[19]

The *Constitutions* were composed in stages, evolving along with the nascent Society. Thus the first drafts, 1547-1550, were concerned exclusively with the education of scholastics. But the success of the college in Gandia, founded in 1545, opened to lay pupils in 1546, achieving university status in 1547, and at Messina prompted Ignatius to add Chapter Seven on colleges and classes for extern students, even those who were not clerks, and Chapters 11-17 on universities in the 1556 version.

The very early colleges were residences for the scholastics at

---

19. **Constitutions**, part 4, preamble, tr. G. Ganss, St. Louis, Institute of Jesuit Sources, pp. 171-72. Further quotes are from Ganss.

the universities as we have seen. Although initially no lectures were held here, as time went on, and university lectures were found unsatisfactory, lectures were offered in the colleges. Opening up the colleges to non-Jesuits, both clerk and lay, came later.

As Ganss points out[20] Ignatius' plans for schools do not claim originality, rather he gathered up the best pedagogical methodology of his times. He was already familiar with the universities of Alcala, Salamanca and Paris. In 1549 he tried to get the constitutions of these universities along with many others to help him in his own determinations. Ignatius' genius was not so much in originating as in editing and organizing. Ganss outlines,[21] five types of colleges that had evolved by 1556. 1. Residences for Jesuits attending the universities; gradually some lectures were held here. 2. Residences in which lectures were given to Jesuits and non-Jesuit students as at Gandia (1546). 3. Colleges founded chiefly for extern students with some scholastics in attendance (Messina, 1548-1549; Rome, 1551). 4. Boarding colleges for aspirants to the priesthood who went elsewhere for lectures (German College, 1552). 5. Boarding colleges for lay students (Vienna, 1553).

Ignatius considered two types of schools for externs, namely, the college and the university, although in actual fact few universities were ever erected. The college had classes in grammar, letters, and rhetoric. Sometimes courses in arts, including philosophy, science and math and even theology were added if there was a demand. But these ordinarily were university subjects. The university in Ignatius' mind included the college of language and literature and faculties of arts and theology. Law and medicine, if added, were to be handled by others. Later a three-fold division developed: gymnasium (language and literature) college (added arts and sometimes theology); and university.

Chapter Seven of the Constitutions deals with extern colleges established after 1546.

20. Ibid., p. 173, n. 7.
21. Ibid., p. 174, n. 7.

> To take care that in our colleges not only our own scholastics may be helped in learning, but also those from outside in both learning and good habits of conduct, where schools (open to the public) can be conveniently had, they should be established at least in humane letters and in more advanced subjects in accordance with the possibility which obtains in the regions where such colleges are situated. The greater service of God our Lord is always to be kept in view. (392)

The morals of the students should be of prime concern with proper instruction in Christian doctrine, confession, sermons, etc. Correction should be handled by an extern.

Teaching should be done without remuneration, freely giving what they have freely received. "However,. for the sustenance of those who serve the common good of the colleges or who study for the sake of it, the endowment which the charity of the founders is wont to assign for divine glory is accepted" (398).

Chapters 11-17 on the universities of the Society were originally separate and inserted into the *Constitutions* before the death of Ignatius.

Ganss summarizes Ignatius' philosophy of education:[22]

1. The Jesuit educator should stimulate the student to relate his studies to his last end: knowledge and love of God and salvation.

2. The immediate object of teacher and student is the student's mastery of secular and sacred science.

3. Capable and zealous leaders are to be trained to take their places in the social order.

4. Branches of learning should be integrated into a whole, into a scientifically reasoned Christian view of life.

5. Theology is the most important branch of learning, helping to gain a Christian outlook, and to tie together all the other branches, consecrating all creatures to God's greater glory.

6. Any faculty should function in a Jesuit university, if it can fit into the general purpose.

7. Formation should be both intellectual and moral.

8. Professors should show interest in their students and their progress.

22. **Ibid.**, pp. 210-11, n. 3.

9. Besides transmitting cultural heritage, the schools should provide for research and creativity.

10. They should use the best educational methods of the day.

11. They should adapt their procedures and pedagogical methods to circumstances, times and places.

In the beginning Ignatius had no intention of fixing the studies of schools newly taken over by the Society. Rather each college sketched a tentative line up or Ratio medeled on that of the Roman College. Eventually these were gathered together including reports, study plans curricula, etc. into the *Monumenta* which give a good background for the *Ratio Studiorum* of 1586.

In 1584 the General Congregation asked for a revision of study plans. A committee was formed whose draft was proposed to the Roman College and the provinces. But national and individual jealousies militated against any universal code of education. Nevertheless, the Ratio was promulgated in 1586 along with six topics for further development, namely: model prelections for the humanities; new methods of classroom discussions and precedures; suggestions for the ceremony and method of the *Renovatio Studiorum* and the distribution of prizes; the Licentiate rite; university officers; and common rules especially concerning discipline.

The Upper German Province sent along their common rules for study. Here are some of them:[23]

1. Love and obey your professor as you would your parents.

2. Pray to God for knowledge; but meanwhile study as if he would not grant your prayer without hard, studious effort on your part.

3. What you learn today, do not put off till tomorrow.

4. Do not think yourself learned before you are so, nor more learned than you are.

5. Do not allow yourself to be outdone by the early morning industry of the artisan, and recall the well-known saying: *Aurora Musis Amica.*

23. Farrell, p. 430.

6. Distribute your day into hours, so as to have a definite time for your tasks.

9. Interrupt long and difficult study with some healthy recreation.

10. Application to books immediately after meals is injurious to health. Hence, give at least half an hour to a game of skill or to music or pleasant conversation or moderate play.

11. Do not study into the night; for if you are diligent, the daytime will suffice for your tasks.

12. Be present in class mentally as well as bodily, and while there sit modestly, applying yourself to the work at hand and banishing all foreign distracting interests.

13. Do not be tardy for class, nor go to it like a slave driven to the mill, but arrive early if possible so as to be ready and eager to begin the day's work.

14. Place more value on the professor's explanation than on private study; and hence never absent yourself, unless forced to do so, even for a day.

15. To sleep in class, to talk, trifle, or disturb the professor is wholly unbecoming a scholar.

18. Just as time spent eating seems long to no one, so, too, you should not think the class tedious; and rather prefer to fill your mind with knowledge than your stomach with food.

20. Converse only in Latin, even with those who have learned to speak it well.

Most of the problems outlined here have plagued education from its earliest days; and although the subjects may change, students and teachers and their interrelationship remain basically the same.

After looking over the suggestions, Father General Aquaviva sent out an amended edition of the Ratio in 1591, less prolix and with definite rules for officials and classroom procedure. But it was not received any more enthusiastically than the previous one. The German provinces in particular were vociferous. Finally Aquaviva issued an ultimate and briefer (200 pp) edition, January 8, 1599, which was to guide Jesuit education until the suppression of the Society in 1773.

Many people contributed to the ultimate Ratio. Besides Ignatius and Aquaviva, there was James Ledesma, an outstanding educator and organizer, Jerome Nadal, great unifier of methodology, and Perpinian, a humanist. The Jesuit system of education was not so much original as well organized and well executed, having the advantage of an international organization, centered in Rome with visitors and other officials to insure uniformity.

Actually the Jesuit plan bears close resemblance to that of Johann Sturm, the German Lutheran master of Strassburg. Another plan which may have influenced both Strum and Ignatius was that of the Brethren of the Common Life who operated a college at Liege and who were influential at Paris and in the low countries.

The early Jesuits were to a man graduates of the universities, mainly from Paris. Ignatius always held Paris in reverence, wanting his young scholastics trained as he had been, in the Parisian manner. Modeling his early colleges on the Paris schools, Ignatius even brought in Parisian alumni to teach in the Roman College.

Certainly the Renaissance affected the development of Jesuit education. The renewed interest in the classics over the medieval dialectic stressed the eloquence of Cicero as interpreted by Quintilian. As McGucken writes:[24] "The Jesuit objective, too, was *efformare ed eloquentiam,* and they took Quintilian's *Institutio Oratoria* as a treasure house from which they drew their pedagogical precepts." The whole Ratio reflects Quintilian: exercises, memory lessons, literary composition, etc. Quintilian was the interpreter of antiquity for the Renaissance as Aristotle had been The Philosopher for the medieval schools. Yet with all the stress on eloquence, Jesuit higher studies did not neglect scholastic philosophy and theology.

Why did the Jesuits go into education? Really no other reason can be given than the crying need in which they saw a top means of spreading the kingdom of Christ. As we have stated many times, Christianity is basically education, beginning with the Rabbi Jesus. So, following in the long line of Christian peda-

24. W. McGucken, **The Jesuit and Education,** Milwaukee, Bruce, 1932, p. 28.

gogues from Jesus and Paul, through Origen, the Cappadocians. Augustine, the Irish monks, Alcuin and the medieval universities, the Jesuits enter a grand tradition at a crucial point in history, the Reformation and the Renaissance.

Ignatius had early seen the value of working with young formable minds, whether at Alcala, Salamanca or Paris. This is where the action is, where the ferment is. This is where Christian leadership is born and built up. Taking the best educational practice of the day, the Jesuits adapted it for the kingdom of God. McGuken sums it up:[25] "Their merit consists, not in the revolutionary rejection of existing educational theory and practice, but in the skillful retention of what was good in the old and in an adaption of this to the needs of the day."

As we have seen, Jesuit education was gratuitous, following the long line of tradition dating back to the early Gaulic councils and before. Certainly it had to be paid for, but this usually was handled by benefices, or by some guarantee from the town fathers. But the price to the individual student was nil, enabling the sons of the poorest parents to come.

The whole system centered around Latin eloquence. And in good Renaissance form, Latin took up most of the curriculum. Students and classes were encouraged by emulation to better their opponents. Repetition was insisted upon as a sure way to learn.

The prelection was an important feature of Jesuit education. In it the master leads the way, first reading the text, explaining and translating it; then the student imitates the master in his own translation and comments. Some have claimed that this causes a certain passivity in the students, but this imitation best served the end of Latin eloquence, both in writing and speaking. Later initiative could be encouraged in the philosophical dialectics.

An objective perfectly defined, namely, the formation of cultured Christian men; a method demanding activity on the part of the pupil by means of exercises carefully graded and adapted to the purpose in hand; a Latin curriculum, sound for its day, however, it may appear to moderns; and through it all the master as the

25. McGucken, op. cit., p. 34.

soul, the vivifying force of the entire system—these seem to be the outstanding features of the **Ratio Studiorum** as it was applied to the schools of Europe during the 17th and 18th centuries.[26]

By the time the Ratio of 1599 went into effect, there were 245 Jesuit schools, increasing to 612 by 1710 and 669 by 1740, plus 176 seminaries. For 200 years little change was made in the Ratio. Meanwhile the Port-Royalists and the Oratorians were introducing French literature, history, mathematics and the sciences into their curricula, as scholasticism waned. Descartes' independent spirit of inquiry after truth for its own sake carried the day.

The Jesuits, too, experimented as in the College of Madrid (1623) with 23 chairs, ranging from Greek and Hebrew to logic, history, math, natural history, moral theology and Scriptures. But it would only last about ten years. While the Jesuits stressed the classics, they also produced great mathematicians and scientists. For example, Clavius, Ricci, Schall, Fabri, Noel, Huet. In general, math and science were limited to the more advanced arts students.

This progression of studies conformed to the psychological unfolding of man. The time when memory was at its best was capitalized in the training of the grammar classes; when imagination mounted high, in poetry and rhetoric: and when reason began to reign, in the exact sciences and philosophy.[27]

Although the vernacular languages did not reach a curriculum status in the Society's European schools till after the middle of the 17th century, yet many great French writers of the 17th and 18th centuries were Jesuit products. For example: Corneille, Moliere, Bossuet, Buffon, Descartes, Montesquieu, Santeuil, Voltaire, etc. And in other countries there were writers and scholar alumni: Goldini, Muratori, Galileo, Canova, Calderon, Cassini. At bottom, any educational system can only be judged by the students it produces.

When political pressures forced the closing down of the

26. Ibid., p. 40.
27. Farrell, op. cit., pp. 373-74.

Society in 1773, Jesuit education ground to a halt, except for a few schools in White Russia. But, of course, many other orders such as the Oratorians and the Benedictines continued to run their fine schools.

When the Society was fully restored in 1814 by Pius VII, the documents gave education top priority as an apostolate. But clearly a new Ratio was needed. In theology, church history and canon law were added. In the arts, Aristotle was removed from his prime position and math and physics were included plus a provision for chemistry and astronomy. In the humanities the vernacular became a main subject. History, geography and elementary math were added. Jesuit education had to change to meet the challenges of the times, for no pedagogy can separate itself from the *zeitgeist*. If education is the communication of ideas through a common language, then the Jesuits must use the language of the day, whether it is the Latin of the Renaissance, or the vernacular of the 17th and 18th centuries or the modern philosophies and the natural and social sciences of the 20th.

Today many pillars of the original Ratio have fallen. For example, Jesuit control, compulsory religion, gratuity, classics and scholastic philosophy and theology. By and large the colleges are being taken over by lay men either as trustees, executives or professors. Gone is the old hierarchy of pope, general, provincial, rector, teacher, student. In its place now, as in the medieval universities, power seems to be settling more and more in the student and faculty senates.

Compulsory religion is no longer a part of the program. Perhaps it never worked anyway. And, indeed, there is evidence that it may have had the reverse effect of its original intent by making religion repugnant to the students.

The high expense of modern religious education has all but eliminated both the gratuity and the poorer student, though much of the cost reflects fringe benefits that have little to do with the rapport between teacher and student.

The death of the classics and scholasticism began in the realism of the late Renaissance. Today they are all but gone, except for vestigial classics departments and a rare scholastic philosopher or theologian here and there like a ghost out of the past. In lieu of Aristotle and Aquinas, we find Heidegger, Hegel or Kierkegaard.

The question is frequently asked: what would Ignatius Loyola do if he were here today? Would he still be drawn to the educational apostolate? Or would he throw his weight into social work or more relevant fields? If Christianity is basically education, then there is a place for the Christian educator. It is true that today public education is really available for all who desire it. But it is largely secular. And there is still a need for an integrated program encompassing both the sacred and the secular including religion, philosophy, social and natural science, helping the student towards his own life synthesis. Since the need is still with us, we may imagine that Loyola would want to fill it, at the same time adapting his pedagogy to the times.

11

LOVE ALL YOUR DAUGHTERS EQUALLY
(Angela Merici, Eighth Souvenir)

A. EARLY WOMEN'S RELIGIOUS EDUCATION

THUS FAR we have been largely concerned with male education. As we have seen, the Jewish synagague and bet ha-midrash
were places of male instruction and wives encouraged their
husbands and sons to study there. This was not so much a case
of male chauvinism as the customs of the time. In Talmudic
times the young Jewish girl was pretty much restricted to the
home until her marriage. There she learned domestic skills and
morals from her mother, and even when married remained a
homebody and so did not need a knowledge of the Law to carry
on her daily duties. As culture progressed, she attended the
synagogue in the balcony and other public events. But a woman
was not allowed to read Torah in the assembly. Certainly women
attended the sermons of the maggid, and Jesus himself instructed
many in this capacity. Moreover, he taught others in the privacy
of their homes, as Mary and Martha. Paul also had women
disciples.

Early Christian women received instructions as catechumens
from the deaconesses and from the bishops in homilies. Later we
find upper class ladies studying Scripture and asceticism in
their homes under such leading mentors as Augustine, Jerome,
Rufinus, Pelagius, and others. Here religious education parallels
the secular, for the wealthy Roman girls were well educated,
and so more capable of appreciating the knowledge of a Jerome
or an Augustine. Indeed, some of these study groups developed
into convents of nuns who read and studied the Bible and
church tradition. Jerome, especially appreciated the interest and
encouragement he received from his virgins. We have already

seen his letter to Laeta on the instruction of young Paula.

Medieval convents continued this love of Scriptures and manuscripts, and probably little instruction of women went on outside the convents and monasteries, and perhaps the castles of the nobles. Sometimes daughters of noble families studied in the convents. But the convents, as the monasteries, were mostly dedicated to the instructing of their own.

B. RENAISSANCE EDUCATION OF WOMEN

From the beginning of the classical revival, women took an active interest in Latin and Greek and also Italian. This began in the ducal palaces and then passed to the convents and eventually to the lower classes. Both boys and girls were taught in the palace schools in classics, grammar, rhetoric, composition, penmanship, literature, religion and ethics.

Morality and religious practices played a large part in the education of the Renaissance girl. And although the schools were not strictly under the church, they were encouraged by her. Daily mass in the court chapel, sacraments, sermons, prayers, etc., were part of the program. Religion and ethics were even more important in the girl's education than in the boy's, for the future mother would have charge of the religious and moral training of her children in their earliest years. Religion was not pursued for its own sake in the Renaissance schools, but was an integral part of the development of the whole man or whole woman in a program that included the classics, music and physical exercise.[1]

Leading educators as Giovanni Dominici, Vittorino da Feltre, the two Gaurinos and Leonardo Bruni D'Arezzo encouraged the education of women.[2] Some learned Renaissance ladies were: Vittoria Colonna, Lucrezia Tornaboni de Medici,

1. For example, see Giovanni Dominici's **Regola del Governo di Cura Familiare**, A. Cote, ed., Washington, 1927.
2. See W. Woodward's **Vittorino de Feltre and Other Humanist Educators**, Cambridge, 1897.

Catherine of Sienna, Marguerite of Navarre, Catherine of Aragon, Isabella of Castile, and, in general, members of the higher families as the Medicis, Gonzagas, Forlis, and D'Estes.

When the wealthy ducal families declined, so did the private palace schools, and the convents became more important as centers of education and religious training. Perhaps the rise and growth of women's religious orders in the Renaissance can be partially attributed to the humanistic training of the upper class women and of the nuns. Renaissance humanitarians taught woman's equality with man in the academy, something that was never admitted in prior civilizations.

In Spain Renaissance girls' schools grew under the patronage of Queen Isabella. For all classes of society, they were directed either by individual humanists or by groups of religious, Augustinians, Benedictines, Franciscans, Dominicans, Tertians, Carmelites. Civil and ecclesiastical princes were often the patrons of these girls schools as they promoted boys' education under the direction of the Jesuits and others.

The education of girls in England was more tardy than that of the boys. But by the reign of Henry VIII, the influence of his Queen Catherine of Aragon and her court mentor Juan Luis Vives with their Spanish-Italian educational traditions was felt in England.

For one, Thomas More educated his son John, his daughters Margaret, Cecilia and Margaret Giggs in the Renaissance ideal. As other Renaissance humanists, More insisted on the complete training of his daughters in the liberal arts and in morals. Writing to their tutor, Gunnell, he said:

> I do not see why learning in like manner may not equally agree with both sexes, for by it reason is cultivated, and (as a field) sowed with wholesome precepts, it brings forth excellent fruit?[3]

After citing examples of Jerome and Augustine instructing women in Scriptures, More continues:

3. More's quotes from F. Watson's **Vives and Renaissance Education of Women**. New York, Longmans, 1912, pp. 177ff.

> Which holy Saints' works you will endeavor, my learned Gunnell, of
> your courtesy, that my daughters may learn, whereby they may
> chiefly know what end they ought to have in their learning, to place
> the fruits of their labors in God, and a true conscience by which it
> will easily be brought to pass that being at peace within them-
> selves, they shall be neither moved with praise of flatterers, nor
> the nipping follies of unlearned scoffers.

More established a Renaissance academy at his chancellor's
manor at Chelsea, perhaps not unlike the ducal schools of Italy.
It was known throughout Europe and praised by men like Vives
and Erasmus. There his children learned Latin and English,
translating back and forth. Moreover, he encouraged them to
study philosophy, physics, Scriptures, and above all virtue and
religion. Writing to their mentor, Gunnell, he speaks especially
of his girls:

> For I esteemed learning, which I joined with virtue more than all
> the treasure of kings. So what does the fame of being a scholar
> bring us, if it be severed from virtue, other than a notorious and
> famous infamy, especially in a woman whom men will be ready the
> more willingly to assail for their learning, because it is a rare
> matter, and argues a reproach to the sluggishness of a man, who
> will not stick to lay the fault of their natural malice upon the
> quality of learning, supposing all their own unskillfullness—by com-
> paring it with the vices of those that are learned—shall be accounted
> for virtue.

But if a woman will join learning and virtue, happiness will be
hers that will exceed Croesus' wealth and the beauty of Helen.
The religious atmosphere pervaded the whole More household
including: family prayer, devotions, instructions, and a spirit
of penance.

More's daughter Meg Roper inherited her Father's love of
learning and virtue, and was recognized as a scholar in her own
right. Her father wrote to her with great pleasure:

> I imagine that nothing can happen to me more fortunate, nothing
> to you my dearest daughter, more happy; for as I have earnestly
> wished that you might spend the remainder of your life studying
> physics and holy Scripture, by which there shall never be helps
> wanting unto you for the end of man's life.

Richard Hyrde wrote in defense of women's education in his introduction to Meg Roper's translation of Erasmus' *Precatio Dominica in Septem Portiones Distributa* (1524), challenging those men who oppose it out of jealousy.

> For if they would look thereon with an even eye, and consider the matter equally, they should find and well perceive that women be not only of no less constancy and discretion than men, but also more steadfast and sure to trust unto than they. . . . For I never heard tell, nor read of any woman well learned that ever was (as plenteous as evil tongues be) spotted or inflamed as vicious. But on the other side, many by their learning take such increase in goodness that many bear witness of their virtue, of which sort I could rehearse a great number, both of old time and of late.[4]

It seems that Renaissance men, or at least some of them, wanted to keep women's education on a low level. No doubt, male chauvinism played a part here, although some claimed that they feared that a learned women could more easily become a bad woman. Men like More, Erasmus, Hyrde, Vives, true humanists, went to great lengths to show the equality of men and women and the value of women's education.

Juan Luis Vives, Valencian friend of More and court educator under Queen Catherine of Aragon wrote his *De Institutione Feminae Christianae* (1523) a landmark in the education of Christian girls. The first book treats of the training of girls before marriage, while the second book is on the married life, and the third for widows. The practical arts should not be neglected, for example, spinning and cooking and above all training in virtue and morality.

> For if she can find in her heart to do naughtily, having so many precepts of virtue to keep her, what do we suppose she should do, having no knowledge of goodness at all (Bk.1, Ch.4).[5]

Vives wanted their reading limited to the Bible, the Fathers and philosophers, Latin readings with solid content. And Latin writing and conversation were practiced. Also he advised educating the girls separately from the boys.

4. Ibid., pp. 165ff.
5. Ibid., pp. 48ff.

Vives, in true humanist manner, calls for equality of education for boys and girls, "The woman's wit is no less apt to all things than the man's is. She wanteth but counsel and strength." And Religious instruction is of the first importance.

> The Lord doth admit women to the mystery of his religion, in respect of which all other wisdom is but foolishness. And he doth declare that they were created to know high matters, and to come as well as men into the beautitude, and, therefore, they ought and should be instructed as we men be.

The girl's training should stress moderation in dress and recreation and above all in the use of cosmetics.

> Verily I would fain know what the maiden means that paints herself. If it be to please herself, it is a vain thing. If it be to please Christ, it is folly. If it be to delight men, it is an ungracious deed. . . . Me thinks it much like, if thou wilt go about to win them with painting, as thou wouldst entice or attempt him with a visor. . . . Thou are but an ill case, if thou have nothing else to please him with, that shall be thy husband, but only painting. (Bk.1, Ch.9)

Vives also warns against extremes of fashion, perfume, and ornaments, kissing and dancing. On kissing, a growing custom, he writes:

> If they do it because of Baptism, that they may seem all as brethren and sisters, I praise the intent. If otherwise, I see not whereunto it pertains to use so much kissing, as though that love and charity could none other way stand between men and women. (Bk. 1, Ch.13)

And he comments on dancing:

> What good doth all that dancing of young women, holden up in men's arms, that they may hop the higher? What means that shaking unto midnight, and never weary, which if they were desired to go but to the next church, they were not able, except they were carried on horseback or in a chariot? Who would not think them out of their wits? (Bk.1, Ch.13)

Chastity is the highest virtue of women. The chaste woman is "Fair, well-formed, rich, fruitful, noble, and all the best things that can be named, and contrary she that is unchaste is a sea and treasury of all (ev)illness" (Bk. 1, Ch. 11).

Although Vives did not favor women teaching in the schools, in the home the mother is the chief educator.

> Wherefore she shall nourish them with her own milk, and obey the commandment of nature. . . Afterwards if the mother can skill of learning let her teach her little children herself that they may have all one both for their mother, their nurse and their teacher, and that they may love her also the more, and learn with better courage and more speed by means of the love that their teacher hath toward them. (Bk 2, Ch.11)

Moreover, the educated woman is not only a joy to her children as their loving and understanding teacher, but also to her husband. Vives remarks in his *De Officio Mariti*,[6]

> A woman well brought up is fruitful and profitable unto her husband, for so shall his house be wisely governed, his children virtuously instructed, the affections less ensued and followed so that they shall live in tranquility and virtue. Nor thou shalt not have her as a servant, or as a companion of thy prosperity and welfare only, but also as a most faithful secretary of thy cares and thoughts and in doubtful matters a wise and hearty counsellor.

All in all, Vives wants Christian girls to be instructed and trained to be as the *mulier fortis* of the Bible, faithful, diligent, strong and moral wives and mothers. This is the whole rationale behind the Renaissance education of women, which is basically a teacher training. *Disce ut doceas.* What the young girl learns in morals and intellectual pursuits, she in her turn can hand on to her family.

Vives was imprisoned in 1528 for speaking out against Henry's divorce of Catherine. After six months he returned to the Netherlands where he took up teaching of letters at Bruges.

Thomas Becon, a contemporary of Vives voices a similar view on the importance of the education of girls in his *Catechisme*.

> Can the mothers bring up their children virtuously, when they themselves be void of all virtue? Can the nurses instill any goodness into the tender breasts of their nurse children, when they themselves have learned none? Can that woman govern her house godly

6. Ibid., pp. 198ff.

which knows not one point of godliness? Who sees not now how necessary the virtuous education and bringing up of the woman-kind is? Which thing cannot be conveniently brought to pass, except schools for that purpose be appointed and certain godly matrons ordained governesses of the same, to bring up the maids and young women in the doctrine and nurture of the Lord.[7]

In Germany about the same time we find Luther concerned for the education of girls.

In like manner, a girl can surely find time enough to attend school for an hour a day, and still take care of her duties at home. She spends much more time than that anyway in sleeping, dancing and playing. One thing only is lacking. The earnest desire to train the young and to benefit and serve the world with able men and women. The devil very much prefers coarse block heads, ne'er do wells, lest men get along too well on earth. (To the Councilmen of Germany, 1524)[8]

And just as the directors of the congregation should choose teachers for the boys,

In like manner the ten directors, out of the common treasury, shall provide an honorable, mature, and blameless woman to instruct young girls under twelve years of age in Christian discipline, honor, and virtue, and at a suitable place to teach them reading and writing in German a few hours daily. (Constitution of the Congregation of Leisnig)[9]

It seems that catechism and the Gospel were taught by the pastors. But although early training in Scriptures, catechism and the vernacular were open to both boys and girls, more advanced education was reserved for young men.

In Italy, France and Spain, new orders of sisters rose up to take over the task of instructing young girls. True, the convents had always been educational centers, first for the training of the young nuns, then for a small number of noble or merchant class girls. In Renaissance times the convent girls studied mostly in the vernacular, but probably learned some Latin also plus

7. F. Watson, **English Writers on Education** (1480-1603), p. 47.
8. T. Tappert, **Selected Writings of Martin Luther**, vol. 3, pp. 62-63.
9. M. Cannon, **The Education of Women During the Renaissance**, Washington, 1916. p. 41.

household skills, religion, good manners. But with the closing of the nunneries in Reformation countries, even this ground to a halt. Clearly the church needed dedicated mistresses to teach the girls, just as she wanted the Jesuit masters to educate the boys.

C. ANGELA MERICI

Italy, the mother of the Renaissance, produced a daughter who was to lead the way in the education of Christian girls. This is Angela Merici, daughter of John Merici of Desanzano in Lombardy. She came from a pious home with daily prayer and good example by model parents. She was a beautiful girl, humble, respectful and pure.

Angela and her sister had a small oratory in their home. It would seem that Angela did not attend a formal school, but studied at home, reading the lives of the saints and sacred history. Perhaps she had a tutor in Latin and Italian for she was fluent in both.

When her sister died, Angela lived in prayerful retirement in her home with another young friend, giving their lives to the teaching of the young and helping those in need. But when this friend also died, Angela was greatly grieved. While living in seclusion at Brudazzo, she had a vision of young maidens descending to earth on a ladder. Then she heard the voice of her dead friend. "Angela, know that our Lord has sent you this vision to inform you that before your death you shall found in Brescia a society like this. Such is his injunction to you." When Angela's spiritual director affirmed the vision as genuine, she set out to instruct young girls.

After a pilgrimage to the Holy Land, Angela with several friends went to Rome to fulfill the conditions necessary for gaining the indulgence. While there (1525) she had an interview with Pope Clement VII, who had heard of her great piety. Clement wanted her to stay on in Rome to care for the schools and hospitals of the city. But Angela felt the call to return to Brescia. Two years later Rome was plundered by German Lutheran troops and Pope Clement imprisoned in the Castle St. Angelo.

In 1533-34, the millennial year of Ignatius' first vows and John Calvin's conversion, Angela had a vision of St. Ursula and her companions, urging her to found a group of religious. The Celtic princess and martyr of Cologne was the patroness of universities and of the education of the young and devotion to her spread rapidly throughout Europe and especially in Lombardy. In response, Angela gathered twelve young ladies about her: Simona Borni, Catherine and Dominica Dolce, Dorosilla Zinelli, Pellagrina Casali, Clara Gaffuri, Paula and Laura Paschieri, Barbara Fontana, Clara Martinengo, Margaret Dell'Olmo, and Maria Bartolletti. Like the very early Christian virgins, they lived in their homes while they devoted their lives to helping the sick and teaching catechism to the poor. And they met regularly in Angela's apartments where she instructed them in love of God and neighbor.

Prompted by the urgent need of reform in both church and society and inspired by a vision of the Lord, Angela set out in 1535 to form a society of young women to attack the problems of the times. Francis Cornaro, cardinal archbishop of Brescia approved her plan. So on the morning of November 25, 1535, Angela and her companions, totalling 28, went to Mass at the church of St. Afra's and then to their private oratory on the cathedral square. It seems that they took no formal vows at this time, but inscribed their names in a book as witnesses to their commitment. Their way of life was based on their virginity. Poverty and obedience were also included.

Angela asked the aid of several older widowed ladies to help in the administration of her young maids, a pattern found in the early church, where older widow-deaconesses supervised the young virgins. Angela divided Brescia into eight districts, and the sisters were to confine their work to the area in which they lived. A directress was in charge of each district. And she had three assistants, one of whom was a spiritual mother to the girls in her area. Each sister continued to live in her own home, while going for counsel to her spiritual mother and cooperating with the others in helping the needy and teaching catechism.

Brescia was in special need of Angela's ministrations for it had suffered sorcery and inquisitions and had been fought over

8. Oxford, Balliol College quadrangle (founded 1263).

and pillaged by both Charles V and Francis I until the peace of Cambray, 1529, sometimes called *La paix des dames* because of the efforts of Louise of Savoy and Margaret of Austria. Angela, another valiant Renaissance woman, led the way in picking up the pieces, aided by other outstanding citizens.

One of the principal needs to rebuild Brescia and all of Europe was the reconstruction of the family. Angela's young companions started in their own homes, giving good example, then concentrating on the religious education of the young girls of the city, the future wives and mothers. Angela's association was the first to be founded specifically for the Christian education of girls. Three things made it successful. First, the Italian Renaissance in which female education flourished. Second, the self-sacrificing young mistresses, devoting their lives to the task. Third, the millennial spirit of the 1530's acting as a catalyst.

The church of St. Afra's was their headquarters where they were inspired and guided by the canons, especially Serafino De Bologna. They attended Mass there and were instructed by Angela. As their numbers increased they moved to a large hall in the home of Elizabeth Prato on the Cathedral Square.

Besides her rules and instructions, Angela's spirit may be found in her final Counsels and Testament. For example:

> One of the chief graces that I owe to God is that he has chosen you to be the true and devoted mothers of so noble a family, to have them in your care and keeping, as if they were your daughters according to nature and even more (Testament, Introduction).[10]

Traditionally education had been a family affair with the mother playing the prominent role in the early years, while male tutors were hired for further education. Angela adopted the family spirit of education of Dominici with the sister as the new mother to her girls. And, indeed, her virginity leaves her especially open to all these adopted daughters.

This family atmosphere was transferred to Ursuline community life when they became canonical nuns. Family education

---

10. Angela's quotes from M. Martin, **Ursuline Method of Education**, Rahway, New Jersey, Quinn and Buden, 1946.

was common in Renaissance upper class homes, which could afford to hire teachers for their children. Since some of the early nuns came from such homes, the family spirit of education could have its origins there.

Angela wanted a personal relationship between her sisters and their spiritual daughters, for the spiritual mother has the advantage over the natural mother. "Love all your daughters equally, having no preference for one rather than another, for they are all God's creatures, and you know not what he may choose to make of them" (Eighth Souvenir).

After the approval of their primitive rule by Paul III in 1544, the Ursulines spread speedily throughout Italy. In 1568 Charles Borromeo invited them to Milan where they took on many of the aspects of a religious order, including vows, living in community and a new rule approved by Gregory XIII in 1585. The children now came to the convent for instruction rather than the former method where the sisters traveled to the children. By 1574 they were in France under the primitive rule, and by 1596 the French communities were adopting the Milan rule. In 1612 Paul V raised the Paris community, founded by Frances de Bremond to the status of a religious order, following the rule of St. Augustine. Soon this privilege was extended to other communities.

Since many of the students were boarders who lived at the convent, a more direct influence could be had by the foster mother, not only in the classroom, but also in the dormitory, refectory and at play. For example, the monastic congregation at Bordeaux had a mistress general of the boarding school who was over the other teachers and was spiritual mother to all the girls, giving them counsel, teaching them catechism and prayer. And the congregation of Paris had mistresses for each division according to age. As a true mother, the mistress wanted her daughters to shine in all the virtues.

Mistresses will give special attention to etiquette at table, helping the children to form habits acceptable in good society. They will give lessons in politeness and courtesy. They will watch over their pupils so that they may develop poise, good manners without affectation, a serene and pleasing face, a soft and moderate voice. They will correct children who are guilty of improper speech. At recreation

> they will train them to delicacy and deference which make relations easy and agreeable. In a word, they will strive in all circumstances to form them to the delicate art of "savoir fair" which religion makes perfect. (Paris Rules 1, 4, 24)

Although humanities were stressed in proper Renaissance form, religious instruction was of primary importance. Religious teaching had traditionally been the province of the clerks and bishops, but in the early church the deaconesses instructed the women catechumens. And, in a sense, the Renaissance virgins are the descendents of the early deaconesses. So there is a precedent for the daughters of St. Ursula to instruct in catechism. "Although religious instruction is the province of the priest, our Constitutions have nevertheless established that mistresses shall teach catechism several times a week" (1, 5). And this is to take place among all the subjects taught, and the lessons should be measured according to the level of the learners.

But catechism is a difficult subject to teach for there seems a natural reticence to study it. Thus the teacher has to make a greater effort to make the matter interesting and applicable to their daily lives. "The teachers shall endeavor to make the catechism classes interesting and agreeable so that the pupils will be pleased with them and will love religious instruction more than other subjects" (1, 5). To form good Christian wives and mothers, pious devotions, school discipline and good example were added to the religious instructions.

Besides the regular three vows of poverty, chastity and obedience, the constitution of the Paris community[11] adds a fourth vow of dedication to the education of girls.

> An express vow of the instruction of young girls, proposing this for their principal aim and end; disposing to this effect all changes and employments, applying to it all their strength and attention, and, in fine, esteeming it as the assured means of complying with their vocation. (1, 1, 1)

So important is this promise that no one should try to escape

---

11. See **Constitutions of the Ursuline Religious of the Congregation of Paris,** New York, Catholic Publication Society, (n.d.).

it by going to another order or using office or honor as a pretext for avoiding the apostolate.

Catechism was taught to the boarders two or three times a week, confession once a month, Holy Communion once a month or oftener if the superior approves. "They will rear their pupils to that civilty and good breeding observable among virtuous Christians, without inculcating anything relative to the religious life; much less must they draw them thereto by words or tacit solicitations" (1, 6, 6). It was natural for the boarders to want to join, but wisdom going to Basil dictates that they should only be admitted with caution.

Besides the boarders, the Paris nuns instructed poor girls from the neighborhood.

> As Ursulines are obliged to instruct not only young ladies, but likewise poor children in piety and the Christian doctrines, as specified in the Sixth Chapter, they may also teach them to read, write and work. (1, 8, 1)

The Ursuline apostolate continued to grow so that by the 18th century there were 350 monasteries with 9000 nuns, cloistered with solemn vows in France. And despite the setback of the French Revolution, they continued to flourish in Europe and on the missions. In 1900 Pope Leo XIII invited them to form a union centered in Rome.

D. FENELON

Another great French educator of Christian girls is Archbishop Fénelon (1651-1715). He was director of the Nouvelles Catholiques, a Catholic sisterhood of converts from the Huguenots under royal patronage and also was the guide of the sons of the royal family. In fact, it was this very connection between royalty and clerical and religious educators which would militate against Catholic education in the 19th century.

In 1685 Fénelon wrote his *On the Education of Girls* at the suggestion of De Beauvillier, the minister of finance, who was concerned about the training of his nine daughters. Actually many of the principles of the book can be applied to boys as well.

Echoing earlier Renaissance writers, Fénelon laments the neglect of girls' education.[12]

> As for girls, it is said, there is no need for them to be learned; curiosity makes them vain and affected. It is enough for them to know how one day to look after their households and obey their husbands without asking why. Reference is invariably made to the numerous women whose intellectual attainments have made them ridiculous. After that it is thought justifiable to hand girls over blindly to the guidance of ignorant and foolish mothers. (Ch.1)

But why should women be educated?

> The world is not an abstraction, it is the sum total of families. And who can civilise it more effectively than women who, in addition to their natural authority and assiduity in the household, have the advantage of being by nature careful, attentive to detail, industrious, attractive and persuasive? But can men hope to obtain any happiness in life if their most intimate association—that of marriage—is turned to bitterness? And what will become of the children, who are destined to be the human race of the next generation, if their mothers spoil them from their earliest years? (Ch.1)

In a word, educate a girl, and you educate a family. Bad education not only harms the girl, but her children and her children's children.

Religion is an important facet of the girl's education. Fénelon devotes chapters seven and eight to hints on how to introduce children gradually to religious ideas, showing them the gospels, ten commandments, sacraments, prayers. But do not bore them.

> After all, it is not a question of making children learn morality by heart, as if it were a catechism. This method only results in turning religion into meaningless language, or at any rate into tedious formalities. Confine yourself to help them to understand it, and put them in the way of discerning these truths for themselves. These will thus make the greater impression. Profit by opportunities to enable them to see more clearly what at present they see only indistinctly. (Ch.7)

Above all they should model their lives on Christ, the object of all Christian education.

12. Fénelon's quotes are from H. Bardard, **Fénelon on Education**, Cambridge, 1966.

Chapters nine and ten outline some of the faults to be corrected in the training of girls, namely: too much affection, inordinate friendships, trivial jealousies, exaggerated compliments and transports, longwindedness, artificiality, false modesty.

The chief fault to be found in girls is vanity. They are born with an eager desire to please. As the avenues which lead men to positions of authority and to glory are closed to them, they try to compensate for this by graces of the mind or of the body. This explains their sweet and insinuating way of talking and why they aim so much at being beautiful, and at possessing a charming appearance, and why they are so inordinately fond of dress. A hat, a piece of ribbon, a curl of hair that is too high or too low, the choice of a color, are for them matters of the highest importance. (Ch.10)

And changing fashions add to the pursuit of vanity.

Make an earnest effort to help girls to understand how greatly honor depends on good conduct and how true ability is more to be esteemed than that which is derived from one's hair or one's dress. Beauty, you will say, deceives the person who possesses it more than those who are dazzled by it. It disturbs and intoxicates the soul. One is more besotted with oneself than the most passionate lovers are with the persons they adore. There are only a few years difference between one woman who is beautiful and another who is not. Beauty can only be harmful unless it can serve to marry off a daughter advantageously. But how can it do that unless it is backed up by merit and virtue? A girl can only hope to marry some young fop with whom she will be unhappy, unless her sensibleness and her modesty make her sought after by men of steady habits and solid worth. (Ch.10)

Above all Christian modesty must be fostered. The girls should be shown examples where immodesty has ruined reputations. "Be horrified at those bare necks and other immodesties."

Since woman is the main teacher of children, especially in their early years, her own education should be aimed at this. Moreover, the practical side should not be neglected, with training in household duties, the management of servants, economics, etc. She must be an expert psychologist to understand the natural aptitudes of each child to prudently gain his confidence and friendship. Besides practical household management, the three "R's" are essential, and something of the principles of law. Selected readings in history, rhetoric and poetry, Latin, music and painting with caution, and design. Above all, each girl should be educated according to her position in society, court, town, or country. Religion, of course, holds the primary place among all the studies.

The governesses should be of top quality.

> It is not to be expected that a good education can be imparted by a bad governess. Doubtless it is sufficient to lay down rules which will make it successful in the hands of an ordinary person. It is not asking too much to expect of her some measure of good sense, a teachable disposition, and a true fear of God. (Ch.13)

Good governesses are important, but good parents are essential for they are the primary teachers.

Fénelon and his contemporaries, Ursuline trained Mme de Maintenon and Claude Fleury agreed that girls' education had been neglected and insisted that the intellectual and moral training of the girls should not be separated. The move away from the classical Renaissance education and towards more practical training with a stress on the vernacular and the three "R's" is clearly seen in Fénelon. But he is writing about a family type of education under a governess. In fact, his little book is written to help governesses.

Urged on by men like Fénelon, the church took more and more interest in the education of girls in 17th to 19th centuries. Many groups of sisters were formed to further the apostolate of teaching children of all classes. Two major factors contributed to the advancement of Christian education of girls, as we have seen. First, the opening up of female education by the Renaissance educators. And second, the dedication of the Christian school-mistresses, living celibate and in community, giving their whole lives to their daughters and sons. Today miriad girls' schools on all levels flourish across the world, combining religion and learning for the future mothers of families, although current trends in coeducation are lessening the separateness of girls' education.

12

THE MEMBERS OF THIS COMMUNITY ARE OCCU-
PIED IN TEACHING IN GRATUITOUS SCHOOLS IN
TOWNS ONLY AND IN TEACHING CATECHISM EV-
ERY DAY. EVEN ON SUNDAYS AND FEASTS (John
Baptist De La Salle, *The Memoir on the Religious Habit*,
1690)

A. REALISM IN EDUCATION

WE HAVE SEEN several outstanding religious teachers of Renaissance times, including Martin Luther, Ignatius of Loyola,
Thomas More, Juan Luis Vives, Angela Merici. In general, they
honored the classical tradition, but also saw the value of practical
training. New inventions and scientific discovery placed a fresh
emphasis on the real in education, including the vernacular and
science. We have seen this tendency before in Reformation Germany and in the France of Fénelon. As the merchant classes rose,
a more universal and practical education was needed. Yet despite
the wave of realism, Jesuit classical schools continued to thrive.

What is realism in education? It stresses the concrete, practical, vocational, the real world, things that will be useful in
man's every day life, including history, politics, law and science.
A reaction to Renaissance classical literature and art, realism
claimed that things are more important than words, and experience takes precedence over theory. The realist curriculum broad-
ened to include modern languages, math, social studies, natural
sciences. The old lecture method of teaching was replaced by
the experimental: direct method language, travel, laboratories,
visual aids, museums.

In many of the utopian views of education in the 16th-
17th centuries the ideal included practical studies. We see this
in More's *Utopia* and Campanella's *City of the Sun*. John Milton's

On Education (1644) stressed education as the principal way for fallen man to get back to God, the very basis of religious education from the beginning.

> The end, then, of learning is to repair the ruins of our first parents by regaining to know God aright, and out of that knowledge to love him, to imitate him, to be like him, as we may the nearest by possessing our souls of true virtue, which being united by the heavenly grace of faith, makes up the highest perfection. But because our understanding cannot in this body found itself but on sensible things, nor arrive so clearly to the knowledge of God and things invisible, as by orderly conning over the visible and inferior creature. The same method is to be followed in all discreet teaching.[1]

Since we are basically sense creatures, we can only go to God through our senses.

Milton points out some of the errors of the past, namely, spending too much time on languages such as Latin and Greek, rather than on the wisdom expressed by the words; and starting out young children with abstract learning such as logic and metaphysics. Milton sets out a plan for the ideal education for the youth of 12-21. "I call, therefore, a complete and generous education, that which fits a man to perform justly, skillfully, and magnanimously, all the offices both private and public, of peace and war."

Then he outlines the school house and grounds and the daily course of studies, beginning with grammar, then some easy and delightful reading on education such as Plutarch, Socrates or Quintilian, with explanations to draw them on to greater learning and admiration of virtue, delighting in the manly and liberal arts. Later math and recreation and after supper religion and Scriptures. Practical science included, besides math, astronomy and geography, architecture, and above all ethics.

> By this time, years and good general precepts will have furnished them more distinctly with that act of reason which in ethics is called **proairesis**, that they may with some judgment contemplate

---

1. Milton's quotes from F. V. N. Painter, **Great Pedagogical Essays**, New York, American Book Company, 1905, pp. 242-54.

upon moral good and evil. Then will be required a special reinforcement of constant and sound indoctrinating, to set them right and firm, instructing them more amply in the knowledge of virtue, and the hatred of vice: while their young and pliant affections are led through all the moral works of Plato, Xenophon, Cicero, Plutarch, Laertius, and those Locrian remnants; but still to be reduced in their nightward studies wherewith they close the day's work, under the determinate sentence of David, or Solomon, or the evangelists and apostolic scriptures.

Milton was both humanist and realist and many of his ideas on education were carried out in the English academies.

The increase of scientific studies also greatly affected education. Two who helped develop the scientific method were Francis Bacon and Rene Descartes, Bacon stressing experiment and discoversies, while Descartes sought proof through reason and mathematics.

Scientific discovery led to a certain optimism among educators. Thus any one applying himself could by the use of reason arrive at scientific truth. John Locke showed this spirit of optimism in his *Some Thoughts Concerning Education* (1693). "I think that I may say that of all the men we meet with, nine parts of ten are good or evil, useful or not, by their education. It is that which makes the great difference in mankind."[2] Locke, as Descartes, believed that reason could and should control man's desires.

Perhaps the most influential seventeenth century educator was Comenius, a Moravian famous for his ladder technique which ranged from the small child to the adult. It led the way to universal education—all studies should be taught to all children. Following nature itself, Comenius advises teaching useful subjects, which appeal to the senses and understanding. Studies should be both understood and remembered; moreover, they should be graded and well-organized.

Comenius underlined knowledge, virtue and piety as the ends of education, and virtue, religion and the Bible played a large part in his program. He writes in his *Great Didactic* (1649).

2. Painter, op. cit., p. 280.

The seeds of knowledge, of virtue, and of piety, are naturally implanted in us; but the actual knowledge, virtue and piety are not so given. These must be acquired by prayer, by education and by action. He gave no bad definition who said that man was a "teachable animal." And indeed it is only by a proper education that he can become a man. (1)[3]

Echoing many Renaissance educators, Comenius claims that education should prepare both for this life and the next.

All who have been born to man's estate have been born with the same end in view, namely, that they may be men, that is to say, rational creatures, the lords of other creatures, the images of their Creator. All, therefore, must be brought to a point at which, being properly imbued with wisdom, virtue, and piety, they may usefully employ the present life and be worthily prepared for that to come. (2)

This Christian education should be open to all. "So that all who are handed over to Christian schools to be imbued with true wisdom, may be taught to live a heavenly life on earth; in a word, where all men are taught all things thoroughly" (4).

We have seen some representative educators of the 17th century. This is a transition period from the Renaissance classical education to the real and practical training of the age of realism. It is an age which would see schooling no longer the privilege of the rich and the clergy, but opening to all, the dawn of universal education, which would not become actual fact till late in the 19th century.

B. JOHN BAPTIST DE LA SALLE

An important person in the furthering of French universal religious education in this period is John Baptist De La Salle (1651-1719). Ordained a priest in 1678, he soon became aware of the wide gulf that separated the rich and the poor in France. So he set about to remedy the situation by founding free schools for the poorer classes.

---

3. **Ibid.,** pp. 258-60.

Education for the poor had always been of some concern. This is one reason the Jewish rabbis did not charge, and we have seen medieval councils urging free schooling. Most medieval university students were subsidized by benefices or wealthy patrons. And Ignatius of Loyola was reluctant to charge tuition. But the fact remained that education was still for the most part the privilege of the upper or professional classes until the Renaissance stress on the equality of all men, translated into practice by men like Comenius.

La Salle was not by nature inclined to schoolmastering.

I felt a repugnance, indeed, when they (masters) used to come to my house for the first two years. It was apparent on that account, that God, who does all things gently and wisely, and does not as a rule force men against their inclinations, brought it about so imperceptibly and gradually, that one engagement led me to another, and I found myself committed to the entire care of schools without having foreseen anything.[4]

The first step to educating the poor was to train teachers, and in 1681 La Salle invited some of them to live with him. These were laymen. The idea of Christian lay teachers is not new. The Jewish rabbis including Jesus and Paul were laymen, as well as the early Christian *didaskoloi* and the monk-teachers. Teaching seems to have become the prerogative of the clergy with the ordination of the *didaskoloi* in the third and fourth centuries, as we have seen.

In 1649 a group of Christian lay teachers was formed in France by Fr. Bourdoise to instruct young children. La Salle joined them as a youth. As Bourdoise observed: "I firmly believe that if St. Paul and St. Denis were to return to the world, they would choose in preference to all other vocations, the vocation of Christian teachers."[5]

In 1679 La Salle met Adrian Nyel who came to Rheims to establish a school for the poor under the patronage of Madame de Maillefer. Soon a second one was opened and La Salle pro-

4. E. Fitzpatrick, **La Salle, Patron of All Teachers,** Milwaukee, Bruce, 1951, p. 65.
5. Fitzpatrick, **op. cit.,** p. 67.

vided for the sustenance of the masters, eventually welcoming them into his own home in June of 1681. Especially in the company of these masters dedicated to the poor, La Salle felt that he should not keep his canonry of the cathedral of Rheims, his benefices or even his personal wealth.

> My mouth is closed. I have no right to speak the languages of perfection to my teachers; nor can I tell them of poverty, while I am possessed of a rich patrimony, which precludes the possibility of want. How can I speak to them of abandonment to Providence, while I am provided against indigence?[6]

In 1684 La Salle and twelve companion masters took a vow of obedience for a year and adopted a habit, calling themselves Brothers of the Christian Schools, Christian lay teachers in the heritage of the early *didaskoloi* and the monk-teachers. Though the monks and clerks had schools, neither seemed well adapted to help the poor and uneducated masses.

Requests came in from many towns and cities for the Christian Brothers to establish grammar schools there: Rheims, Laon, Guise, Chateau-Porcien, Rethel, Paris, etc. In response to the request of the town fathers of Chateau-Porcien, La Salle wrote (1682):

> Gentlemen, even were I to take but little interest in what pertains to the glory of God, I must needs be very callous to remain untouched by the earnest prayers of your dean and by the courteous manner in which you have done me the honor of writing to me this day. In view of the eagerness and zeal you assure me you have for the Christian instruction and education of your children, it would be very wrong on my part, gentlemen, if I refused to send you school masters from our community.[7]

These requests were not just for secular schools, but for Christian schools that would help heal the problem of religionless children. Thus the priests of Chartres wrote to their bishop of conditions there (1699):

---

6. **Ibid.,** p. 83.
7. W. J. Battersby, ed., **De La Salle, Letters and Documents,** New York, Longman, 1952. p. 6.

Having frequently met together to confer on this matter, we are agreed that one of the principal causes of the indocility, lack of reserve, ignorance and dissipation of most of the children of this town, both boys and girls, comes from the lack of poor schools, and from the fact that the schoolmasters and mistresses have hitherto had no other end in view than to earn their own living and have failed, either from inability or from want of zeal, to do their work properly. . . . It is essential that this grave evil be remedied by the provision of free schools, for without them, the children, lacking instruction and without discipline, run the streets, become corrupted and incorrigible.[8]

La Salle's schools stressed the religious side with daily mass, periods of recollection, rosary and religious instruction.[9]

Christian civilty was not neglected as the *Conduite des Ecoles Chrétiennes* (Conduct of the Christian Schools) says:

When the pupils know how to read French perfectly and are in the third section of Latin, they will be taught . . . to read the book of Christian Civilty. This book contains all the duties of children towards their parents, and of decorum and of good manners, Christian as well as civil. (1, 3, 9)[10]

Christian civilty is nothing more than the outward expression of the Christian love of the gospels.

One of the books of pedagogy which had a great influence in the latter half of the 17th century and which was probably known by La Salle and his companions is *Escole Paroissiale,* the instruction of parish children by a Parisian priest. It was widely used by the schoolmasters of Paris. Its first part describes the ideal schoolmaster, classroom conditions and students, while the second section outlines religious instruction; exercises of piety, including divine office, vespers and other prayers; and catechism. And the concluding section stresses the three "R's," Latin and daily school exercises. The classroom 26 by 18 by 12 held 100 students and was adorned with crucifix, statues, etc. Books recommended as texts: *Life of the Saints, Diocesan Catechism,*

8. Fitzpatrick, op. cit., pp. 91-92.
9. Ibid., p. 141
10. Quotes from the Conduite from The Conduct of the School of Jean Baptiste de La Salle, ed., F. de la Fontainerie, New York, McGraw-Hill, 1932.

The Paradise of Young People, Bonaventure's *Little Book of Meditations, and Christian Pedagogy, The Guide to Sinners* by Louis de Grenade, and a Latin grammar. Some Jesuit customs such as the use of decurions is also described.[11]

La Salle's *Conduite des Écoles Chrétiennes* built upon the *Escole Paroissiale,* but he also consulted the daily experience of his brothers in the classroom. Like many of the great documents of Christian pedagogy, it is based on experience, synthesizing suggestions and practices. The first edition of *Conduite* appeared in 1705-1706. Further changes were made following suggestions of the masters in 1717-1718 version published in 1720.

The first part of the *Conduite* deals with the daily activities of the grammar school from its opening to closing, including meals, studies, three "R's," spelling, religious practices: prayers, Mass, catechism. As the *Escole Paroissiale,* La Salle advocated simultaneous teaching with the large classes needed for the charity schools. Also he wanted French to be the language of instruction. Promotions are based on individual needs.

Almost a third of the *Conduite* is devoted to religion, showing its importance in the curriculum. For example, the day should begin in a prayerful manner:

> It will be instilled into them that they must enter the classroom with profound respect, but of consideration for the presence of God. When they have entered the center of the room, they will make a low bow before the crucifix and will salute the teacher if he is present. Then they will kneel to adore God and to say a short prayer to the Blessed Virgin, after which they will arise again, bow before the crucifix in the same manner, salute the teacher, and go sedately and silently to their regular places. (1, 1, 1)

The day is literally sprinkled with prayers:

> There will always be two or three pupils, one from each class, kneeling in some place in the school which has been chosen by the Brother Director or the inspector and arranged for this purpose, who will recite the rosary in turn. At each hour of the day some short prayers will be said. These will serve to call the teacher's attention to themselves and to the presence of God and to accustom the

11. Fitzpatrick, op. cit., pp. 221-22.

pupils to think of God from time to time and to offer him all their actions, so as to draw upon them his blessing. (1, 7, 1)

At the beginning of each lesson, a few short Acts are recited to ask God's grace. Also morning and evening prayers are repeated at the proper times. When they attend Mass, the young who cannot read pray the rosary, while the older children read a book of prayers (1, 8, 3).

Catechism is taught for a half an hour at the end of the day.

> One of the principal tasks of the teacher during Catechism is to conduct the lessons in such a manner that all the pupils will be very attentive and may easily retain all he says to them. To this effect, he will always keep all his pupils in sight and will observe everything they do. He will take care to talk very little and to ask a great many questions. (1, 9, 3)

The teacher should speak on the subject, be serious, dynamic, practical, teaching morals by question and answer, and postpone punishments till after the lesson. "He may, however, sometimes but rarely, when he considers it unavoidable, give a few blows of the ferrule during this time."

> During the time the catechesis is being taught, pupils will be seated, their bodies erect, their faces and eyes turned towards the teacher, their arms crossed and their feet in order. (1, 9, 4)

When called upon by the teacher, the pupil rises, makes the sign of the cross, crosses his arms and answers.

> All the pupils will be very attentive during the entire catechism lesson. The teacher will take care that they do not cross their legs and that they do not put their hands under their garments, in order that they may not do the least thing contrary to good behavior. He will not permit any pupil to laugh when another has not answered properly or any one of them to prompt another who is unable to answer a question. He will take care that the pupils go out of the room the least number of times during the catechism, and only in case of great necessity. (1, 9, 4)

Both in La Salle's and in earlier treatises on catechetics, we find some common themes, namely, keep it short, relevant, serious, dynamic, pleasant, towards the end of the day (perhaps the students are less prone to resist for they are tired).

Part two of the *Conduite* is disciplinary, "The Means of Establishing and Maintaining Order in the Schools," including vigilance of the teachers, signals, registers, rewards, punishments, absences, holidays, holy days and general construction and arrangement of the school. It ends with the virtues of a good teacher: seriousness, silence, humility, prudence, wisdom, patience, restraint, gentleness, zeal, watchfulness, piety and generosity.

La Salle used his theological background to write *Devoirs d'un Chrétien*, three volumes on doctrine, morals, sacraments, prayer, liturgy, Mass, office, etc.

As we have seen, in the beginning he had no intention of founding a community of religious teachers. But as he saw the necessity, he invited some of the teachers to live with him. And for forty years he had his rule under practical study with formulations in 1695, 1705 and 1717. Above all, the community was to be poor, depending on Divine Providence. "The members of this community are occupied in teaching in gratuitous schools, in towns only and in teaching catechism every day, even on Sundays and feasts" (*The Memoir on the Religious Habit* (1690).[12]

La Salle's community were laymen, and he was anxious to preserve the lay aspect. So he was cautious in accepting seminarians or clerics.

> Youths who have started their humanities, however, will not be refused. But they will be received only on condition that they give up the study of the classics, because, in the first place, this will not be necessary for them: secondly, because it might subsequently become an enticement for them to leave their state; and thirdly, because the community exercises and the occupation of teaching require one's whole attention.[13]

Their distinctive habit was to be neither secular nor clerical

> Lest the masters would have the appearance of those evil-minded

12. Battersby, **op. cit.**, p. 241.
13. **Ibid.**, p. 243.

clerics (abbez incubes). And it was feared that they might take on their airs. Thirdly, they would have looked like ecclesiastics dressed according to the fashion, although they were no such thing.[14] (Memoir on the Habit, 1690.2)

La Salle felt that the religious habit underlined the Brothers' separation from the world and helped bolster vocations.

Since the adoption of this habit, no one has applied to enter with any other idea than that of joining a community and of remaining there for the rest of his life. Salaries are unheard of, and it is esteemed a great honor to be accepted. The habit alone has produced these results. (5) [15]

The Brothers' dedication to the education of youth can be seen in their rules as approved by Pope Benedict XIII in 1725. Here are a few in summary form.

5. That the said Brothers teach children gratuitously, and that they receive neither money nor presents, when offered by the pupils or their parents.
6. That they be always associated in keeping schools, and that there be at least two together in the direction of each school.
7. That none of the Brothers ambition the priesthood, or aspire to ecclesiastical orders.
9. That the vows of the Brothers be those of chastity, poverty, and obedience, and stability in the said institute, and also of teaching the poor gratuitously.
17. That the Brothers not only teach the children reading, writing, orthography and arithmetic, but that they chiefly imbue their minds with the precepts of Christianity and of the gospels; that they teach them catechism for one half an hour every working day, and for these latter days they take them to church to assist at Mass and Vespers; that they teach them how to say their morning and evening prayers, and impress on their hearts the commandments of God, the laws of the church, and other things necessary for salvation.[16]

Though the first members to join La Salle's group do not seem to have been of the highest quality, the order was soon attracting excellent men, completely dedicated to the education of poor boys. Besides a novitiate for the brothers, normal schools

14. **Ibid.**, pp. 245-47.
15. **Ibid.**, p. 253.
16. Fitzpatrick, **op. cit.**, pp. 158-59.

for the training of lay masters were opened at Rheims and Paris. With the opening of Paris schools the institute became national and would soon become international under papal approval.

But all was not success, for there was opposition from jealous writing masters and teachers of the *petites écoles,* because their paying students were being attracted to the free schools of the brothers. In response Parliament in 1706 forbade La Salle to establish charity schools or training schools in the Paris area without the permission of the *Ecolâtre.* It seems that the clerics at St. Sulpice were also jealous of the brothers' success. In 1702 La Salle was removed as superior. Also Fr. Baudrand curé of St. Sulpice wanted the brothers to wear the priest's soutane, and another curé, de La Chetardye, wanted De Brou, one of his priests to assume the position of superior to the brothers. La Salle himself had his faculties removed on his death bed (1719) because the students of the reformatory at St. Yon were attending Mass in the brothers' chapel instead of the parish church.

But despite this opposition, or perhaps because of it, the brothers' schools were more and more in demand. Besides the grammar and normal schools already mentioned, *écoles dominicales* were started where young workers and apprentices could learn reading, writing, spelling, arithmetic, geometry, architecture and design. Also there was a school for seamen in Calais, a boarding school in Rouen which taught practical studies for the sons of bourgeois, contrasting with the classical colleges of the Jesuits and the Oratorians. La Salle started a school for delinquents at Rouen.

At his death in 1719, there were 27 houses, 274 brothers, and 9000 pupils. Driven from France by the Revolution, they dwindled to 20 brothers living in Italy by 1798. But by 1822 they were back up to 950 brothers in 310 schools with 50,000 students and by the 1960's numbered 15,000 teaching brothers with half a million students throughout the world.

Of his many contributions to education including simultaneous teaching, strict discipline, vernacular, specialized schools, practical course vis a vis the classical, perhaps La Salle's greatest is the primacy of religion. For religious and moral training of youth were his principal reason for going into education in the first place. The whole school day was centered around religion, with catechism, sacraments, Mass, Bible, prayers. Perhaps no one before or since has been successful at integrating sacred and secular learning.

Popular education was not only growing in France under the leadership of men like La Salle, but also in Germany with the Pietists and in Great Britain by the Church of England, all concerned about the ignorance and immorality of the masses of the people.

C. THE STATE AND UNIVERSAL EDUCATION

As nationalism grew, church and state competed and sometimes cooperated in education. Church schools were gradually replaced by those of the state. With the rise of nationalism and the decrease in papal power, came a new stress on national culture, customs, language, religion, origins and history, all traditions passed on by education either at home or in school. Nationalism developed fast in France with an accompanying absolutism, reaching a peak under Louis XIV whose ministers stimulated intellectual life in art, literature and science for the greater glory of the king.

Rousseau (1712-1778) in questing liberty and equality set the stage for the swift growth of nationalism. In his *Political Economics* (1755) he advocated public education which "Under the rules prescribed by the government and under magistrates established by the sovereign is therefore one of the fundamental maxims of popular and legitimate government." Moreover, the educators should be the best men available, outstanding leaders and exemplars to the young. Otherwise the people will not believe that education has high priorities in the state. Private education can only be valid where family authority is strong as in ancient Rome.[17]

In his *Emile* (1762) Rousseau outlines a naturalist approach

---

17. R. Masters, **The Political Philosophy of Rousseau**, Princeton, 1968, p. 384.

to education, following man's nature and developing it to maturity.[18]

> We are born weak, we need strength; we are born destitute of all things, we need assistance; we are born stupid, we need judgment. All that we have not at our birth, and that we need when grown up, is given to us by education. This education comes to us from nature itself, or from other men, or from circumstances. The internal development of our faculties and of our organs is the education nature gives us; the use we are taught to make of this development is the education we get from other men; and what we learn, by our experience, about things that interest us, is the education of circumstances. (1, 1)

Rousseau is not interested in vocational training, but in man training. "In the natural order of things, all men being equal, the vocation common to all is the state of manhood. And whoever is well trained for that, cannot fulfill badly any vocation which depends upon it" (1, 2). Rousseau was to be a stimulus to educational reform with a student centered approach, on a national scale.

Other 18th century educators who promoted national education were La Chalotais and the Marquis de Condorcet. In 1763 La Chalotais wrote his *Essay on National Education*, showing the inadequacy of the old ecclesiastical system of instruction.

> Without entering too deeply into the consequences which result from so enormous an error, should we be astonished if the vice of monasticism has infected our whole education? A foreigner, to whom its details had been explained would imagine that France wished to people seminaries, cloisters and Latin colonies. How would it be possible to suppose that the study of a foreign language, and the practices of the cloister could be the means of training soldiers, magistrates and heads of families, fitted to follow the different callings which, united, constitute the strength of the state . . .

> Why indeed, should the colleges be administered by monks or by priests? Under what pretext should the teaching of letters and sciences devolve exclusively upon them? The ecclesiastics will always assign the motive of instructing the children in their religion. It is certain that of all instruction this is the most important. But is it true that only ecclesiastics can teach them the catechism, instruct

18. Painter, op. cit., p. 280.

them in French and Latin, explain to them Horace and Virgil? (50-51)[19]

La Chalotais had little faith in the outmoded Jesuit classical education.

The Jesuits were convinced that the plan of studies (**Ratio Studiorum**) drawn up under Aquaviva in the 16th century and the feeble opuscule of Jouvency (**Magistris Scholarum Inferiorum Societatis Jesu de Ratione Discendi et Docendi**, 1703) were masterpieces of literature. Dominated by old prejudices, they were the last to abandon them and they resisted all reform. They admitted no books except their own, and they began to adopt Cartesianism only when others began to abandon it. (62)

The Jesuits were blamed for the unreformed condition of education in France. Some felt that their pupils were more loyal to the Pope than they were to France.

According to La Chalotais, the state has the right and duty to teach its own.

I claim the right to demand for the Nation an education that will depend upon the State alone; because it belongs essentially to it, because every nation has on inalienable and imprescriptible right to instruct its members, and finally because the children of the state should be educated by members of the state. (53)

Even the teaching of morals is the duty and right of the state. "The teaching of the Divine Law concerns the Church, but the teaching of the moral law belongs to the State, and has always belonged to it" (149).

Though La Chalotais wanted to limit the number of unproductive clergy and lawyers, he also felt that too much education for the working classes would make them dissatisfied. In this area he laid the blame on the Christian Brothers.

The Brothers of the Christian Doctrine, who are called Ignorantins (Because they taught lower grades) have appeared to complete the ruin of everything. They teach reading and writing to people who ought to learn only to draw and to handle the plane and the file,

---

19. Quotes from La Chalotais and Condorcet are from **French Liberalism and Education in the Eighteen Century**, F. de La Fontain, ed., New York, 1932, pages in parentheses.

but who no longer wish to do so. They are the rivals or the successors of the Jesuits. The welfare of society requires that the education of the common people should not go beyond its occupations. Any man who looks beyond his trade will never work at it with courage and patience. It is hardly necessary that any of the common people should know how to read and write except those who earn their living by these arts, or whom these arts help to earn their living. (60)

So although La Chalotais wanted a national education rather than an ecclesiastical one, he was by no means in favor of universal schooling.

In 1775 Turgot, for a while finance minister under Louis XVI, proposed a Council of National Education with control of all the French schools and Diderot suggested universal schools open to all and taught by paid public teachers.

The Marquis de Condorcet (1743-1794) wrote his Report on Public Instruction (1792). In fifty pages he gave a complete outline of a national educational system in the spirit of the French revolution, stressing freedom, self-realization and happiness. Convinced of man's basic perfectibility, he saw education as the best means of perfecting his natural talents. Moreover, equal education is the best means of bringing about equality of the citizenry.

He felt that man's basic needs obliged the government to furnish a universal education.

Education should be universal, that is to say, it should be within the reach of all classes of citizens. It should be equally shared insofar as compatible with the necessary limitations imposed by the cost, by the distribution of the population, and by the greater or less amount of time that children can devote to it. (326)

But the schools are not to be instruments of governmental propaganda, but rather to help the individual citizen develop the fullness of his powers.

The Marquis' system included primary and secondary schools, institutes of applied science, lycees and universities. He was sure a man could advance if only he were given the opportunity to learn. Thus the lower schools were free, while scholarships aided the needy to attain a higher education. Overall was a national board of scholars called The National Society of Sciences and Arts.

Ethics was an essential part of his curriculum, and he made an important distinction between ethics and religion.

The principles of ethics that will be taught in the institutes will be those which, being founded on natural sentiments and on reason, are common to all men. The Constitution, by recognizing the right of each individual to choose his religion, by establishing a complete equality among all the inhabitants of France, does not permit the introduction into public instruction of any teaching which, by excluding the children of a part of the citizens, would destroy the equality of social advantage, and give to particular dogmas an advantage contrary to the liberty of opinions. It is then absolutely necessary to separate ethics from any special religion, and not to permit in public instruction the teaching of any religious creed . . .

Each religion should be taught in its own temples and by its own ministers. Parents can then, whatever may be their opinions concerning the necessity of one religion or another, send without reluctance, their children to the national schools; and the government will not have usurped the rights over consciences under the pretext of enlightening and guiding them. (347)

In 1790 the French Revolution imposed the oath of the Civil Constitution on the clergy. Religious orders refused to take the oath and were driven from their schools. Some were imprisoned and even put to death, for the revolutionaries felt that the church was alligned with the upper classes and the monarchy.

During the Revolution many educational plans were drafted. In general, they supported a universal, free, state supported education with a realist curriculum including practical arts, civics and science, administered by the state, with normal schools for teacher training.

But the revolutionary days were too chaotic to start any new system of state education. Government finances, taxes and the low state of the teaching profession militated against it. But the seeds were sown for egalitarian education. Educational reform had a slow start after the Revolution, but some schools were established by the bourgeoisie in 1795. Also some technical schools opened in Paris under the sponsorship of the Convention.

When Napoleon came into power (1799) he made peace with the church (Concordat of 1801), so the clergy and religious who had been expelled in the revolution returned to reestablish their schools.

Napoleon was most interested in secondary and technical education, founding four military schools and 400 colleges and lycees, whose curriculum included Latin, French, science and mathematics. This was the beginning of public education in France, although private schools flourished on the primary level, many of them taught by the newly restored Christian Brothers.

In 1802 Fourcroy, a chemist, was made Director General of Public Instruction, and schools of arts, trades, engineering mining, medicine, law and science were founded. and also institutes for the handicapped. Napoleon founded the University of France in 1808. Including a Grand Master and a council of 26, it had overall charge of education in the country, embracing schools, curricula, teachers, funds, exams. And no school could be established or run outside the jurisdiction of the University.

Napoleon set the stage for later developments when he insisted that education was a prime prerogative of the state with his teachers as civil servants, professionals, disinterested, learned in the arts and sciences. Two major contributions of Napoleon to French education were, first, a continuation of the classical tradition with both Latin and French letters and his centralization of the system.

But progress especially in the lower schools was slow, for only one half the communes had primary schools by 1830, many of these were taught by the Christian Brothers who resisted government control. The industrial revolution would bring the money to establish the type of universal education that the earlier political revolution had in mind. The July Monarchy of Louis Phillipe with its primary school law of 1833 insured primary and higher primary education for the lower classes, whereas the old colleges and lycees continued to serve the upper classes, so the higher professions were still closed to the common people.

Besides increasing the appropriations for the primary schools, the new government required all teachers to be certified, even those belonging to religious orders. But church schools were to be allowed if their teachers were certified and the schools inspected. And religious teachers were to be represented on local school committees. But no child was to be given religious instruction unless his parents approved. But by 1851 still 2500 communes were without schools, though there were over 61,000 primary schools and 1500 public and private secondary schools in France.

The Loi Falloux (1850) of the Second Republic gave many concessions to the church, abolishing the state monopoly on education, freeing the schools from any absolute state control which would prevent free association, but still allowing some measure of government supervision. Napoleon's University's powers were curtailed. The free schools could be inspected by the state to insure morality, hygiene, and conformity with the constitution and law, but with the Loi Falloux denominational schools were encouraged in France and achieved equality with the common schools.

But the competition between public and private schools encouraged a division in French youth leading to the eruption of 1880 of the Third Republic. In 1875 a law was passed limiting the monopoly of the University so that denominational schools of higher education could begin and the French Catholics had a complete school system.

In the days of the Third Republic things came to a head. Jules Ferry, an active Free Mason, was appointed Minister of Public Schools in 1879. He and his colleagues believed that education was the prerogative of the state. By this time Catholic religious in France had grown to 160,000 teaching in 1900 schools of which only 980 were legally authorized.

Two bills, called the Ferry Bills, suppressed the free universities, hereafter called free faculties, and restricted private education. Article Seven of the second Ferry Bill read: "No one who is a member of a non-authorized religious congregation shall be permitted to take part in public or free teaching, nor to direct an establishment of any type whatsoever."[20] Though Article Seven was subsequently removed from the law, it gives a good idea of the attitude of Ferry and his colleagues vis a vis Catholic education.

Early in 1880 religious communities of France decided to fight the government demands and regulations for they rightly

20. See N. Predovich, **Leo XIII: On Education**, unpublished MS, Woodstock, 1962, pp. 57ff.

felt that state authorization could be used as a weapon against them. But the problem was not only one of education, but also political for most Catholics sided with the monarchy. A compromise was attempted by Prime Minister De Freycinet asking that the religious communities sign a declaration of political neutrality. But popular reaction replaced De Freycinet with Jules Ferry, and anti-clericalism closed over 250 religious schools.

The concept of public schools funded by public taxes brought a new look to French education and competition for the private schools. Allied was the compulsory primary education law of 1882. A rider in the bill proposed by Bert and Ferry forbade the teaching of religion in the schools in the name of freedom. Instructions in morals and civics were substituted, echoing the thoughts of Marquis de Condorcet.

But French Catholics feared the new "L'ecole sans Dieu," for they had no doubts that Ferry's proposed neutral schools were in fact atheistic. Anticlericalism grew along with Roman opposition.

By the Organic Law of 1886 members of religious communities were forbidden to teach in public schools. So gradually the teaching state, "L'etat enseignant," had developed a complete system of public education, compulsory, gratuitous, universal, secular, free of all religious influence. But the private Catholic schools were far from dead, and within ten years 5000 new schools opened in France with over a million students.

Leo XIII tried to achieve a rapproachment between the French Catholics and their government, a "ralliement," with a full integration of Catholics into national life. But he received little support from the monarchists. Both the republicans and the Catholics used their schools against each other, firmly convinced of the error of the other side.

In 1901 the Freedom of Association Act was passed, requiring all religious communities to have their rules approved by the Chamber. Only five communities met the standards. Thousands of communities either closed down or left for foreign lands. But France's loss was to be the gain in religious education in many other lands. By 1904 almost 14,000 religious schools were closed.

Finally in 1905 the Law of Separation declared the French

government separate and free from the church. But this was not just a separation of church and state but also of private and state education.

Similar battles between church and state over educational rights were being fought in Austria, Hungary, Italy, Prussia, England and the United States. In Prussia Bismark's Kultur-kampf ousted the Jesuits, withdrawing all schools from church control. But he made a truce with Leo XIII.

Since earliest times education had been under the care and direction of the church, yet the church could handle only so much, training her clergy, monks and nuns, educating a certain small percentage of the youth, often of the upper classes, although some inroads were made into the instructing of the poor from time to time. But once the universality of education was the norm, encouraged by the Renaissance and the revolutions, weakening the class structures and supporting the equality of all men, then only the state could handle it with its right to tax and use tax monies for the benefit of the people. The battle over whether religion should be allowed in these schools, or if so, how much, was to be waged in just about every country.

13

ENCOURAGE THE ESTABLISHMENT OF CATHOLIC
SCHOOLS, MAKE EVERY SACRIFICE (American Bishops, Pastoral Letter, 1852).

A. EARLY AMERICAN EDUCATION

THE GROWTH of religious and public education in America in
many ways parallels that of France. But except for the early
missionaries, most of the founders of the new country were
Protestants, many of whom had fled the established churches
of Europe. As in Europe in the 17th and 18th century, most
education in America was done under religious auspices.

The Spanish and French missionaries were the first religious
teachers in North America, that is, outside of the handing on
of native traditions among the Indians themselves. The Spanish
missionaries gathered the Indians around their churches, teaching them sheep-herding, farming and trades. They also taught
them religion, liturgy and Spanish and tried to make their
native languages into some sort of a system. Since the padre was
the best educated man in the new settlement, schooling of the
natives was his natural jurisdiction. Sometimes a few youths
would even be trained in letters, especially if they showed promise
of a vocation to the priesthood.[1]

In 1516 the Spanish passed the Law of the Indies, requiring
a school to be attached to each mission church, where a sacristan
was to teach the natives the fundamentals, usually including
vocational training. Carlos IV commanded that schools be established in all the towns of New Spain, and Diego Borica, governor
of California (1794) attempted unsuccessfully to start schools
in which Spanish would be taught to the Indians. The French

1. X. J. Harris, "Education, U.S.," NCE 5, pp. 128-148.

missionaries in some ways paralleled the Spanish, teaching the natives trades and some fundamentals of the Christian religion.

In the early 1700's the Capuchins opened a small school for boys in New Orleans, and the Ursuline nuns a convent. Other schools opened in Maine, Detroit, St. Louis, Montreal, Quebec, etc. And most of the missions had small schools for native and immigrant children.

In the southern colonies education was a privilege of the rich who could afford a private school or tutor. But the rural sections of the South did not even have these.

In the North, the Massachusetts Bay Colony decreed compulsory literacy (1642) and compulsory schools (1647). Massachusetts Bay had a cultural heritage from mother England with many university trained ministers and professional men, including leaders like Cotton Mather and John Winthrop. By 1700, 39 Latin grammar schools and Harvard college were founded.

There were no state, public or neutral schools in the later sense of the word. As in Europe of the time, the early colonial schools were church sponsored—Congregational in new England, Anglican in the South, and of various denominations in the middle colonies. The Jesuits started the first Roman Catholic schools in the middle colonies, a college in Maryland in 1660 and an elementary school in New Town, Md., 1640-1688. But due to legal restrictions, they had to be closed. Similar schools were started in New York (1662-1689) and Pennsylvania (1704-1765).

New England's schools weakened along with its religious fervor. But the Great Awakening under the leadership of Jonathan Edwards (1732-) saw four new ministerial colleges, Princeton, Brown, Rutgers and Dartmouth. Also academies sprang up as middle schools.

Most of the colonies had established or preferred religions, for example; Virginia, Carolinas and Georgia, The Church of England; New England, Congregationalism; and New York originally Dutch Reformed. By the time of the American Revolution ten colonies (not Rhode Island, Pennsylvania or Deleware) had established or favored religions. This situation favored a federal disestablishment when the time came for a union of the colonies.

9. **Old South Building, Georgetown College (1789), founded by John Carroll. George Washington spoke to the students from its steps. (Georgetown).**

When the states called conventions to ratify the Constitution, they were strong for religious liberty, for they wanted little federal interference, especially in religious matters. The Bill of Rights, ratified in 1791 read, "Congress shall make no law respecting an establishment of religion, or prohibiting the free exercise thereof."

The states themselves eventually disestablished, but it took some of them a long time. Mullaney[2] discusses some of the reasons why they gave in. First, it was seen that religion thrived in the non-established states such as Rhode Island and Pennsylvania. Secondly, the established churhes had grown stagnant and were not about to oppose disestablishment. Thirdly, immigration swelled the ranks of the minority churches, especially the Roman Catholics, sometimes overshadowing the established demoninations. The Bill of Rights, ratified by the state conventions, finally led the way to a general disestablishment.

The Revolutionary War decimated colonial education. But the Continental Congress of 1787 left little doubt of the need of good schools to keep the morality of the country. The Ordinance of 1787 for the organization of the Northwest Territory (article 3) reads: "Religion, morality, and knowledge, being necessary to good government and the happiness of mankind, schools and the means of education shall be encouraged." As the ancient Romans, the Americans saw religion and morality as the foundations of good government. In its survey ordinance of 1785 Congress had set aside section 16 of each western township for the support of schools. Ohio, admitted to the union in 1803, was the first state to gain from this law. Some states managed their school lands well, while others sold it off quickly.

Public education grew slowly in the United States. Jefferson had a plan in Virginia whereby the state would pay tuition for needy students to attend the already existing schools. And in 1825 his idea of a state university materialized at Charlottesville.

New England led the way in public education for they already had a tradition of civil responsibility for education. The

2. "Church and State," NCE 3, p. 747.

Middle Atlantic states with their denominational schools were slow to adopt a public system, but allowed state funds to go to the private schools. Southern states endowed private academies and colleges and pauper schools.

When new states came into the union, they followed the pattern set by their immigrants. Thus Ohio and northern Indiana, settled by New Englanders, soon adopted a public system of education. In other states there was either no public involvement in education or else there was state support of private and parochial schools. So there was no set pattern in early American schooling.

The Anglicans were active in church schools in the South as they were in England through two main organizations, namely, The Society for the Promotion of Christian Knowledge and the Society for the Propagation of the Gospel. Also Sunday schools were growing.

And the academy with its practical courses and vernacular stress was gradually replacing the Latin school as middle education. Moreover the colonial colleges, initially started to train clergy, swerved from the classical to the practical with modern language, history, math and science, and the beginnings of university level professional schools of law, medicine and engineering. The Dartmouth College Case (1819) restrained the states from taking over private denominational colleges and encouraged their growth.

The freedom of religion guaranteed in the U.S. Constitution opened the way for religious education. Roman Catholics were in the tiniest minority with less than two percent of the churchgoers at the time of the Constitution. Many of the early Catholic clergy and bishops were either French or trained in France and so showed the French interest in religious education.

B. CATHOLIC BEGINNINGS

John Carroll of Maryland, a Jesuit trained in France, was chosen the first Roman Catholic bishop of the U.S.A., with his see in Baltimore (1790-1815). The First Synod of Baltimore (1791) stressed the importance of Catholic education, as reflected in Carroll's letter (1792).

> Knowing, therefore, that the principles instilled in the course of a Christian education are generally preserved through life, and that a young man according to his way, even when he is old, will not depart from it (Prov 22:6), I have considered the virtuous and Christian instruction of youth as a principal object of pastoral solicitude.[3]

Exhorting parents to be exemplars in morals and religious practice, he tells them of a new religious college which he and some others had started at Georgetown two years previously. "I earnestly wish, dear brethren, that as many of you as are able, would send your sons to this school of letters and virtue." But he knew many could not afford this. "At least it may reasonably be expected that some, after being educated at Georgetown, and having returned to their own neighborhood, will become, in their turn, the instructors of the youths who cannot be sent from home."

Though under the sponsorship of the Catholic church, the school was open to boys of other denominations. For example, Augustine and Bushrod Washington, grandnephews of the president attended. And Washington himself once addressed the students from the steps of Old North. Besides Georgetown, the French Sulpician Fathers opened St. Mary's seminary in Baltimore (1791).

Harris outlines[4] several problems that early Catholic education faced. First of all, it was dependent on Europe for both teachers and money. Secondly, despite the federal guarantee of religious freedom, there was still danger of persecution in certain states with established religions. And the trustee system, modeled on the Congregational government, gave the lay elders control of the finances.

One of the earliest forms of Catholic elementary education in the United States was the free school attached to a boarding school for the upper classes. For example, St. Angela's founded by the Ursulines in New Orleans in 1727 on the Paris model.

---

3. Carroll's quotes from P. Guilday, ed., **The National Pastorals of the American Hierarchy** (1792-1919), Washington, 1923, pp. 3ff.

4. "Education, U.S." **NCE** 5, p. 132.

Later free schools were attached to Georgetown Visitation Academy (1798) and St. Joseph's Academy, Emmitsburg, Md., by Mother Seton.

The first parish school was Philadelphia St. Mary's (1782). Two more were opened there by 1808. In Baltimore St. Patrick's common school started in 1815 and St. Mary's free school in 1817, and 17 more by 1838. New York had one school, St. Peters, in 1800 and nine more by 1840 taught by the Sisters of Charity of Emmitsburg, laymen, and helped by priests. By 1840 the Boston Diocese had schools in five New England cities, with five in Lowell Massachusetts, supported by public funds.

Of course without the teaching sisters, the religious education of American Catholic youth would have been impossible. Some of the early religious teaching congregations came from Europe, many driven out by the French Revolution and its aftermath, while others were native congregations. The high demand for their services was prompted both by the desire of parents and church that Catholic youth be brought up by religious teachers and also by the gratuity of their labors in a period when tax-supported schools were not yet in existence.

The Carmelite nuns came from Belgium to found a convent at Port Tobacco, Md., under the guidance of Fr. Charles Neale in 1790. Bishop Carroll wrote to Rome to get permission for them to teach and eventually they opened a school in Baltimore in 1830. In 1792 some Poor Clares came from France to Frederick, Md., and then to Georgetown in 1801 to open a school, but returned to Europe in 1804.

Fr. Leonard Neale, president of Georgetown College, obtained the Poor Clare's property and asked a group of pious women to take over. Eventually they became a convent of the Visitation order in 1816. Their academy was a pioneer in the education of working girls in the U.S.A.

A second American teaching community was founded by Mrs. Elizabeth Bayley Seton, a young widow who went with her three daughters to Baltimore at the invitation of Rev William Du Bourg. When several other young women joined her by 1809 they took the name of the Sisters of Charity, founded by Vincent De Paul. Mother Seton founded her house near Emmitsburg Md., starting a boarding school for young girls there. Her prime aim was to staff free common schools for the needy, the first of which opened at St. Joseph's Parish, Emmitsburg in 1810. But they had to run academies for the wealthy in order to subsidize their work with the poor. By her death in 1821 Mother Seton had fifty sisters and six schools.

An early pioneer in religious education in the Michigan Territory was Sulpician Father Gabriel Richard, who opened a seminary in Detroit in 1804. Concerned about the education of girl's he trained four young ladies as teachers. He hoped they would become a congregation of sisters, but a fire that destroyed Detroit in 1805 thwarted his plans.

Richard is most famous for his contributions to Michigan education. He wanted universal education and in 1805 petitioned public funds. In 1809 he submitted a plan for education in the Michigan Territory, stressing the practical to prepare youth for life and including the teaching of the Indian youth, which was to be adopted by the War Department ten years later. Besides his schools, six for boys and two for girls, Richard pioneered in school books, setting up a press in Detroit in 1809.

Richard's plans included a university or Catholepistemiad which he founded with the aid of a Protestant clergyman John Monteith and Judge August Woodward. Monteith was president and Richard vice president and professor of intellectual science, mathematics and astronomy. Appreciative of Richard's pioneering in education, the people of Michigan elected him to Congress as territorial delegate in 1823.

Another state of early educational progress in the midwest was Kentucky. Even before Kentucky became a state in 1792, Catholics had migrated from Maryland, in the hope of a freer and more opportune life. In 1793 John Carroll sent Stephen Badin to care for the Kentucky Catholics. Badin's interest in education was encouraged by his colleague Charles Nerinckx recently arrived from Belgium. The Dominican Fathers led by Edward Fenwick came to Kentucky with Carroll's permission to open a school in 1807. It was called St. Thomas College, but closed in 1820.

Benedict Joseph Flaget was consecrated the first bishop of the Diocese of Bardstown (1810), which covered the states of Kentucky, Tennessee and Ohio and the territories of Indiana,

Illinois and Michigan with 6000 souls and seven priests. Flaget had John David his coadjutor begin a seminary and St. Joseph's College in 1819. St. Mary's College of Marion County was started in 1821.

In 1812 Flaget approved two new religious communities of women, the Sisters of Loretto and the Sisters of Charity of Nazareth. And the Dominican Sisters came in 1822. By 1825 the Loretto Sisters had five schools in Kentucky and one in Missouri. Other schools were opened by the Sisters of Charity and the Dominicans. But Nerinckx was unsuccessful in establishing a society of brothers to teach the boys.

Flaget had been a professor in France and at Georgetown College and brought his ability and interest with him to the wilderness. St. Joseph's College in Bardstown flourished, rivaling the best schools of France. The customary free school was attached to teach poor Catholic boys who had not made their First Holy Communion. St. Joseph's received high praise in Congress in 1832.

> This college without the aid of government endowment, brought into existence and sustained by individual enterprises, will lose nothing in comparison with any college in the union. . . . Its portals are open to all denominations. Religious bigotry does not extend its unhallowed influence over the consciences of the professors or their pupils. The benevolence of its founder and its conductors is felt in all ranks of society. The orphan and the destitute find ready access to the benefits of this institution. And when there is inability to pay the moderate charges of board and instruction, none are made.[5]

By 1825 the diocesan seminary at Bardstown had 19 seminarians and St. Thomas preparatory seminary had 15. Besides St. Joseph's College, there was St. Mary's country school with 120 boys. The Sisters of Loretto were now 100 in number with their five schools in Kentucky and one in Missouri; while the Sisters of Nazareth had 60 members with four schools plus one in Vincennes.

Although Catholic education had met with some success

5. Quoted in H. Buetow, **Of Singular Benefit,** New York, Macmillan, 1970, pp. 79-80.

in French-oriented Detroit and in Maryland-colonized Kentucky, it received stiff opposition in Puritan established New England. The first bishop, John Cheverus, had only 720 Catholics and three scattered churches and one small school attached to the Boston church by 1804.

Stephen Blyth defended the need for Catholic schools in his letter to the Massachusetts Senate in 1806, asking permission to hold a lottery to help defray the costs of religious schooling.

> Catholics have an involuntary and afflicting scruple of sending their children to the common schools, where the integrity of their faith is apt to be shaken by heedlessness or design. Nor are instances infrequent of Catholics preferring the inconveniences and scantiness of domestic education and even the want of any, to the hazard of this exposure.[6]

In 1820 the Ursulines, trained in Three Rivers, Quebec, opened a school for girls in Boston, moving to Charleston in 1826, where they took in boarders, both Catholics and Protestants. And although there was no evidence of proselytizing, Protestants feared the nuns, burning their school and convent to the ground in 1834 and forcing them to return to Canada.

Bishop Benedict Joseph Fenwick, consecrated second bishop of Boston in 1825, did much for Catholic education, founding a day school for boys and girls, a seminary and a classical school for boys.

Other schools were established in New York, Philadelphia, New Orleans, Charleston, etc. New York had a melange of charity schools sponsored by the Dutch Reformed, Episcopal, Presbyterian and Catholic churches. St. Peter's Catholic school dates as a free school from 1800, obtaining state aid in 1806. In 1805 the Free School Society was founded by major De Witt Clinton to take care of needy students who did not attend the religious schools; the Society was to be the predecessor of the New York public school system. But, although non-demoninational, the society stressed the importance of religion, giving religious instruction on Tuesday afternoons and assembling the

6. H. Buetow, op. cit., p. 82; Lord, Sexton and Harrington, **Archdiocese of Boston,** vol. 1, pp. 597-98.

students on Sunday morning to see that they went to church. There is little doubt that early American education, both denominational and public, had the religious and moral formation of the children foremost in mind. But the secularization of the New York schools began in 1825 with the Free School Society becoming the Public School Society of New York (1826).

In 1808 Father Kohlman, a Jesuit, was sent to New York to administer the new diocese. With five companions he founded the New York Literary Institute (1809), a classical college; in 1813 they turned it over to the Trappists. The Ursulines from Ireland opened a school for girls in 1812, but due to financial problems had to return to Ireland. In 1817 the Sisters of Charity of Emmitsburg started an orphan's asylum, a pay school to support themselves and finally in 1820 a free school.

The development in other dioceses was parallel with small religious schools starting out under the guidance of the nuns, with academies, seminaries, convent pay schools and free schools rising up. So by 1829 the American bishops could report to Rome: six seminaries, nine colleges three of which were chartered as universities by the state legislatures, 33 monasteries or houses of religious women including Ursulines, Visitandines, Carmelites and others whose main occupation is the education of Christian girls, houses of Dominicans, Jesuits, Congregation of the Mission, Sulpicians, missions, schools and hospitals, all within the space of a few years.

But these foundations were not without their problems, for they met with opposition in some states with established religions. Also since most Catholics were of the poorer classes they could ill afford a separate school system. But the generosity of European mission societies such as the Propagation of the Faith in France and the Leopoldine Society in Austria came to their aid. Catholics were a small minority in a Protestant country so their religious education was aimed at preserving their identity. But the schools also sought to prepare the children for life in the world by the humanities and the practical arts.

Catechism was an important part of the Catholic schools, using texts by Butler or Challoner or a translation of the Catechism of the Council of Trent, which became sources of the later Baltimore catechism. Other books were produced by men like Molyneux of Philadelphia and Richard of Detroit.

The secondary Catholic schools followed the classical tradition for the boys, whereas the girls' academies stressed the more practical home arts, as well as religion and morality.

The teaching staffs were largely sisters, with some priests in the academies and a few lay teachers. The nuns made the difference for the Catholic schools; their celibacy, dedication, spiritual lives, and gratuitous services put the Catholic schools way ahead of those of other denominations and enabled them to continue when the others failed due to economic or other problems. Indeed, it was not unusual for Protestant parents to send their children to the Catholic schools. But still in the first part of the 19th century, a small percentage of American youths went to school, and the secondary schools, as in Europe, were largely for the upper classes. The trend towards universal education was to change all this and make a public supported school system a necessity.

C.   CHURCH AND STATE

Perhaps it would be good to mention something here about the federal situation, after having seen the local conditions in various states, some favorable to Catholic education, others unfavorable. As we have seen, from the beginning there was no established federal religion, even though several states had their own denominations. The situation of religion was so diverse in the several states and territories that it would have been impossible for the federal government to adopt any one religion. Religion was a local, not a national matter.

The First Amendment forbidding Congress to make laws about religion or prohibiting the free exercise thereof did not express a national disinterest in religion or the wish to set up a secular or atheistic state. Quite the opposite. It wanted to guarantee disestablishment in order to safeguard individual rights in the practice of religion.

But federal disestablishment did not preclude the giving of aid to various religious schools, hospitals and missions, which could help the common good. However, the federal government could not subsidize one religion exclusively. Congress actually provided land for churches in the western frontier because it felt that churches furthered the common good. And the War Department subsidized the missions to help educate the Indians and paid chaplains to minister to the nation's soldiers.

So the United States was disestablished, allowing freedom of religious practice. This was not separation of church and state, but rather a prohibition of the government's protection and support of any one religion. So the federal government was not neutral to all religion or atheistic or areligious. In fact, the modern term "separation of church and state" did not even occur in federal documents until the Supreme Court decision of 1879 with the particular meaning that religion does not excuse a man who practices polygamy against the law.[7] As we have mentioned, the individual states gradually disestablished absorbing the free atmosphere of the Bill of Rights.

D. PUBLIC SCHOOLS

The changes that Europe saw in the middle of the 19th century and which brought it to universal education, were also at work in the U.S.—first the democratization of the American Revolution, secondly the advances of the Industrial Revolution, opening up new possibilities for all alike, and the accompanying intellectual and scientific revolution, questioning the old religious myths and dogmas.

Industrialization and humanitarianism both prompted American universal education under the leadership of men like Horace Mann, James Carter, Henry Bernard and others. Mann, especially through a series of reports, convinced Americans that they were ready for and needed a public system of education, free, tax-supported, universal and non-sectarian, stressing social civil and moral virtues.

Mann was the first secretary of the Massachusetts State

7. Buetow, op. cit., p. 98.

Board of Education. His schools were non-denominational and some felt anti-religious. But he responded strongly in favor of religious education in his 12th and last Annual Report (1848):

> But it will be said that this grand result in practical morals is a consummation of blessedness that can never be attained without religion, and that no community will ever be religious without religious education. Both these propositions I regard as eternal and inmutable truths. Devoid of religious principles and religious affections, the race can never fall so low but that it may sink still lower. Animated and sanctified by them, it can never rise so high but that it may ascend still higher. . . . The man, indeed, of whatever determination or kindred or tongue he may be, who believes that the human race, or any nation, or any individual in it, can attain to happiness or avoid misery, without religious principle and religious affections, must be ignorant of the capacities of the human soul, and of the highest attributes in the nature of man.[8]

But what should be the function of the government in religious education? Mann answers:

> The government should do all that it can to facilitate the acquisition of religious truth, but shall leave the decision of the question, what religious truth is, to the arbitrament without human appeal, of each man's reason and conscience. In other words, the government shall never, by the infliction of pains and penalties, or by the privation of rights and immunities, call such decision either into prejudgment or into review.

Massachusetts law at this time protected all sects and religions without any subordination or preferential treatment. This is clearly disestablishment, but not irreligion or areligion.

As in Europe, the new American public schools were stressing the practical vis-a-vis the classical—science, mathematics, geography, economics, history, with the Prussian graded system recommended by Mann. Other European influences were Pestalozzi's spirit of inquiry and observation and Froebel's kindergarten. Compulsory education soon became common with Massachusetts first in 1852. In 1867 was established a federal department of education. And normal schools blossomed after the Civil War.

High schools evolved from the academies and concentrated

---

8. Mann's quotes from Painter's **Great Pedagogical Essays**, pp. 395ff.

on the practical. And the colleges grew with 182 colleges and universities by 1860, with technical and women's colleges rising after the Civil War. Charles Eliot introduced the elective system at Harvard in 1869.

E.   IMMIGRANTS AND NATIVISTS

While public education was growing in the mid 19th century, Catholic schooling advanced especially with the large Irish and German immigrations. The Germans especially wanted their own parishes and schools. Sisters and priests joined the migrations. Notable were the German Jesuits, expelled by Bismark's Kulturkampf, who founded the Buffalo mission in 1869 with schools in Buffalo, Cleveland, Toledo, Prairie du Chien and Mankato. But hostility to the immigrants grew in the native American parties of the middle 1800's.

Though American education became public and non-sectarian, it still was Protestant and religiously oriented with Bible reading and school prayer. Protestants supplemented this with denominational Sunday schools. But minority Catholics wanted their own schools to preserve both cult and culture. Moreover, they feared not only the Protestant orientation of the public schools, but also their growing secularism. The Council of Baltimore (1852) reiterated the need for Catholic schools.

> If your children, while they advance in human sciences are not taught the science of the saints, their minds will be filled with every error, their hearts will be receptacles of every vice, and that very learning which they have acquired, in itself so good and necessary, deprived of all that could shed on it the light of heaven, will be an additional means of destroying the happiness of the child, embittering still more the chalice of parental disappointment, and weakening the foundations of the social order. . . . Encourage the establishment of Catholic schools, make every sacrifice which may be necessary for this object.[9]

Even a Catholic university is encouraged, following the example

---

9. P. Guilday, **The National Pastorals of the American Hierarchy,** pp. 190-91.

of the Irish bishops, uniting religious and secular instruction at the highest level.

In 1875 an instruction from the Propaganda in Rome urged the American bishops to establish a Catholic educational system. Finally the Third Plenary Council of Baltimore in 1884 insisted that within two years each parish should have a school to which parents were obliged to send their children.

> Two objects, therefore, dear brethren, we have in view, to multiply our schools and to perfect them. We must multiply them till every Catholic child in the land shall have within its reach the means of education.

But these schools are to be in no way inferior. "Let them push their praiseworthy ambition still further, and not relax their efforts till their schools be elevated to the highest educational excellence."[10] Thus Catholic education grew in the United States with strong support from the bishops, priests, nuns and laity. To staff the schools 44 orders of teaching sisters and 11 of teaching brothers came to the United States in the years 1829-1884, not to mention the already established orders of nuns and priests.

As the Nativist opposition to Catholic schools grew, they withdrew into a state of siege. Anti-Catholic riots, convent burnings and the proposed Blaine amendment (1876) which would forbid federal aid to sectarian institutions, added to the confusion. Blaine's proposal read:

> No state shall make any law respecting an establishment of religion or prohibit the free exercise thereof; and no money raised by taxation in any state for the support of the public schools, or derived from any public fund therefore, nor any public lands devoted thereunto shall ever be made under the control of any religious sect or denomination; nor shall any money so raised or lands so devoted, be divided between religious sects or denominations.

Although the Blaine Amendment was defeated in the Senate, its philosophy is reflected in amendments in 29 state constitutions. Even though there was plenty of opposition to Catholic schools, there were some islands of cooperation as at Savannah, Hartford, Lowell, Poughkeepsie and parts of Minnesota. Sometimes in very Catholic areas nuns even taught in the public schools.

10. Guilday, op. cit., pp. 246-47.

As the 19th century progressed, Catholic education fought new battles with positivism, nationalism, Darwinism, A.P.A. Compulsory education laws and the recommendations of the Baltimore Councils helped pack the Catholic classrooms, with consequent shortages of teachers and space. Then there was the ferment over progressive teaching methods and the state's right to teach. Fresh interest was shown in the education of minority groups, besides the new immigrants—the Negroes and Indians. Court cases by both Catholics and Protestants tested the validity of bible reading in the public schools, nuns teaching in the public schools, released time, etc.

Two outstanding religious educators of the period were John Ireland, archbishop of St. Paul and John Lancaster Spalding of Peoria. Ireland saw the impracticality, not to say the impossibility of having all Catholic children in Catholic schools. So he proposed cooperation with the public schools. Although he praised the public system, he found it lacking, as he said in his address to the National Education Association in 1890.

> There is dissatisfaction with the state school as it is at present organized. The state school tends to eliminate religion from the minds and hearts of the youth of the country. . . . In our fear lest Protestants gain some advantage over Catholics, or Catholics over Protestants, we play into the hands of the unbelievers and secularists.[11]

It is because of this lack of religious instruction and consequent secularism that the parochial schools were made necessary.

One proposal of Ireland was that the state would reimburse the denominational schools for secular teaching. Another plan would emulate Poughkeepsie where the public school system rents the parish school from 9 AM to 3 PM, thus religious instructions may be given outside the rental time. A controversy raged among Catholics over Ireland's ideas for some felt he was endangering the parochial school system which was just coming into fruition. And the debate continued over who had the right to educate—state, church or parents.

11. J. Ireland, **The Church and Modern Society,** Chicago, McBride, 1897, pp. 203-204.

John Lancaster Spalding, another eloquent advocate of religious education spoke to the International Congress of Arts and Sciences in St. Louis in 1904. "The Christian religion is education—the deepest and most far-reaching educational force in the world—the power which more than all else originates and sustains the impulse to conduct which is three fourths of life."[12] Spalding decried the secularized education of his time.

Shall we in our schools set aside days to commemorate some mediocre patriot, poet, orator, and make it an offence to do homage to Him who has given His name to our civilization. . . .
This faith (in Christ) lies at the root of modern civilization. It is the vital principle of the Christian home and the Christian church; and if the State and the School organize themselves on a purely secular or utilitarian basis, our social and political life will undergo a radical change. We may increase our commercial efficiency; may so manipulate the natural resources of our continent that the markets of the world pay tribute to us; we may heighten the level of intelligence and raise the standard of living of the multitude; but little by little we shall lose the power to believe in the absolute worth of truth and goodness and beauty of justice, and purity and love. We shall become the richest of nations, but shall have no supreme men and women. The poet's vision, the saint's rapture, and the patriot's lofty mind will be made impossible. Existence will cease to have for us a spiritual content, and we shall come to hold that a man's life consists in the abundance of the things he possesses, and not in the faith, hope, and righteousness which make him a child of God and a dweller in eternal worlds.[13]

Spalding did much to encourage religious higher education and normal schools to train teachers. He encouraged the formation of the Catholic University of America in Washington in 1887. Moreover, under his leadership the church turned new energy towards the education of Indians and Negroes.

F.   THE TWENTIETH CENTURY

The turn of the century witnessed new waves of immigration principally from Austria, Hungary, Russia and Italy, swelling the number of Catholic elementary schools to 6,551 by 1920. Moreover, other sects showed new interest in beginning parochial

12. **Religion and Art,** Chicago, McClurg, 1919, p. 103.
13. **Ibid.,** pp. 105, 110-111.

schools for many of the same reasons the Catholics had. Most Protestant denominations had abandoned their primary and secondary schools in the mid 1800's in favor of colleges and Sunday schools. However, with the secular trend in the public schools, the 20th century saw a modest growth of Protestant elementary and secondary schools chiefly sponsored by the Lutheran, Episcopal and some Methodist churches. Seventh Day Adventists, Baptists and Jews also found the public schools inadequate for the type of religious formation that they needed.

Catholic schools in the 20th century have been affected by many of the trends that have hit the public system, for example, a more child-centered concept of education. In high school and college the elective system has been promoted. Experimental methods of learning, self-direction, less authoritarianism and more democracy were promoted by men like Edward Pace, Thomas Shields and George Johnson.

After World War II emphasis was placed on life adjustment through Christian social living. Special programs for the retarded, handicapped vocational schools, adult education, sister formation were encouraged.

The financing of Catholic schools had always been a problem. In the beginning some money had come from Europe, then the sisters subsidized the poor schools with tuition from well-to-do boarders in the convent schools. Today both public and Catholic schools are in financial problems, the former because of shrinking tax bases and allergies to new school levies, the latter because of diminishing vocations, increasing costs, and the reluctance of some Catholics to support the system.

The probability of state or federal aid to Catholic schools appears to be slim due to the many state laws against it, and the Supreme Court's affirming the wall between church and state. One possibility remains, that of helping the schools under the supposition that they are aiding the public welfare, which was the earliest basis of government support. Modern applications of this have been The GI Bill of Rights (1944), released time (1952) and The National Defense Education Act (1958).

Supreme Court bans on the teaching of religion in the public schools has by no means stopped interest in it. In fact, the interest in religion in public academic circles is probably greater than it has ever been. But the new approach is rather teaching *about* religion than teaching religion in a sectarian manner. Religion is such an important part of man that one would hardly be fully educated if he did not know something about religion, even if he did not practice it. For example, much of the world's literature is religious, and one's education would, indeed, be greatly truncated if this were bypassed. Consequently many private and state universities and colleges now have thriving religion departments. This could easily develop on lower levels as well.

In catechetics new breakthroughs, using some of the latest in educational expertise, have all but eliminated the old rote memory so necessary in the days of low literacy. Participation and relevance are the keynotes. Indeed, in churches where the liturgy is full and participation great, catechetics have never played a very large part. The famous Baltimore Catechism (1886) worked on by Bishop Spalding and Monsignor de Concilio and modeled on earlier texts—perhaps Bellarmine's, Butler's or others—was an attempt at simplicity and uniformity in a time when the educational level was not yet high. Although it was not meant to be used as a textbook, it soon became one and supplementary texts were issued to help both students and teachers.

Chief criticisms of early catechisms, including the Baltimore, are: they are too abstract and deductive for children, too expository with little chance of children's participation, and not easily adaptable to different groups of learners with varied capacities.[14] As we have seen, these were criticisms faced by catechists from earliest times. Make it relevant, participatory, concrete, experiential etc.

New religion texts since Vatican II have stressed the kerygmatic approach with a salvation history reminiscent of early Christian writings and catechisms. Christocentricity, liturgy, personal commitment to Christ and a relevant value-centered

---

14. See Pierre Ranwez, "General Tendencies in Contemporary Catechetics," in **Shaping the Christian Message**, G. Sloyan, ed., New York, 1948. pp. 112ff.

approach have helped. The Christian anthropology of men like Karl Rahner and Urs von Balthasar has underlined the basic relationship between anthropology and Christology, manhood and Christhood. Many new catechisms have appeared including, *Come to the Father, Dutch Catechism, Loyola Religion Series,* etc. But in the end the teacher is more important than the book, and although great strides have been made in updating religion and CCD teachers, much more remains to be done.

Vatican II renewed the long tradition of religious education in the church. Actually the whole council was a learning experience for bishops, theologians, laity and ecumenical observers alike. The Declaration on Christian Education plots the basic position, leaving the working out of details to post-conciliar commissions.

Christian education is to be integrated into the whole pattern of modern life. Far from separating children from the world, Christian education should prepare them to work out their salvation in the world along with their fellow men. Although the council recognized the rights of the state in education, it was against a public monopoly. "Parents who have the first and the inalienable duty and right to educate their children should enjoy true freedom in their choice of schools" (6).

The church has the unique title of educator.

> Not merely because she deserves recognition as a human society capable of educating, but most of all because she has the responsibility of announcing the way of salvation to all men, of communicating the life of Christ to those who believe, and of assisting them with ceaseless concern so that they may grow into the fulness of that same life. (3)

As a mother, the church must educate her children, permeating their lives with the spirit of Christ, at the same time developing the whole person towards the building up of the whole society.

Besides the council, recent sociological surveys have been a stimulus in religious education, for example, Notre Dame's *Catholic Schools in Action* (1966) and the Greeley-Rossi, *The Education of Catholic Americans* (1966). Greeley and Rossi found some evidence that Catholic schooling increased religious values of children from highly religious homes, but did not make a lasting impression on those from moderately religious or non-religious families. Further they felt that, at present CCD is not an adequate substitute for Catholic schools.

On the positive side, they found moderate but significant association between Catholic education and adult religious behavior. This was strongest among those who had attended Catholic colleges, many of whom had had 16 years of religious education.

Of course, there are problems with the Catholic schools, as there are with the public. And often the problems are parallel, including finance, personnel, and curriculum, and some parents are unhappy with the progress being made. But, many, parents still seem to prefer to send their children to the religious school.

It is extremely difficult to measure value. Too many evaluations are really devaluations. How can one measure the effectivity of the Catholic schools by the number of times the alumni go to Communion or how they respond to questions on social attitudes? Perhaps the greatest proof of the effectivity of the Catholic school system is the alumni who want their own children to attend Catholic schools.

And the American Catholic bishops continue the firm support of religious education. Their 1972 Pastoral "To Teach as Jesus Did" urges Catholic educators and parents to clearly define their pedagogical goals, to cooperate with other schools on all levels and to practice "fiscal, professional, academic and civic accountability." It also places a high priority on an excellent CCD program. So despite the problems of a shrinking school system, the American Catholic Church is still strongly committed to the apostolate of religious teaching.

14

CHRISTIANITY MIGHT PROVE MORE ATTRACTIVE IF THE CHURCH COULD CONVEY ITS MESSAGE MORE BY STORIES, BY PARABLES AND BY DRAMATIC ACTIONS (A. Dulles, "Church as Multimedia," 1971)

A. SUMMARY

THUS FAR we have seen some vistas of western religious education, beginning with the Jewish rabbis and Jesus, the founding rabbi of Christianity and his leading disciple, Paul. Jesus, as the other rabbis, had his own school with his own oral torah, based on the fundamental law of love. He felt that in their valiant struggle to preserve the divine teaching, some of the Pharisees had all but smothered it with their oral traditions. Jesus' disciples spread out to start their own schools, James, Matthew, John, Peter, Paul. Paul was largely responsible for opening up the messianic and eschatological school of Jesus to non-Jews. But Paul saw the danger of different schools of Christianity, always insisting that Jesus is *The* Teacher, and all others including himself, his disciples.

As Christianity became a Roman religion, the rabbi was replaced by the *didaskolos* and the Greek-Roman *paideia* became a model for Christian teaching. We see it in Rome in the schools of Justin and Hippolytus and in Alexandria with Clement and Origen. Many Roman rhetors became converts and bishops in Christianity. For example, Basil, the two Gregories, Augustine, leaving off their pagan books to concentrate on the Bible and religious writings.

With the barbarian invasions, education suffered along with the empire, though the clash of barbarian mind and classical tradition was to be a catalyst of the medieval synthesis.

The Christian monks taught their own novices to read and write, training them in the classics and Scriptures. Some extern students were taught, but it seems that their number was never great, and probably included many who were interested in the monastic life. The monks preserved the classical traditions in their libraries, scriptoria and in teaching. Besides the Celtic monastic educational tradition of men like Columba and Columban, we see the Anglo-Saxon strain of Bede and Alcuin, the latter organizing the Carolingian schools into a workable order.

The growth of the towns in the Middle Ages saw the rise of cathedral, guild and town schools. The medieval universities perhaps grew out of the cathedral schools under teachers like William of Champeaux and Abelard. Guilds of teachers and students formed the heart of the medieval universities. Whereas the monasteries had concentrated more on literature, the universities were centers of philosophy and the professions. Besides their arts curriculum, many universities had schools of medicine, law and theology. It seems that most of the students were clerks, many of whom were supported by benefices. To protect themselves from local interference, many medieval universities sought papal patronage.

While the medieval doctors pored over theological problems in the universities, the illiterate or semi-literate peasants were instructed by homilies, liturgy, plays, stained-glass windows and statues in the cathedrals. And there was episcopal fear that the new university doctrines might shock the laity.

The Italian Renaissance of the 14th and 15th centuries was the logical outgrowth of medieval classical studies, with more of a stress on language and literature. Giants were Dante, Da Vinci, Michiavelli, Celini. The Renaissance humanism came to the North countries a century later under the leadership of men like Erasmus, Vives and Ramus.

In Reformation times a growing rationalist humanism was felt. And a collapse of education was seen in Germany and elsewhere due to the closing of the monasteries and advancing materialism. In response, Luther encouraged the study of the Bible and catechism by the children and a learned corps of ministers, enlisting the aid of the princes in achieving his goals.

The communications breakthrough of printing made both the Reformation and Renaissance education possible. Thus the bible and other religious writings became available to all, opening the road to universal literacy and individual interpretation

Over at the University of Paris a middle-aged student named Inigo of Loyola was convinced of the value of religious activity on campus. Gathering together a college of disciples, he soon found himself in educational work with houses of studies on the campuses and continual calls from city fathers for more colleges to educate their children. Soon a Ratio was developed for the guidance of these schools, outlining a classical Renaissance program along with a thorough training in religion and morals.

With Renaissance humanism came increasing educational opportunities for girls. The girls of the wealthy families had always been educated by tutors but with the rise of the merchant classes came a new cry for a more universal schooling of women with a special emphasis on religion and morality, for the Christian girl is the future mother and teacher of her children. Some leaders in the field of girls' education were More, Vives, Silvius, Luther, Merici, L. Bruni D'Arezzo and Fénelon.

Although the convents had always been educational centers, they usually taught their own or girls from the upper classes. But with the Renaissance the older orders of nuns plus some new ones began to teach middle and lower class young ladies. Angela Merici's Ursulines were the first order founded specifically to teach girls, although this was the traditional occupation of the early deaconesses, the nuns' predecessors. Angela's family type of education spread rapidly and was emulated by other sisters in the 17th to 19th centuries.

A growing reaction to Renaissance classics and idealism was seen in a new realism in education, stressing the practical. Actually there had been preludes to this among some of the Renaissance educators such as More and Vives. Realists and naturalists taught the importance of sense knowledge. Also universal education as proposed by Comenius and others was increasing.

John Baptist De La Salle was a leader in religious education especially for the poor in the 17th and 18th centuries, training teachers and organizing them into an order, The Brothers of the Christian Schools. He soon had more requests for schools than he could fill.

With the French Revolution came a push for state schools, eventually resulting in a system of compulsory, gratuitous, secular schools, free from all religious influence. Some religious schools continued, but in a lesser role.

The situation in America paralleled that in France in some ways. For example, in the early days all education was religious. Since colonies had their preferred religions, federal disestablishment was decided upon by the founding fathers. Early Americans were convinced of the value of religious education and did all they could to foster it.

Catholic education in the United States was pioneered by men like, Carroll, Flaget, Fenwick and Richard. Parish schools increased gradually, staffed by teaching sisters from home and abroad, with some opposition in established areas.

Parallel to Europe, public education came to America led by Horace Mann. And Catholic education increased with new waves of immigration and encouraged by the Councils of Baltimore.

The twentieth century saw new growth into a system educating millions of students under the leadership of a couple hundred thousand dedicated teachers, religious and lay. The 19th and 20th centuries saw new attempts at the expression of old truths, with existentialism, the search for the historical Jesus, neo-orthodoxy, neo-scholasticism, the biblical-kerygmatic and modern secular Christian opproaches.

Vatican II was an attempt at synthesizing the biblical-kerygmatic theology of Roman Catholic ecumenism with the hierarchical scholastic theology of the seminaries on the Roman model. Dulles comments:[1]

> The two theologies are difficult to harmonize, since they reflect different visions of revelation, of the church and of theological communication. For the older seminary theology, revelation is to be found, first of all, in dogmas. The church is seen primarily in

1. See A. Dulles, "Church as Multimedia" in New Catholic World, Jan/Feb, 1972, pp. 24ff.

terms of office; the members of the church are the docile subjects of the pope and the bishops in union with him. Theological truth is communicated by the dissemination of magisterial teaching, with suitable commentary from the theologians, to the less educated laity. For biblical-kerygmatic, on the other hand, revelation is to be found, primarily, in the proclamation of the infant church as attested to by the New Testament. The church is seen more in terms of charism then of office, more in terms of event than of institution. The ecclesiastical magisterium is made subordinate to scripture. Theological communication is found by preference in the context of liturgy, when the people of God are assembled in faith to hear the proclaimed word.

That there is fundamental, though, hidden agreement, is shown by the many ecumenical dialogues which have flourished after the council.

At present both methods have been outstripped by the popular Christian secularism illustrated by Teilhard de Chardin and Dietrich Bonhoeffer and which may be seen in the Pastoral Constitution on the Church in the Modern World of Vatican II and many current authors too numerous to mention.

Revelation according to radical-secular theology, is not something confined to the Bible or to the church. It is neither an authoritative message on the lips of a preacher nor a set of truths enshrined in official documents. Rather, it is a dimension of our contemporary experience, as God addresses us through the signs of the times. For proper discernment of these signs there must be prophets in the world today—persons who, through the illumination of the Holy Spirit, are able to arouse men from their apathy and awaken the church itself from its dogmatic slumbers.[2]

Secular theology is more future-oriented than past. It subordinates the church to the future messianic kingdom which man must begin today by his social and political action in the world.

Just as the new media of the printed word changed religious teaching in Renaissance times, so the modern electronic media have revolutionized the paideia, opening up a "post-literate" culture. Modern electronic communications stress the "cool media" of Marshall McLuhan[3] with personal participation, spon-

2. **Ibid.,** p. 24.
3. M. McLuhan, **Understanding Media, the Extension of Man,** New York, McGraw-Hill, 1964, pp. 22ff.

ιaneity, immediacy, relevance over the old "hot media" of the printed word with its facts, logic, metaphysics and scientific abstractions. The new media include the oral, visual, auditory, tactile, personal.

The medium and the message are closely allied. And the teaching church as she has over the centuries, must adapt the gospel to the modern media. But the new media resist the old dogmatic absolutes and kerygmatic proclamation in favor of the tentative, the relative, the existential and personal. Dulles comments,[4] "The church in its striving to elicit faith from all men must be on guard against creating unnecessary obstacles by proposing faith in patterns that are out of phase with contemporary culture."

Dulles feels that the secular-dialogue style is more viable with modern communications, for it can work without texts, absolutes, categories, abstractions, definitions, etc., and is more personal, participative, informal, spontaneous, more gut and less brain, less past-oriented and more for the present and future. In fact, many of these techniques were used by the early Christian teachers going back to Jesus and the didaskoloi, as we have seen. Certainly The Master was most concerned with present and future problems in his dialogues and parables and audience participation. Perhaps the advent of scholasticism with its emphasis on the hot media along with the printed word often addressed to an imaginary audience hastened the dichotomy between thought and practice, ideal and real.

Dulles observes[5] "Christianity might prove more attractive if the church could convey its message more by stories, by parables and by dramatic actions." Of course the modern liturgy and catechetics have moved in this direction, the methodology of the post-literal age moving back to that of the ante-literal era.

B.   QUESTIONS FOR TODAY AND TOMORROW

Many questions are being asked about religious education

---

4. A. Dulles, "The Church as Multimedia," NCW, Jan/Feb, 1972, p. 45.
5. Ibid., p. 45.

today and they concern all from the pope and bishops to the teachers, parents and students. Most would agree that the parents are the principal educators of the children. It is ultimately the parents who will decide whether to have religious schools or not, and if so, of what type. For the parents keep the religious schools going with their financial contributions and by insisting that their children attend. As has been pointed out in recent surveys, unless the parents are involved with the religious education of the children in the home, the Catholic schools can do little of lasting import. Many parents today are active in parish CCD programs, while some others prepare their children for the sacraments at home.

Still others suspicious of the cool media approach of the new catechetics are trying to teach their offspring through the hot media of the old Baltimore Catechism, but with little success, needless to say.

There is growing evidence that young parents are unwilling to build new schools in suburban parishes and refuse to send their children to some of the parish schools already in operation. This is especially true in the suburbs where the public schools are of the highest quality. Many of these parents feel that the Catholic school no longer serves the protective function that it had for them and their parents, guardian of cult and culture, language and faith. Moreover, with fewer nuns in the classrooms and often in non-religious garb, with mounting salaries and tuitions, class and school closings, more and more parents are losing faith in the system. This could move the whole religious education program in a different direction with more stress on catechetical centers and some type of home instruction either by television or by visiting teachers.

Who are the teachers of the church today? Bishops teach from the cathedra and priests from the pulpit. But is anybody listening? There certainly is a large gap between teaching and practice. What is the relationship between parents, lay teachers, nuns and brothers, and the bishops and priests? In the early church the presbyter-guardians watched over tradition, while the lay *didaskoloi* searched out new ways of expressing the old truths, adapting to the times and the students. Although as the educated classes were converted to Christianity, the *didaskoloi* were often chosen as bishops, nevertheless there always remained a rank of non-episcopal teachers, monks, friars, nuns, regular clerks, brothers. Historically the bishops have guarded the simple laity from new and sometimes disturbing trends. But today as the laity becomes more educated and sophisticated, perhaps this function is less needed and might partially explain the gap between episcopal teaching and lay observance. Also as the church becomes less structured with Pentecostalism and other experiential groups, less stress is needed on the noetic in religious education and more on experience.

Newest example of the lay *didaskolos* is the parish religious education coordinator who is gaining in importance as the religious schools close and more and more students are placed in the public system and as the need for adult religious studies is recognized.

The *didaskolos,* lay or religious, must adapt his message to his hearers in a common language between teacher and student. This has been a problem in education from the beginning as we have seen. And the modern teachers in grade, high, or CCD school know how important it is. So they are constantly experimenting with new methods in order to speak to easily bored youths—new prayers, liturgies, catechisms, using all the latest methodology to stimulate the senses.

But what about the students? In many recent surveys young people have clarified their interests, needs, relationships, likes and dislikes. One such study was done by the Department of Research and Planning of the Religious Education Office of the Diocese of Davenport, reported by Thomas A Downs.[6] Here teen-agers were asked to relate five psycho-social needs with seven kinds of groups. More important to satisfying their psycho-sociological needs were their relationships to God, family, friends and society, less important were their ties with school and church. This has probably always been true, but is being brought out more clearly by modern surveys.

6. T. Downs, "Turmoil in the Classroom," **NCW**, Jan/Feb, 1972, pp. 20ff.

The students also showed a preference for psychological over theological discussions, which would seem to dovetail with their need of personal relationships with God, family, friends, etc. For example, they rated friendship, love, careers, personality, sexuality, communication ahead of theological topics as Christ, charity, faith, heaven and hell, sacraments, commandments and Bible. Questioned on methodology, those in the psychology-oriented curriculum preferred activity first, followed by discussion, planning, and lastly—lecture and reading. In the theology-oriented curriculum the order of methodology preferences showed a bit of variation: activity, discussion, reading, planning and lecture.

One might conclude that the students need to be actively involved in the teaching-learning process. And they want man-centered topics over the dogmatic, the personal over the abstract, active participation over passive listening and reading. Augustine and other early teachers drew similar conclusions. But we need modern educators and psychologists to remind us of the ancient truths, always mindful, as Augustine was, that the student is taught interiorly by God and that the human teacher is here to aid this divine *paideia*.

But there are other problems in religious education besides the purely methodological ones, as any teacher will readily verify, who has tried all the latest methods to arouse the deadening passivity of adolescent pupils of religious education. Some of these problems stem from the times, others from the individual student. Here are a few of them: creeping secularism, adolescent faith crisis, a rejection of early compulsory, fundamentalist and moralist catechetics, the yen for freedom, adult pharisaism, the generation gap, the apotheosis of modern science, laziness—it's easier to be non-religious than to be religious, peer pressures, anti-institutionalism. As usual, there are faults on both sides, the youthful laziness and desires for free and easy life and adult obstinacy and self-righteousness. Only honest dialogue and prayer between parents and children, teachers and students will lead to a meeting of minds.

We have seen glimpses of past traditions in Western religious education, the present we are well aware of with its pluses and minuses, but what of the future? This is the day of the prophets and the pseudo-prophets, for a prophet is never proved out until what he foretells comes true. About all we can do is contemplate some big "if's". If present trends continue, there will be higher costs, perhaps as high as $1000 per pupil by 1980. There will be fewer Catholic schools on all levels, grade, high and college, but more released time and catechetical centers. There will be fewer priest and religious teachers and more lay instructors. For example, one large midwest archdiocese expects a drop of 800 teachers about half religious and half lay by 1975 and a drop of 16,000 grade school pupils.

The President's Commission on School Finance (1971) projects enrollment of American Catholic elementary schools (1970-3.4 million) at 1.4 million by 1980, a 60% drop, while high school enrollment (1970-1 million) will slip to 700,000 in 1980, a 30% loss. Thus by 1980 only 20% of Catholic children will be in Catholic grade schools in contrast to 54% in the peak year of 1958. Catholic education on all levels seems to be a buyers' market into the foreseeable future. And Catholics are asking whether a large proportion of funds should be spent on only 20% of the children.

There are many causes of the dropping enrollment including: our mobile society, dropping birth rate, rising tuition, improved quality of public schools, lack of confidence in the Catholic schools, etc.

Will Catholic education slip into the Protestant pattern of the 19th century, namely, abandoning its religious schools for the public system, supplemented by Sunday schools and strategically placed colleges? By and large, the Catholic CCD program has been about as successful as its Protestant counterpart. There is a real contrast between the professional, paid, semi-autonomous educators in the full-time religious schools and the more pastorally oriented amateur catechists of the CCD program, guided by the clergy to prepare children for Holy Communion and Confirmation. Whether or not the present volunteer pastoral approach to catechetics can be or should be professionalized, and whether it will be viable apart from a regular school system remains to be seen. Moreover, there is some evidence that the CCD enrollment does not rise proportionately when the parish schools close. It also seems likely that no longer can CCD classes be held under dire threats, e.g. unless the pupil attends, he will not be confirmed.

We should not underestimate the value of the religious college as an important keystone in a system of Christian education, and not only for ministerial training. The colleges and universities have always been seminaries of new religious movements. Christianity itself began in the college of Jesus, and numerous early Christian doctrines spread from the schools of the didaskoloi. Later the Friars, Reformation, Pietism, Jesuits, Methodism, and modern liturgical reforms, Pentecostals, Jesus Movement, transcendental meditation have risen from the fertile ground of the colleges. And, as in the past, these youth movements will continue to influence future trends in the church as a whole.

Finances have always been a problem in religious education. So religious teachers have often supported themselves from the Jewish rabbis to the Christian nuns and the modern lay catechist. Certainly the donated services of priests, nuns and laity have helped make religious education viable in the past. For example, in 1970 $340 million was contributed by religious in salaries to the parish and diocesan schools, not to mention the millions of dollars invested in buildings, etc.

Due to a drop in vocations and transfers of religious to other work, the teaching religious are fewer each year. Some estimate that there will be a total of 40-50 thousand by 1975 (85,000—1970). Not only is this tremendous subsidy rapidly disappearing, but many older religious who supported the system in the past face the prospect of a pensionless retirement because the whole plan of having the retired nuns supported by the younger ones is collapsing.

Besides rising tuition and private donations, perhaps there may be some hope of governmental aid indirectly to the schools, although, so far, law suits have hindered it in most states. Most likely possibilities are tax rebates, tuition reimbursement, scholarships, or perhaps a separate school system such as thrives in some countries and which was advocated by some of our early founding fathers. Without some sort of state help, the private school system, as we now know it may not last out the decade.

More and more educators and legislators today are seeing

the value of a pluralistic system of education, abandoning the long fight for a state monopoly in teaching. Early America had pluralistic education, and modern historians tell us that the results were not bad. A monopoly in anything can be evil, but governmental domination of education has led to the enslavement of more than one country in modern times and it could happen again.

Secularization of education has been the trend during the last couple of centuries as we have seen. And it is still going on. For example, each year colleges which formerly were denominational are being abandoned by their supporting churches to become private or state schools. Also further closings of lower schools and the transferral of the students to the public system may be expected.

But the church remains basically a teaching church. And as any old teacher, she must change her language and methodology to fit the students of the times. She teaches through her healing doctors and her instructing doctors, through her guardian bishops and her guiding deaconesses. And if she is not a teaching church, she is nothing at all. "Go and make disciples of all nations" (Mt 28:18).

In conclusion, our purpose here has been to study some of the outstanding religious teachers in western tradition. These are our exemplars, the hero teachers of days gone by, our rabbi-fathers, beginning with the Master Jesus, Paul and coming down to our own day. The Christian religious teacher today, as his predecessors, is an existential representative of the Master, trying to find a common language between the Rabbi Jesus and contemporary society, just as Jesus sought stories and wisdom sayings to get his message across.

The future will see further syntheses, further incarnations, further attempts to bridge the gap between the sacred truths and students who have known only the secular. And there will be continual battles between the conservatives who hold onto the old ways, the old liturgies and the old catechisms, and those who want to try new modes of expressing the sacred truths in today's language. But there must be dialogue, participation, spontaneity, freedom, openness, a profaning of the sacred or a

10. Modern religious education at college level. (John Carroll).

consecrating of the profane. Either this or no communication at all.

In some form or other religious teaching will perdure as long as man is religious man and so desires to penetrate the mysteries of the sacred from the primordial hierophanies to the future eschaton.

SELECTED
Bibliography

I. THE RABBIS.

Abrahams, I., **Studies in Pharisaism and the Gospels**, New York, KTAV, 1967.

Adler, M., **The World of the Talmud**, New York, Schocken, 1963.

Baron, S., and J. Blau, **Judaism, Post-Biblical and Talmudic Period**, Indianapolis, Bobbs-Merrill, 1954.

Bokser, Ben Zion, **Wisdom of the Talmud**, New York, Citadel, 1962.

Bowker, J., **The Targums and Rabbinic Literature**, Cambridge, 1969.

Finkelstein, L., **The Pharisees**, 2 vols; Philadelphia, The Jewish Publication Society, 1966.

——————— **New Light from the Prophets**, New York, Basic Books, 1969., **The Mishnah**, tr. H. Danby, Oxford, 1964.

Montefiore, C., and H. Loewe, **A Rabbinic Anthology**, Cleveland, World, 1963.

Neusner, J., **A Life of Yohanan Ben Zakkai, ca 1-80 C.E.**, Leiden, Brill, 1970.

Newman, J., **Halachic Sources from the Beginning to the Ninth Century**, Leiden, Brill, 1969.

Pirke Aboth, The Ethics of the Talmud, R.T. Herford, ed., New York, Schocken, 1962.

The Talmud, London, Soncino Press, 1935.

The Targums of Onkelos and Jonathan Ben Uzziel on the Pentateuch, J. W. Etheridge, ed., New York, KTAV, 1968.

II. R. JESHUA B. JOSE.

Aron, R., **The Jewish Jesus**, Maryknoll, Orbis, 1971.

Cohon, H., **Men at the Crossroads** Between Jerusalem and Rome, Synagogue and Church, The Lives, Times and Doctrines of the Founders of Talmudic Judaism and New Testament Christianity, New York, Yoseloff, 1970.

Dalman, G., and H. Laible, **Jesus Christ in the Talmud, Midrash, and Zohar**, Cambridge, 1893.

——————, **Jesus-Jeshuah; Studies in the Gospels**, New York, KTAV, 1971.

Davies, W.D., **The Sermon on the Mount**, Cambridge, 1966.

Derrett, J.D., **Law in the New Testament**, London, Darton, Longman and Todd, 1970.

Gerhardsson, B., **Memory and Manuscript**, Uppsala, 1961.

Herford, R.T., **Christianity in Talmud and Midrash**, Clifton, N.J., Reference Book Publishers, 1966.

Jeremias, J., **Rediscovering the Parables**, New York, Scribners, 1966.
———————, **New Testament Theology**, New York, Scribners, 1971.
Jerome Biblical Commentary, R. Brown, J. Fitzmyer and R. Murphy, eds., Englewod Cliffs, Prentice-Hall, 1968.
McKenzie, J., **Dictionary of the Bible**, New York, Crowell-Collier, 1965.
Montefiore, G., **Rabbinic Literature and Gospel Teachings**, New York, KTAV, 1970.
More, G.F., **Judaism in the First Centuries of the Christian Era**, Harvard, 1927-1930.
New Testament, Revised Standard Version, New York, Nelson, 1965.
Perrin, N., **Rediscovering the Teaching of Jesus**, New York, Harper, 1967.
Rengstorf, K., "Didasko, Didaskolos, etc." TWNT, vol 2, pp. 135-165.
Robinson, J., and H. Koester, **Trajectories Through Early Christianity**, Philadelphia, Fortress, 1971.
Stendahl, K., **The School of St. Matthew**, Philadelphia, Fortress, 1968.
Thompson, W., **Matthew's Advice to a Divided Community**, Rome, 1970.

III.   PAUL.

Bertram, G., "Paideuo, Paideia, etc.", TWNT, vol. 5, pp. 596-625.
Bonsirven., **Exégèse rabbinique et Exégèse Paulinienne**, Paris, 1939.
Bornkamm, G., **Paul**, New York, Harper and Row, 1971.
Bultmann, R., **Theology of the New Testament**, New York, Scribners, 1955.
Davies, W.D., **Paul and Rabbinic Judaism**, London, SPCK, 1958.
Ellis, E., "Paul and His Co-Workers," NTS, July, 1971, pp. 437-452.
Fitzmyer, J., **Pauline Theology**, Englewood Cliffs, Prentice-Hall, 1966.
Fraser, J., "Paul's Knowledge of Jesus," NTS, Mar. 1971, pp. 295-313.
Klausner, J., **From Jesus to Paul**, Boston, Beacon, 1961.
Lebreton, J., and J. Zeiller, **The Church in the New Testament**, New York, Collier, 1962.
Le Dant, R., "Traditions Targumiques Dans Le Corpus Paulinienne," Bibl 42 (1961) pp. 28-48.
Mohler, J., **Dimensions of Faith**, Chicago, Loyola, 1969.
Montefiore, C. G., **Rabbinical Judaism and the Epistles of Paul**, 1930.
Parkes, J.W., **Jesus, Paul and the Jews**, New York, Herder and Herder, 1964.
Schoeps, H.J., **Paul**, Philadelphia, Westminster, 1959.
Sheets, J., "St. Paul as Teacher," Bible Today, March, 1971, pp. 284-290.
Thackeray, H.S.J., **The Relation of St. Paul to Contemporary Jewish Thought**, London, 1900.

IV.   ROMAN TEACHERS, JUSTIN AND HIPPOLYTUS, EDESSA AND NISIBIS

The Apostolic Fathers, AF, ANF.
Barnard, L., **Justin Martyr**, Cambridge, 1967.
Bauer, W., **Orthodox and Heresy in Earliest Christianity**, Philadelphia, Fortress, 1971.

Berger, A., **Encyclopedic Dictionary of Roman Law**, Philadelphia, The American Philosophical Society, 1953.

Camphausen, H., Von, **Ecclesiastical Authority and Scriptural Power In The Church in the First Three Centuries**, Stanford, 1969.

Filson, F., "The Christian Teacher in the First Century," Life Spir., 12 (1957), pp. 22-29, 64-73.

Gwynn, A., **Roman Education from Cicero to Quintilian**, New York, Russell and Russell, 1964.

Hippolytus of Rome, **Apostolic Tradition**, G. Dix, ed., London, SPCK, 1968.

Lebreton, J., and J. Zeiller, **The Emergence of the Church in the Roman World**, New York, Collier, 1962.

Marrou, P., **A History of Education in Antiquity**, New York, Sheed and Ward, 1956.

Quasten, J., **Patrology**, 3 vols, New York, Paulist/Newman, 1962.

The Theodosian Code, C. Pharr, ed., Princeton, 1952.

Voobus, A., **History of The School of Nisibus**, Lavain, 1968.

Wilkins, A.S., **Roman Education**, Cambridge, 1914.

V.   CLEMENT AND ORIGEN.

Alexandrian Christianity, LCC.

Clement of Alexandria, **Works**, ANF.

Danielou, J., **Origen**, New York, Sheed and Ward, 1955.

Eynde, D. van den, **Les normes de l'enseignement chrétien dans la littérature patristique des trois siecles**, 1933.

Gauche, W., **Didymus the Blind, An Educator of the Fourth Century**, Catholic U. Press, 1934.

Jaeger, W., **Paideia, The Ideals of Greek Culture**, Oxford, 1943-45.

————, **Early Christianity and Greek Paideia**, Oxford, 1969.

Lebreton, J., "La désaccord de la foi populaire et de la théologie savante dans l'Eglise chrétienne au IIIe siècle," RHE, 1924, pp. 481ff.

————, and J. Zeiller, **Heresy and Orthodoxy**, New York, Collier. 1962.

————, **The Triumph of Christianity**, New York, Collier, 1962.

Origen, **Works**, ANF, ACW, SC.

Wolfson, H., **The Philosophy of the Church Fathers**, Harvard, 1956.

VI.   THE CAPPADOCIANS AND JEROME.

Basil, **Works**, LCL, NPNF, FOC.

Cassidy, F., **Molders of the Medieval Mind**, St. Louis, Herder, 1944.

Clarke, W., **St. Basil the Great**, Cambridge, 1913.

Festugiere, A-J., **Antioche paienne et chrétienne**, Paris, De Boccard,.

———— , **Les moines d' orient. I, culture ou sainteté** Paris, Cerf, 1961.

Gregory of Nazianzus, **Works**, FOC, NPNF.

Gregory of Nyssa, **Works**, NPNF, ACW, FOC.

Jerome, **Works**, ACW, LCL, NPNF.

John Chrysostom, **Works**, NPNF.

Lainster, M.L.W., **Christianity and Pagan Culture in the Later Roman Empire**, Ithaca, Cornell, 1951.

Libanius, Selected Works, LCL.
Ruether, R., Gregory of Nazianzus, Oxford, 1969.
Steinmann, J., St. Jerome and His Times, Notre Dame, Fides, 1959.

VII. AUGUSTINE.

Augustine, Works, ACW, FOC, NPNF.
Brown, P., Augustine of Hippo, University of California, 1967.
Hagendahl, H., Augustine and the Latin Classics, Göteborg, Elanders, 1967.
Howie, G., Educational Theory and Practice in Augustine, London, Rout-
    ledge and Kegan Paul, 1969.
Marrou, H., S. Augustin et la fin de la culture antique, Paris, Editions E.
    de Bollard, 1958.
Meer, F. vander, Augustine the Bishop, New York, Sheed and Ward, 1961.
O'Meara, J., The Young Augustine, Staten Island, Alba House, 1965.
Portalie, E., A Guide to the Thought of S. Augustine, Chicago, Regnery,
    1960.

VIII. THE MONKS.

Adomnan's Life of Columba, A. and M. Anderson, tr., New York, Nelson,
    1961.
Alcuin, Works, PL.
The Rhetoric of Alcuin and Charlemagne, ed. W. Howell, Princeton, 1941.
Bede, History, LCL.
Bieler, L., Ireland Harbinger of the Middle Ages, Oxford, 1963.
Blair, P., The World of Bede, NY, St. Martin's Press, 1970.
Cassiodorus, An Introduction to Divine and Human Readings, tr., L.W.
    Jones, New York, Columbia, 1946.
Chadwick, N., Poetry and Letters in Early Christian Gaul, London, Bowes
    and Bowes, 1955.
————, Studies in the Early British Church, Cambridge, 1958.
————, The Age of the Saints in the Early Celtic Church, Oxford, 1961.
Duckett, E., Alcuin, Friend of Charlemagne, New York, MacMillan, 1966.
Haaroff, T., Schools of Gaul, Oxford, 1920.
Healy, J., Ireland's Ancient Schools and Scholars, New York, Benziger,
    1912.
Hughes. K., The Church in Early Irish Society, London, 1966.
Leclercq, J., The Love of Learning and the Desire for God, New York,
    Fordham, 1960.
McCormick, P., Education of the Laity in the Early Middle Ages, Wash-
    ington, Catholic University, 1912.
MacManus, F., St. Columban, New York, Sheed and Ward, 1961.
Martianus Capella, De Nuptiis Philologia3 et Mercuril et de Septem Arti-
    bus Liberalibus, Frankfurt, 1836.
Mohler, J., The Heresy of Monasticism, Staten Island, Alba House, 1971.
Mullinger, J., The Schools of Charles the Great, New York, Stechert, 1911.
Ryan, J., Irish Monasticism, Dublin. Talbot. 1931.

IX. MEDIEVAL UNIVERSITIES.

Adamson, J., The Illiterate Anglo-Saxon, Cambridge, 1946.
Aquinas, Thomas, The Teacher, The Mind, tr. J. McGlynn, Chicago, Regnery, 1963.
Cartularium Universitatis Parisiensis, H. Denifle, ed., Brussels, 1964.
Daly, L., The Medieval University, New York, Sheed and Ward, 1961.
Donahue, J., Thomas Aquinas and Education, New York, Random House 1968.
Gabriel A, Student Life in Ave Maria College, Medieval Paris, Notre Dame.
Glorieux P., Les Origines Du College De Sorbonne, Notre Dame.
Haskins, C., The Rise of the Universities, New York, Peter Smith, 1940.
Pieper, J., Scholasticism, London, Faber and Faber, 1960.
Rashdall, H., The Universities of Europe in the Middle Ages, 3 vols, eds, F. Powicke and A. Emden, Oxford. 1936.
Sanderlind, E.D., The Medieval Status of the College of Autun, University of Paris, Notre Dame.
Thompson, J., The Literacy of the Laity in the Middle Ages, New York, Burt Franklin, 1963.
Thorndike, L., University Records and Life in the Middle Ages, New York, Columbia, 1944.
William of Tournai, De instructione Puerorum J. Corbett, ed., Notre Dame.

X. LUTHER AND LOYOLA.

Donahue, J., Jesuit Education, New York, Fordham, 1963.
Dudon, St. Ignatius of Loyola, tr. W. Young. Milwaukee, Bruce, 1949.
Eby, F., Early Protestant Educators, New York, McGraw-Hill, 1931.
Farrell, A., The Jesuit Code of Liberal Education, Milwaukee, Bruce, 1938.
Ganns, G., St. Ignatius' Idea of a Jesuit University, Milwaukee, Marquette, 1956.
Goulet, R., Compendium of the Magnificence, Dignity and Excellence of the University of Paris, 1517, Pennsylvania, 1928.
Ignatius of Loyola, Constitutions of the Society of Jesus, tr. G. Ganss, St. Louis, Institute of Jesuit Sources, 1970.
————, Letters, tr. W. Young, Chicago, Loyola, 1959.
Luther, M., "To the Christian Nobility," "A Sermon on Keeping the Children in School," Selected Writings of Martin Luther, T. Tappert, ed., vol. I, Philadelphia, Fortress, 1967.
McGucken, W., The Jesuits and Education, Milwaukee, Bruce, 1932.
Monumenta Historica Societatis Jesu, Madrid, Lopez del Horno, 1903-.
Painter, F.V.N., Luther on Education, St. Louis, Concordia.
Ratio Studiorum et Institutiones Scholasticae Societatis Jesu, 3 vols, Berlin, A. Hofmann, 1887.
Rose, S., Ignatius Loyola and the Early Jesuits, New York, The Catholic Publication Society, 1891.

XI. RENAISSANCE EDUCATION OF WOMEN.

Aeneas Silvius, **Del Liberorum Educatione.**
Aeneas Silvius, W. Boulting, London, 1908.
Aron, M., **Ursulines,** New York, MacMillan, 1947.
Bainton, R., **Erasmus of Christendom,** New York, Scribners, 1969.
Bertolotti, G., **St. Angela Merici,** Brescia, 1950.
Cannon, M., **The Education of Women During the Renaissance,** Washington, 1916.
Charlton, K., **Education in Renaissance England,** London, Routledge and Kegan Paul, 1965.
Constitutions of the Ursuline Religious of the Congregation of Paris, New York, Catholic Publication Society, (n.d.).
Dominici, G., **On the Education of Children,** A. Cote, ed., Washington, 1927.
Erasmus, Christian Humanism and the Reformation, ed., J. Colin.
Fenelon on Education, ed., H.C. Barnard, Cambridge, 1966.
Hay, D., **The Italian Renaissance in Its Historical Background,** Cambridge, 1962.
Maphei Vegii Laudensis, **De Educatione Liberorum et Eorum Claris Moribus Libri Sex,** M. Fanning, ed., Washington, 1933.
Martin, M., **Ursuline Method of Education,** Rahway, Quinn, and Boden, 1946.
Monica, M., **Angela Merici and Her Teaching Idea,** New York, Longmans, Green, 1927.
More, T., **The Correspondence of Sir Thomas More,** Princeton, 1947.
Reynolds, M., **The Learned Lady in England, 1650-1760,** New York, Houghton, Mifflin, 1920.
Vives and the Renaissance Education of Women, F. Watson, ed., New York, Longmans, 1912.
Vives on Education, intro. F. Watson, Totawa, N.J. Rowman and Littlefield, 1971.
Woodward, W.H., **Studies in Education during the Age of the Renaissance,** Cambridge, 1906.
——————— , **Vittorino da Feltre and Other Humanist Educators,** Cambridge, 1912.

XII. REALISM, LA SALLE AND UNIVERSAL EDUCATION.

Battersby, W.J., **De La Salle, Three Volumes,** New York, Longmans, 1949.
Comenius, J., **The Great Didactic,** London, Black, 1923.
Fitzpatrick, E., **La Salle, Patron of Teachers,** Milwaukee, Bruce, 1951.
Fontaine, F., de la, ed. and tr., **French Liberalism and Education in the Eighteenth Century,** New York, McGraw-Hill, 1932.
——————— , **Conduct of the Schools of Jean Baptiste de la Salle,** New York, McGraw-Hill, 1932.
Masters, R., **The Political Philosophy of Rousseau,** Princeton, 1968.
Painter, F.V.N., **Great Pedagogical Essays,** New York, American Book Co., 1905.
Pestalozzi's Educational Writings, ed., J. Green, New York, Longman's, 1912.
Predovich, N., **Leo XIII on Education,** unpublished dissertation, Woodstock College, 1962.

Rousseau, J., **Emile,** New York, Dutton, 1961.
————— , **Social Contract,** L. Crocker, ed., Cleveland, Case Western Reserve, 1968.
Sadler, J., **Comenius and the Concept of Universal Education,** London, Allen and Unwin, 1966.
Zeldin, T., ed., **Conflicts in French Society; Anticlericalism, Education and Morals in the Nineteenth Century,** New York, Humanities Press, 1970.

XIII. THE UNITED STATES.

Brownson, O.A., **Works,** 20 vols, Detroit, 1882-1887.
Buetow, H., **Of Singular Benefit; The Story of Catholic Education in the U.S.,** New York, MacMillan, 1970.
Cordoba, P. de, 1482-1521, **Christian Doctrine; for the Instruction and Formation of the Indians,** Miami, 1970.
Cremin, L., **American Education, the Colonial Experience, 1607-1783,** New York, Harper and Row, 1971.
Ellis, J.T., **American Catholicism,** Chicago, 1956.
————— , **A Guide to American Catholic History,** Milwaukee, Bruce, 1959.
————— , **Documents of American Catholic History,** Milwaukee, Bruce, 1962.
England, J., **Works,** 7 vols, Cleveland, 1908.
Fichter, J., **Parochial School, A Sociological Survey,** Notre Dame, 1958.
Good, H.J., **A History of American Education,** New York, MacMillan, 1962.
Greeley, A., and P. Rossi, **The Education of American Catholics,** Chicago, Aldine, 1966.
Guilday, P., ed., **The National Pastorals of the American Hierarchy (1792-1919),** Washington, NCWC, 1923.
————— , **A History of the Councils of Baltimore** (1791-1884), New York, MacMillan, 1932.
Hanley, J., et al, "Church and State in the U.S. (Legal History)", NCE, vol 3, pp. 742-758.
Harris, X.J., "Education, United States," NCE, vol. 5, pp. 128-148.
Ireland, J., **The Church and Modern Society,** Chicago, 1897.
Mather, C., **Magnalia Christi Americana, or The Ecclesiastical History of New England,** New York, Ungar, 1970.
McCluskey, N., **Catholic Education in America, A Documentary History,** New York, Columbia, 1964.
McGrath, J., **Church and State in American Law,** Milwaukee, Bruce, 1962.
McLoughlin, W., **New England Dissent, 1630-1883; The Baptists and the Separation of Church and State,** Harvard, 1971.
Phelan, J., **The Millennial Kingdom of the Franciscan in the New World,** U. of California, 1970.
Spalding, J.L., **Means and End in Education,** Chicago, 1897.
————— , **Education and the Higher Life,** Chicago, 1903.
————— , **Things of the Mind,** Chicago, 1905.

———— , Religion, Agnosticism and Education, Chicago.

XIV. CONCLUSION.

Bruner, J., The Relevance of Education, New York, Norton, 1971.
Butler, R., God on the Secular Campus, Garden City, Doubleday, 1963.
Cully, C., ed., Does the Church Know How to Teach? New York, Mac-
    Millan, 1970.
Di Giacomo, J., Faith, New York, Holt, Rinehart and Winston, 1968.
———— , Conscience and Concern: Teacher's Guide, New York, Holt,
    Rinehart and Winston, 1970.
———— , See You in Church, New York, Holt, Rinehart, and Winston,
    1971.
Downs, T., "Turmoil in the Classroom," NCW, Jan-Feb, 1972, pp. 20ff.
Dulles, A., "The Church as Multimedia," NCW, Jan-Feb 1972, pp. 22ff.
Gary, L., The Collapse of Non-Public Education, Rumor or Reality, Newark,
    1972.
Greeley, A., The Changing Catholic College, Chicago, Aldine, 1967.
———— , and W. Brown, Can Catholic Schools Survive, New York,
    Sheed and Ward, 1971.
Gustafson, J. et al., Moral Education, Harvard, 1970.
Jones, R., Fantasy and Feeling in Education, New York, Harper and
    Row, 1970.
Kay, W., Moral Development: Moral Growth from Childhood to Adoles-
    cence, New York, Schocken, 1969.
Lee, L., and P. Rooney, Toward a Future for Religious Education, Day-
    ton, Pflaum, 1970.
McLuhan, M., Understanding Media, the Extension of Man, New York,
    McGraw-Hill, 1964.
———— , and Q. Fiore, The Medium is the Massage, New York, Ban-
    tam, 1967.
McKenzie, L., Christian Education in the 70's Alba House, 1972.
Moran, G., Visions and Tactics Towards an Adult Church, New York,
    Herder and Herder, 1968.
———— , Design for Religion: Towards Ecumenical Education, New
    York, Herder and Herder, 1971.
Neiman, J., Coordinators; A New Focus in Parish Religious Education, St.
    Mary's College, 1971.
O'Neil, M., New Schools in a New Church, Collegeville, Liturgical Press.
Raths, L.E., et al, Values and Teaching, Columbus, Merrill, 1966.
Silberman, C., Crisis in the Classroom: The Making of American Educa-
    tion, New York, Random House, 1970.
Sloyan, G., ed., Shaping the Christian Message, New York, 1948.
———— , Speaking of Religious Education, New York, Herder and
    Herder, 1968.
Strommer, M., ed., Research on Religious Development: a Comprehensive
    Handbook, New York, Hawthorne, 1971.
Wiencke, G., ed., Christian Education in a Secular Society, Philadelphia,
    Fortress, 1970.

INDEX OF NAMES

John of Beverley, 130, 131.
John Chrysostom, 92ff, 105.
John the Scot, 136.
Joshua B. Perahyah, 20.
Judah the Prince, 15, 18.
Julian, Emperor, 55, 88.
Justin, xi, 55f, 58, 253.

Lachalotais, 222f.
Lainez, D., 170, 172.
Lainster, M. L. W., 95ff.
LaSalle, J. B. De, 212ff, 255f.
Locke, J., 211.
Loewe, H., 7 (37), 13f, 17 (11).
Logos, 56f, 68, 79, 89.
Luther, M., 22, 141, 163ff, 198, 254.

Mann, H., 243f.
Marrou, H., 50, 52, 53, 65 (8).
Martianus Capella, 127, 132.
Matthew, Apostle, xi, 28, 30, 34, 43.
McGucken, W., 185, 186, 187 (26).
Melanchthon, 166.
Merici, A., 199ff, 255.
Milton, J., 210.
Montefiore, C., 7 (3), 12 (4).
More, T., 193f.
Moses, 3, 8, 10, 13, 14, 43, 47.

Nadal, J., 178, 180, 185.
Napoleon, 225f.
Narsai, 63ff.

Origen, 55, 67, 68, 71ff, 81, 85, 91, 97, 99, 156, 186.

Painter, F. V. N., 210 (1), 222 (18).
Paul, Apostle, xi, xii, 34, 35ff, 53ff, 119, 186, 213, 253.

Paul III, Pope, 172f, 175, 203.
Paula, 98, 100.
Pestalozzi, 244.
Philo, 14, 18, 36.
Pieper, J., 137, 158 (20).
Pippin, 133, 134.
Polanco, J., 175, 179.
Predovich, N., 227 (20).

Quintilian, 51, 117, 185.

Rabanus Maurus, 112, 136.
Rashdall, H., 157.
Richard, G., 238.
Rose, S., 169 (8 &9), 176 (13).
Rouseau, 221.
Ruether, R., 87 (1), 88, 89 (4).

Seton, E. B., 237f.
Spalding, J. L., 247f.
Spirit, 44, 86f, 90, 91f.
Steinmann, J., 98f.
Sturm, J., 166, 185.

Tappert, T., 163ff.
Tempier, E., 141, 157.
Tertullian, 57, 61.
Theodore of Mopsuestia, 63.
Theodoric, Emperor, 124, 125, 137.
Thorndike, L., 139 (6), 143 (8), 146 (12), 149 (14).

Ursula, 200.

Vives, J. L., 195ff.
Voobus, A., 63ff.

William of Champeaux, 141.
William of Occam, 157.

SUBJECT INDEX